DEMOCRATS, DINNERS, & DOLLARS

A History of the Democratic Party, its Dinners, its Ritual

Dinners for Democrats as we

for dollars renew faith in the old democracy of Jefferson and Jackson.

DEMOCRATS,

A History of the Democratic Party,

By

With an Introduction By

THE IOWA STATE UNIVERSITY PRESS,

DINNERS, & DOLLARS

its Dinners, its Ritual

RONALD F. STINNETT

HUBERT H. HUMPHREY

PRESS BUILDING, AMES, IOWA, U.S.A., 1967

Ronald Floyd Stinnett, Assistant to the Vice President of the United States, Hubert H. Humphrey, has a background of managerial experience in politics ranging from mayoral campaigns to national. He is a graduate of the State University of New York and holds the M.A. and Ph.D. degrees from the University of Minnesota, the latter in speech and political science. In 1963–64 he served as Research Director of the Democratic Senatorial Campaign Committee.

© 1967 The Iowa State University Press
Ames, Iowa, U.S.A. All rights reserved

Composed and printed by
The Iowa State University Press

First edition, 1967

Library of Congress Catalog Card Number: 66–21644

DEDICATION

To the man and woman who "showed me the way"—
who influenced my life the most:

My Father, OWEN E. STINNETT

My Mother, LILLIAN STINNETT

To the Citizen of the United States who taught me that to
work for my Fellow Citizen is the greatest reward on earth:

My Mentor, My Friend, My Inspiration

HUBERT H. HUMPHREY

Vice President of the United States

THERE is high political wisdom in the custom yearly to revive the memory of civil virtue and national glory in the mind of the living generation, because nothing is more efficient to keep alive the spirit of patriotism . . . that powerful genius which, like the angels of Scripture, guards with flaming sword the paradise of national liberty and independence.

"Happy the land where the history of the past is the history of the people and not a mere flattery to kings; and doubly happy the land where rewards of the past are brightened by present glory . . . present happiness . . . and where the noble deeds of the dead, instead of being a mournful monument of past greatness that saddens the heart, though it ennobles the mind, are a lasting source of national welfare to the age and to posterity." ★

LEWIS KOSSUTH, HUNGARIAN PATRIOT
Speaking at the Jackson Day Banquet
January 8, 1852

FOREWORD

AS ONE who has devoted his life to politics and public service, I am deeply aware of the influence the American political party ultimately exerts on the lives of our citizens and our national policies.

The United States government is the working instrument of the people. The policies it formulates and executes flow from the public will, and the public will is most directly expressed through political parties and their candidates.

Our American political parties are our vehicles of popular expression and our means to power. They are places, too, where national conflicts may be channeled toward peaceful and responsible resolution.

Our oldest operating political party is the Democratic Party, founded in 1792 by Thomas Jefferson.

This book shows a stream of that party's history by uniquely examining the annual political dinners of the party. Dr. Stinnett's descriptions of these dinners—the personalities involved, the issues discussed, their changing role of party usefulness—present a picture of our country's political evolution. These annual ritualistic gatherings of the Democratic Party reveal, perhaps as much as the party's platforms, how our democratic system has managed to make change its ally and a force for good.

One cannot read this book without concluding that our parties have served us well and that, imperfect as they may sometimes seem, they are an effective means indeed of making self-government work.   ★

HUBERT H. HUMPHREY
Vice President of the United States

PREFACE

POLITICAL parties, like any organized group of people, try to preserve their identity, promote unity within their own group, and propound vital principles of self-preservation and self-promotion. The two major American political parties have survived the trials of tempestuous times and the scars of more than a century's scourging struggles. Law and order, the reasons for party survival, have dictated the orderly change of American government from control by one party to control by the other throughout America's history.

Although the Constitution of the United States does not provide for the establishment of political parties, which actually were thought to be divisive and schismatic by our Founding Fathers, parties have performed the function of a necessary catalyst in the successful operation of the United States' form of democracy.[1]

From disputes over our basic form of government, expressed in disagreements within the first President's Cabinet, political parties were created. Parties in our country today make possible in practice the theoretical principles of rule by the people expressed in the Declaration of Independence and the United States Constitution. The inevitability and necessity of political parties in American democracy have been apparent for more than a century and a half.[2]

Although parties are of major importance in the American constitutional system, it is less evident why and how a party is able to keep itself energized and vital. The Democratic Party, for example, has existed for 175 years.[3] It is obvious that self-preservation and self-promotion become as vital motivations to a political party as they do to an individual person.

As in religion, certain formal or ceremonial acts or procedures are developed by political parties for their propagation. For major parties, no political oracles set down these rites; usually no formal plans are drawn for observing such ceremonies. Yet every successful party gradually develops a set of traditional observances that helps it express and deepen the faith of its followers.

Like the origin of political parties themselves, political ritual grew irregularly, but steadily, out of the seeds of party needs, tradition, pride, and reverence for leaders. With the passage of time and as an acknowledgment of its heritage, the Democratic Party developed a ritual designed to unify the party and to renew faith in its fundamental principles.

More than a quarter of a century passed from the founding of the Democratic Party in 1792 until it had accumulated the quality of endurance, a sense of history, enough success to merit a measure of pride, and a perspective far enough removed to permit the veneration of the respected leaders of history. By 1827, thirty-five years after its birth, the Democratic Party was rich in history, inured to the control of the government, and ripe for fruition of its ritual.

For the preservation and promotion of a political party, among the several actions and feelings of party members ideally sought are:

1. Each member must identify himself with the party, its principles, its positions, its patriarchs. He must feel as though he is a significant part of the party, that the party accepts him and his talents, however great or small. He must become as one with the party; its actions must become his actions in his eyes. Nearly total empathy of the individual with the party must be induced. By possessing such identification of the individual with the party, the party preserves and promotes itself.

2. Each member, though disagreeing with other members on certain matters, must feel the necessity for joining hands within the party when threatened from without. Unity, a quality necessary for continued existence of a party, is most needed in times of danger. During those times, each member must accept a higher appeal for cohesion and unity and must reject any predilections to disagree. In other words, party preservation must rank higher than petty differences within the party.

3. Each member must be ready to submit himself and his energies to the all-important party. The functions, activities, principles, and actions accepted by the party must be assimilated and acquiesced to by the member. Self-sacrifice by the member is expected in case of conflict with the total party positions and actions.

4. Each member, being completely immersed and identified with the party, must feel a sense of pride and reverence for the party's accomplishments throughout its history, and for the leaders and heroes held high by the party. Ego involvement and identification of each member with the historic deeds and actions of the party's patriarchs provide for party continuance, promotion, and cohesion.[4]

Given these basic requirements, a political party is capable of continuing its work and promoting its policies. Once the identification of the members with the party can no longer be maintained, the party becomes crippled, emaciated, and finally defunct. An excellent example of the demise of such a party is the Federalist Party, which withered away after the War of 1812 when its affiliates no longer cared to identify with it and its un-American actions during that war.

How are these vital qualities endowed in a political ritual? What form or shape does the ritual take?

Without recognizing the psychological results of the identification process and without its ever being formally explained by party leaders, many people participate in such rituals several times a year. The characteristics of the ritual are usually present each time: a large gathering of members of the party, the presence of several high party officials, the delivering of toasts or public addresses, the use of several symbols or decorations evoking identification of a member with his party, an appeal to protect the party and its principles from some common enemy or scapegoat, an appeal to each member to promote the party's interests as other leaders have in the past, an appeal for self-sacrifice, and a reassurance that the party, and thereby the individual member, will be victorious and successful.

The Democratic Party has a long history of political ritual in the nature of its Jefferson-Jackson Day celebrations. These occasions, beginning after the War of 1812 and continuing almost annually to the present, serve as vehicles for the ritual of reaffirming the party's principles, renewing acquaintances and faith in the party, revitalizing the party members, remembering and revering the party's past and present leaders, and rededicating itself to the aims and objectives of the party.

The complete history of the Jefferson-Jackson Day affairs is traced in this book simply as a historical study rather than an analytical one. However, the recurring pattern of the events, the actions, the party members, the speakers, and the speeches lead inevitably and indisputably to the conclusion that such celebrations are a cardinal element in the political ritual of the Democratic Party.

Throughout the description of the Jefferson-Jackson Day Dinners in these chapters is woven the thread of political ritual. Without explaining the ritualistic meaning of each dinner, speaker, and speech, the analysis may easily be ascertained by the reader. The primary purpose of this book is revelation, exposition, or narration of the history of the $100-a-plate dinners and the Jefferson-Jackson Day celebrations. The annual occurrence of such affairs, the tie which binds these events together, highlights the need of a political party for political ritual. ★

ACKNOWLEDGMENTS

THE LIBRARY OF CONGRESS and its employees were very helpful in providing me with all Washington, D.C., newspapers from 1815 through 1966. These newspapers proved to be the most valuable single primary source for reconstructing the story of Democratic Party dinners held in the nation's capital. The century-and-a-half newspaper record of the Jefferson-Jackson Day celebrations provides a vivid account of Democratic Party history in all its glory.

All photographs were printed through the courtesy of the Library of Congress, except certain photographs printed with the permission of the Worcester Art Museum, Underwood and Underwood, the City News Bureau of Washington, D.C., and the White House photographers.

A special note of gratitude is given to those reporters and news analysts of Washington, D.C., newspapers who provided the basic data throughout the past century and a half and made this book possible.

In collecting data from the Franklin D. Roosevelt Library in Hyde Park, New York, from the Harry S. Truman Library in Independence, Missouri, and from the Sam Rayburn Library in Bonham, Texas, I was graciously and efficiently aided by Herman Kahn, Philip C. Brooks, and H. G. Dulaney, the respective directors of these libraries. Also, I wish to acknowledge the assistance given by the staffs of these libraries in obtaining materials pertinent to this history.

I wish to give a very special word of appreciation to those people who were kind enough to be interviewed personally: Hon. Harry S. Truman, former President of the United States; the late Hon. Sam Rayburn, Speaker of the House of Representatives; James A. Farley, former Postmaster General and former Chairman of the Democratic National Committee; the late Hon. Estes Kefauver, Senator from Tennessee; Mrs. India Edwards, former head of the Women's Division of the Democratic National Committee; Oscar Ewing, former adviser to President Truman and also former head of the Federal Security Agency; Samuel C. Brightman, former Deputy Chairman of Public Affairs of the Democratic National Committee; Hon. Orville Freeman, former Governor of Minnesota and presently Secretary of Agriculture; Edward Roddan, former Washington news correspondent.   ★

Washington, D.C.   R.F.S.
January, 1967

CONTENTS

DEMOCRATS, DINNERS, & DOLLARS

A History of the Democratic Party, its Dinners, its Ritual

Chapter 1

A PARTY IS BORN

THE DEMOCRATIC PARTY, the oldest political party in America, was born almost simultaneously with the birth of our nation. The Federal Constitutional Convention of 1787, which created the framework for the type of government the United States would have, also laid the cornerstone for its political institutions. One political faction, composed of the followers of Thomas Jefferson, became known as the Republican Party; the other, made up of the supporters of Alexander Hamilton, was called the Federalist Party. Republicanism versus monarchy or aristocracy—government *by* the people or government *of* the people—these were the basic issues of this period, the Republican Party espousing the former and the Federalists the latter on each issue.[1]

Thomas Jefferson, as our first Secretary of State, fresh from France as our ambassador, was filled with a fear of monarchies and a fever for democratic ideas. The French Revolution in 1789 had gained the sympathy of the American minister. Traveling throughout France, Jefferson saw that the French peasants were extremely poor and had few rights, while the nobility had virtually all of the privileges and lived in luxury.[2]

As author of the Declaration of Independence thirteen years earlier, Jefferson had displayed for posterity his philosophy of governments in relation to the people. Governments, as he saw them, were servants of the people—not people the servants of governments.

When Jefferson assumed his role as our first Secretary of State, he found that the capital city of New York abounded in antidemocratic attitudes. He reported that at social gatherings he often was the only one present holding to a democratic philosophy. Although America had just won its independence from a monarchy, many powerful men in government believed that George Washington should rule in an aristocratic manner similar to the roles played by kings in European monarchies.

In addition to Alexander Hamilton, the founder of the Federalist Party, other proponents of a government by aristocracy to rule over the common people were Gouveneur Morris, who believed that the Senate should be appointed by the President for life from the rich and aristocratic classes; George Cabot, the Senator from Massachusetts who feared democracy; and John Jay, Chief Justice of the Supreme Court, who felt that the people did not really have the ability to govern themselves and should be governed by the aristocrats.

The Democratic Party, disavowing despotic rule by any class and long touted as the party of the common man, has had a long succession of Presidents who have fought the "Economic Royalists" or the "special interests." From its beginning, the party has tried to represent the large class of people who cannot afford special representation and who desire only a fair, honest, and effective government.

The seeds of the Democratic Party were sown in conversations at the dinner tables of New York during these first few months of the government under its newly ratified Constitution. Thomas Jefferson wrote:

> I cannot describe the wonder and mortification with which the table conversations filled me. Politics were the chief topic, and a preference of kingly, over republican, government was evidently the favorite sentiment. An apostate I could not be, nor yet a hypocrite; and I found myself, for the most part, the only advocate on the republican side of the question.[3]

Alexander Hamilton, although respected by Jefferson, bore the brunt of Jefferson's antipathy for the advocates of aristocracy. Continual clashes between Hamilton and Jefferson created confusion and discontent in Washington's Cabinet. These two men symbolized the polar views of the road the young American government should take—aristocracy versus democracy.

Hamilton had become the cogent spokesman of the "rich and well-born" in America. He feared the common people, called them a "great beast," held the poor and lower classes in contempt, and felt that they were incapable of

controlling or ruling themselves.[4] He had no particular admiration for the wealthy but did think that the wealthy
were a safer depository of power than the equally selfish
common people.

His followers became known as the Federalists and believed in a strong federal or national government similar
to the British government. John Adams, the other principal
Federalist leader, called Hamilton's followers the "rich, the
well-born, and the able." They soon labeled Jefferson's followers as Anti-Federalists, a term which improperly suggested that they were against federalism and for a more
anarchial kind of government. The Federalists were primarily made up of merchants, creditors, and financiers. By
warning these groups that the failure of the the new government would ruin them economically, Hamilton was able
to get them to throw their full support behind ratification
of the Constitution. As Secretary of the Treasury, Hamilton
displayed facility and success in making his measures of
funding, assumption, and banking work for the benefit of
the new country.

The Anti-Federalists, the group supporting the ideas
of Thomas Jefferson, assumed the name of "Democratic-
Republicans" or simply "Republicans." This first Republican Party—later, ironically and paradoxically, to become
known as the Democratic Party—was composed mainly of
farmers and workers. Their major strength came from the
South and the West while the Federalists' strength came
from the industrial Northeast. The Republicans favored
farming over manufacturing, the rural over the urban.

In the early days of the Washington Administration,
neither Jefferson nor Hamilton actively sought to form and
organize political parties. However, it was inevitable that
factions would evolve out of this basic philosophical issue.
Feelings on the fundamental nature of the United States
government could hardly be kept from formalizing into
dissenting political parties.

Hamilton and Jefferson fought fiercely in Washing-

ton's Cabinet; their followers attacked each other bitterly
in and out of Congress; rival newspapers were organized and
aligned with one side or the other.

The newly born party, composed of the followers of
Jefferson and his philosophy of government, received its
name from its parent and founder, Thomas Jefferson, when
he wrote to George Washington on May 13, 1792: "The Republican party, who wish to preserve the government in its
present form, are fewer in number than the monarchial
Federalists."[5] Not only did Jefferson give the name to the
newly founded party, called the Democratic Party today, but
he also characterized his followers' opposition by calling
them "monarchial Federalists."

George Washington, appreciative of the talents and
efforts of both Alexander Hamilton and Thomas Jefferson,
acted as a mediator in the philosophical arguments and
bitter personal fights carried on about him. He had great
praise for Hamilton's financial abilities and for what he
had done to make the young government's financial situation sounder and more respected. On the other hand, his
admiration was great for Thomas Jefferson who had the experience, knowledge, and ability to represent the United
States in its foreign affairs.

At first the Democratic-Republican Party was not
really a party at all but simply a conglomeration of countrymen possessing similar ideas and expressing their thoughts
in letters to each other. Nor did the Hamiltonians gather to
form a political party. In fact, the Federalists feared dissent,
organized as factions or parties, more than anything else in
the new government. Gradually, however, this conglomeration became more closely knit and united.

Political parties are mentioned nowhere in the Constitution, and it is a matter of record that those framing the
Constitution feared factionalism. Even Washington in his
Farewell Address warned against the "baneful effects of the
spirit of party." It was felt that political parties or factions
would split the country asunder and cause confusion and

dissension among the people. For example, James Madison, writing in *The Federalist,* feared factionalism, but he recognized that political parties were bound to come since "the regulation of these various and interfering interests forms the principal task of modern legislation, and involves the spirit of party and faction in the necessary and ordinary operations of government."[6] John Adams also expressed fear of the growth of political parties and the divisiveness which would result. "[There] is nothing I dread so much as the division of the Republic into two great parties, each under its leader. . . . This, in my humble opinion, is to be feared as the greatest political evil under our Constitution."[7] And John Marshall said: "Nothing I believe more debases or pollutes the human mind than faction."[8]

It is very clear that the Republican Party founded by Jefferson gave itself the name to escape the negative connotation of Anti-Federalists. Anti-Federalists were those who fought the ratification of the Constitution in 1789. Jefferson strongly supported the Constitution and did not want to be identified with the term "Anti-Federalists." He wanted to emphasize that he and his followers favored a republican, or anti-monarchial, form of government.

Jefferson became so embroiled in the battles with Alexander Hamilton over the policies the United States government should follow that he resigned as Secretary of State in 1793. But being a man of high purpose and principle, and destined to become a leader, he could not step out of his office and retire to his plantation for very long. He led the Republicans to their victories in Congress in 1795 and became their candidate for the Presidency in 1796 and 1800.

Part of the reason for the birth of the Republican Party was Jefferson's objection to the power which the wealthy merchants, manufacturers, and financiers were getting as a result of subsidies from the government. He felt that these groups of "special interests" were becoming even wealthier as a result of their manipulation of the coupons of the government bonds, the dividends on their bank stock, and the protective tariff on their goods. Jefferson believed that these businessmen were not very interested in liberty and equality; all they wanted was government help in making more money. He saw the government becoming corrupt and gradually falling into the hands of the financiers and speculators with whom Hamilton dealt.

Out of all these rumblings arose the present-day Democratic Party. In 1796, just a few years after this group of Jeffersonians became known as the Republican Party, they exhibited their growing strength by electing a majority in the House of Representatives and losing the Presidency by only a narrow margin.

The Federalists noticed that Jeffersonians were beginning to criticize the Federalists in power and to increase their strength by including the many recent immigrants from Europe. Therefore, fearing a loss of power to the accelerating growth of Republican strength, the Federalists inspired the passage of the Alien and Sedition Acts of 1798. These four acts were aimed at punishing those who criticized the government and directed toward making it difficult for foreigners to become American citizens, many of whom were French and most of whom were Republicans. The acts had sharp political overtones and were even disapproved of by such leading Federalists as Adams, Hamilton, and Marshall.[9] The Republican Party countered with the Virginia and Kentucky Resolutions, prepared by Madison and Jefferson. The resolutions declared that the remedy for an unconstitutional act of Congress was nullification by the state sovereignties. Primarily, the resolutions served as campaign material against the Federalists in the election of 1800.

The battle of parties had begun. By 1800 Jefferson had proved that the Republican Party was truly national in character and had the sympathy of the masses.

Thomas Jefferson occupied the executive mansion from 1801 to 1809, followed by Madison and Monroe who held the Presidency from 1809 to 1825. This was the real measure of the strength of the movement started by Jefferson in 1792. The Federalist Party was ultimately destroyed by its resistance to the War of 1812 and by its participation in the Hartford Convention. For one very brief period in American history, 1812 through 1825, there was really only one political party in the United States, the Republican, or Democratic, Party started by Thomas Jefferson. Instead of uniting the country, the decline of Federalist opposition led to chaos, thus making it more apparent that party organization is a vital principle of representative government.

Democrats today look upon Thomas Jefferson much as an offspring looks upon his parent. Jefferson's mind and actions gave birth to the Democratic Party. For this and a multitude of other reasons, Thomas Jefferson is remembered and revered by Democrats each year in thousands of Jefferson-Jackson Day celebrations throughout the country.

Bitterness erupted in the Presidential election of 1824 when John Quincy Adams was elected President. Although the Presidential contest of 1824 was not a contest of parties, since the Federalist Party was dead, it was a struggle between sections of the country to get control of the government. The candidates were John Quincy Adams of Massachusetts, Andrew Jackson of Tennessee, Henry Clay of Kentucky, John Calhoun of South Carolina, and William Crawford of Georgia. Since none of the five candidates received a majority of the electoral college, the House of Representatives chose the President from the three highest names on the list. Clay, not being one of these three, threw his support to John Quincy Adams, thereby giving Adams the election. The Jackson supporters cried "corrupt bargain" after Clay was appointed as Adams' Secretary of State. From that moment onward, Jackson and his supporters worked to win the election in 1828. They harped on the theme that Jackson was unjustly deprived of the Presidency in 1824. They argued that he was "the people's choice" since he had received the greatest number of popular votes and the greatest number of electoral votes.

Jackson went on to win the Presidency in 1828 and again in 1832. He was the embodiment of the principles which Thomas Jefferson promoted. Unlike the Presidents before him, Jackson was a man who had deep faith in the common people. Although Jefferson had an abiding faith in inalienable natural rights and an inherent system of moral values, he believed that education and training were desirable to fit the common man for his part in government. Jackson, on the other hand, disregarded such requirements and stated: "The duties of all public officers are . . . so plain and simple that men of intelligence may readily qualify themselves for their performance."[10] Jackson believed that every American, no matter what his background or education, was capable of holding any job in government. He challenged existing government practices and made room for his supporters. The common man was going to run the country.

Jacksonian democracy was given added impetus by the growing population and the addition of new states in the West. The laboring man, the farmer, the common man attained their zenith—they received recognition of their abilities, their intelligence, and their contributions to the fast-growing country.

The Jacksonian era probably gave America its greatest flourish of democratic changes. It gave more people the right to vote; it extended free discussion on the platform, the pulpits, and in the rapidly multiplying newspapers. It was an era when the number of elected officials was expanded, when many state constitutions were revised, and when the national nominating convention came into being.

It was in Jackson's time that labor started to organize, that inventions in industry and commerce flourished, and that such major means of transportation as the steam locomotive and the ocean steamship became successful.

And the Jacksonian era was a period of humanitarian reform in many areas—debtor's laws, prisons and asylums, and the elementary schools. It was in Jackson's time that agitation for the abolition of slavery was begun.

Jackson, like Jefferson, will long be regarded as one of America's greatest Presidents. Also like Jefferson, Jackson is remembered and revered in the thousands of Jefferson-Jackson Day celebrations held annually throughout the United States.

Thomas Jefferson, the Virginia scholar and statesman, believed that the competent should rule, always subject to the suggestions and criticisms of the total public. He established the Democratic Party on this basis. The victory in 1800 of the Republican Party over the Federalists gave the common man new hope.

Andrew Jackson, the dynamic, self-made frontiersman from Tennessee, believed that government should be *by* the people as well as *for* the people. The United States was pushing its frontiers farther west, farther from the aristocratic customs and traditions of the Old Continent. This added strength to the concept of democracy which was being widely accepted at that time. The party's victory in 1828 was a triumph for the people in a most practical way.

Jefferson gave the Democratic Party its being; Jackson gave it its full meaning. Jefferson was the champion of democracy and its theorist in the formative stages of America. He created the rationale of a broad-based party. Jackson was the practitioner of democratic government. He brought theory to life for the people. They participated. They understood. They *were* the government of the United States.

The Democratic Party, full-grown and mature today, celebrates and commemorates the happy compatibility of theory and practice through the Jefferson-Jackson Day Dinners held annually throughout the nation. Theory and practice, thought and action—in the Democratic Party these mean Jefferson and Jackson. ★

Chapter 2

THE HISTORY OF
AN EXPENSIVE MEAL

"JAMES A. FARLEY is a better merchant than Andrew Jackson since Farley is the only political manager who has ever been able to sell $5 worth of groceries for $100,"[1] remarked O. Max Gardner, Chairman of the 1939 Jackson Day Dinner Committee and former Governor of North Carolina; Farley is credited with being the founder of the $100-a-plate fund raisers on the national level.

Since 1936 the Democratic National Committee Dinners have been known as Jackson Day Dinners, Democratic Victory Dinners, Washington Dinners, Jefferson Day Dinners, and, more recently, Jefferson-Jackson Day Dinners. These annual affairs became known officially as the Jefferson-Jackson Day Dinners in 1948, the year of the celebration of the 100th anniversary of the Democratic National Committee. Similar dinners are given throughout the United States, sometimes at the suggestion of the National Committee, sometimes on the initiative of the local party, always for the main purposes of raising funds and renewing faith in the party.

From 1936 to the present time, official national Jefferson-Jackson Day celebrations have been held in Washington except in the years 1941, 1945, and 1953. Even in those years, Jefferson-Jackson dinners were held throughout the country. For example, in 1941, the Washington, D.C., Jefferson-Jackson Day Dinner was cancelled because President Roosevelt could not attend. He did, however, bring his ship into a Florida port long enough to deliver a radio address to those attending dinners throughout the country. In 1945 the dinner was cancelled because Roosevelt died the day before it was to be held. In 1953, after Adlai Stevenson's resounding defeat in his bid for the Presidency, there was no dinner held in Washington.

The origin of these dinners as fund raisers came from the quest of James A. Farley, Democratic National Committee Chairman in 1936, to find ways and means of reducing the large Democratic Party debt which resulted from the Presidential campaigns of Alfred E. Smith in 1928 and Franklin D. Roosevelt in 1932. The Democratic National Committee had a several hundred thousand dollar debt at the beginning of 1936, a Presidential election year, when more and greater expenses would be incurred. Faced with this difficult situation, Farley had to find ways of eliminating the old deficit and of obtaining money for the forthcoming campaign.

In an interview with James Farley in 1958, the former Democratic National Committee Chairman stated that it was his idea to hold these $100-a-plate dinners.

> I wanted to do it in order to rid ourselves of the deficit. Also, we thought that more people would pay $100 a plate for a dinner and contribution than we could get from large contributions. It is a little funny now that we look back on the idea. However, at the time Roosevelt was not too keen on the idea. Also, others laughed and scoffed at the idea, such as the Republicans. Now everybody is having dinners to raise campaign money, including the Republicans. I was working on the idea with W. Forbes Morgan. We thought it was worthwhile, and we took a chance. We started the dinners in 1936. Prior to this the Democratic National Committee Dinners were held once every four years.[2]

As for other reactions to this radical plan of charging high prices for a dinner, Marie Chatham wrote in her doctoral dissertation:

> Often credited with inaugurating the $100 dinner, Farley disclaims the honor. What he originated was the dinner for revenue. When he suggested his scheme to put the dinner to work, as a direct money-making device, he suggested $25 per plate as the price and "they" thought it was "terrible." The even more "terrible" price of $100, however, has been very successful. In 1940 Oliver Quayle, the Treasurer of the Democratic National Committee, to whom, incidentally, Farley gives most of the credit for the success of the scheme, reported that over $400,000 had been collected through the device of the campaign dinners. At first, the dinner tickets seemed to be control proof inasmuch as the purchase of the ticket was voluntary, at least on the surface. However, after the passage of the Hatch Act, the plan had to be changed somewhat. No longer were the tickets sold at $100 apiece, but the guests were "invited" to the dinner, the $100 donation being the understood price.[3]

It has been reported recently that Matthew McCloskey, former Ambassador to Ireland, held a $100-a-plate dinner in Philadelphia in 1935. He is credited with starting the dinners on a local level while Farley made the idea successful on the national level.

Actually, the first Democratic National Committee Dinner in 1936 cost the participants $50 apiece. Since 1937, the price has been $100 per plate. Of course, lower and varying prices are found at the Jefferson-Jackson Day Dinners held in other cities throughout the country. In order to evade taxation on the admission to the dinners, the potential participants at the dinners are appealed to for funds prior to the banquet. To everyone contributing $100, an invitation (not a ticket) is sent, and he is considered a dinner guest of the Democratic Party.

The first dinner was an obvious financial triumph and was equally acclaimed for its political effect. In a *New York Times* article a few days after the dinners were held, W. Forbes Morgan, the Secretary of the Democratic National Committee, said:

> Proceeds from Jackson Day Dinners throughout the country will total nearly $250,000 and will wipe out the party's deficit. . . . The dinners were not only successful from a financial standpoint, but the reports of enthusiasm shown in every section of the country, not only with regard to the dinners themselves, but also for President Roosevelt's magnificent Jackson Day address, was an evidence of the respect, admiration, and faith which the whole country has for the great leader of the party he heads.[4]

Thus, these $100-a-plate Democratic National Committee Dinners or Jefferson-Jackson Day Dinners had their origin in a problem of economics rather than in a desire to provide the setting for political speechmaking. President Franklin D. Roosevelt was the only speaker at the first great dinner, and he was chosen because he would be the biggest attraction for the $50 contributors.

Remarking about the dinners, Secretary of Agriculture Orville Freeman stated that this method of raising funds is "a relatively painless way to raise money without incurring any kind of obligation, for there is a return to the participant in terms of a dinner and a social evening."[5]

Speaker Sam Rayburn of Texas said:

> The purposes of the dinners are first of all to generate enthusiasm within the party and to raise money for the coming campaign. The public speeches present an opportunity to recount the accomplishments of the party upon which to strive for even better results. The speeches should not be eliminated because a person is not going to pay one hundred dollars for a meal without some kind of entertainment, and this is the type of entertainment which is best—and it is the type that is needed at these functions.[6]

Stephen A. Mitchell, a Chicago lawyer and former Democratic National Committee Chairman, commented, "It is to my mind the best known method of raising money, extracting a substantial sum of money from a goodly number of people."[7] He said also that these dinners provided the "principal source of the funds with which we paid off the Democratic National Committee deficit after the '52 campaign."

There is no doubt that these dinners are a major means of raising money for the party. Although getting access to information on the actual sums of money raised at these Jefferson-Jackson Day Dinners, nationally and locally, is an impossible task, some idea of the amounts raised can be obtained by noting how many people attend the affairs, since the price of the dinner is known. The usual range of financial intake for the national dinner until the 1960's was between $200,000 and $600,000. In the past six years, some of the affairs have hit the million dollar mark.

Although the major purpose of these dinners remains that of fund raising, there are other purposes almost as important. More and more attention is being given to the platform provided for the principal speakers at such affairs.

Concerning these other purposes for the celebrations, Secretary Freeman has said that the Democratic National Committee Dinners provide a "springboard for sharpening

*James A. Farley, Democratic National
Party Chairman and Postmaster General in
the Roosevelt days, deserves more credit
than anyone else for making the $100-a-
plate dinner a reality, a success, and
an annual affair.*

the issues and commanding publicity and attention," and "they give an opportunity for people within the party to gather together, come to know each other, and to develop a closer working relationship."[8]

The late Senator Estes Kefauver stated that an important purpose of the dinners is to "activate the Democrats, to instill within them a team spirit, and to get publicity and statements of principle from the top down to the individual worker."[9]

Stephen A. Mitchell added: "I think these dinners were given, in my time, at least, for the purpose of bringing party adherents together to develop and exchange ideas and opinions, to bring cohesion among the members of the party, to give a public display of strength and vigor as well as to raise money."[10] Other people have remarked that the affairs are very important in rallying the faithful and giving them the arguments that will be used in the campaign, setting forth the fundamental opinion.

Thus, it is generally to be recognized that whipping up party enthusiasm, giving party workers arguments which they can use in their home areas, building greater party cohesion, getting publicity and attention for the current issues of the party and for the leading personalities within the party, providing a good social evening for party people from all over the United States, portraying what the party principles are and how the party is upholding these principles, shaping opinion within the party, and proclaiming the virtues and achievements of past and present Democratic leaders while condemning certain Republicans and their actions are all important reasons for holding the Jeff-serson-Jackson Day events.

I think the prime importance of these dinners is to articulate the party position at that moment in a way demonstrating its strength and willingness to stand forth and be heard and to be able to gather a group of people for that purpose. It is an articulation of party policy in a public way of far-reaching effect.[11]

STEPHEN A. MITCHELL
Former Democratic National Committee Chairman

They're important for shaping opinion within the party. They're important to the extent that they reach the public and affect its opinion either directly through radio and television or through an accounting in the mass media. They are important to individuals within the party insofar as whether they are favorably received by those in the party. Their effectiveness is controlled by their content and by the way they are delivered.[12]

SAMUEL C. BRIGHTMAN
Former Public Affairs Director,
Democratic National Committee

First, obviously they [speeches by party members to party members] serve the purpose of stimulating people's enthusiasm and interest, their feeling of cohesiveness, their loyalty to the party, and every kind of contact is good, very good. Secondly, the interchange between people is a healthy thing and tends to build a team spirit. . . . This is an opportunity to try to stimulate their [party workers'] more active participation in campaigns.[13]

ORVILLE FREEMAN
Secretary of Agriculture

Former President Harry S. Truman summed it all up when he said that the speeches help to set forth party policies and that these dinners provide the only way large amounts of money can be raised by the Democratic Party since "the Democratic Party has no economic royalists to pay their way."[14]

Thus, in addition to the legislative and administrative innovations of the New Deal era, there came innovations for raising funds for the Democratic Party. From the $50-a-plate dinner in 1936 to the $100-a-plate dinners starting in 1937 to the $1,000 President's Club fund-raising device discovered in 1962, the Democratic Party has found its major means of financing its campaigns. Political banquets and suppers are as old as political parties, but political banquets and suppers as fund-raising devices are relatively recent.

The general type of people attending these affairs can be labeled sociologically as "ingroup" in composition and "friendly" in attitude. They are usually composed of Democrats who view themselves as a group which gives favorable treatment and acceptance to its own members while denying such treatment and acceptance to members outside the group. This group of people also has values and goals in common.

By attitude of the people is meant the predisposition of the majority of the members to react in a certain way toward the speakers and their ideas at these events. Since by definition an ingroup is composed of members who look favorably upon their own members with whom they generally share values and goals, the attitude of an ingroup listening to a speaker who is a member of that ingroup will generally be friendly. This is not to say that every idea of the speakers will be agreed to and accepted by the members of the ingroup, but it does mean that the members of the ingroup (in this case, the Democratic Party) will usually feel friendly to the speakers and their ideas. If this were not so, a speaker who continually met hostile audiences in a supposedly ingroup situation would soon be classified as a member of the outgroup (such as the Republican Party).

The composition and attitude of the people attending these dinners has been very consistent. From the first Jackson Day Dinner in 1827 to the one given this year, the core of the audience has been made up of Congressmen, federal employees, state and local executives, and state legislators—with various nonofficial party contributors filling out the rest of the audience.

One of the general purposes of speakers who deliver the major addresses at these affairs is to reinforce the traditional beliefs and values of the party by repetition of the virtues of these beliefs and values. Since a high degree of identification with the audience already exists in this type of speaking, the main task of the speaker in this situation is to present variations on the common beliefs and values and to demonstrate how any proposed course of action is the most expedient (the aim of political speaking) and is in harmony with the ideology held by the party. The immediate purpose is identification or persuasion; the ultimate purpose is social cohesion.

More specifically, and in summary, the general purposes of the speaker are:

1. To articulate and reaffirm the principles, ideals, and beliefs of the ingroup, the Democratic Party, as well as to praise the party's great leaders.
2. To attack the ideas and beliefs of the outgroup, the Republican Party, in order to effect greater ingroup cohesion.
3. To enunciate the current postures of the Democratic leaders on certain current issues, often by demonstrating how their postures correspond to similar situations handled by former leaders of the party.
4. To whip up enthusiasm among the listeners for getting more interest and work out of them.
5. To seek party and popular support for the speaker's position on current issues.
6. To promote greater party cohesion or unity.

At the national Jefferson-Jackson Day Dinners or the Democratic National Committee dinners in Washington, D.C., from 1936 through 1965, the major speakers have been President Franklin D. Roosevelt, President Harry S. Truman, President John F. Kennedy, President Lyndon B. Johnson, and Speaker Sam Rayburn. Besides these principal speakers, there have been other speakers on some of the programs. A list of the speakers and their official positions is presented below in the chronological order of the dinners.

1936—FRANKLIN D. ROOSEVELT, President of the United States
 JAMES A. FARLEY, Postmaster General and Democratic National Committee Chairman, Master of Ceremonies

1937—FRANKLIN D. ROOSEVELT
 JAMES A. FARLEY
 JOSEPH P. TUMULTY, Secretary to President Wilson, presided.

1938—FRANKLIN D. ROOSEVELT
    JAMES A. FARLEY
    WILLIAM B. BANKHEAD, Speaker of the House of
        Representatives
    L. W. ROBERT, JR., Secretary of the Democratic Na-
        tional Committee, presided.

1939—FRANKLIN D. ROOSEVELT
    JAMES A. FARLEY
    WILLIAM B. BANKHEAD
    O. MAX GARDNER, former Governor of North Car-
        olina, Chairman of Jackson Day Committee, pre-
        sided.

1940—FRANKLIN D. ROOSEVELT
    JAMES A. FARLEY
    WILLIAM B. BANKHEAD
    HOMER S. CUMMINGS, former Attorney General,
        Chairman of the Jackson Day Committee
    L. W. ROBERT, JR., presided.

1941—FRANKLIN D. ROOSEVELT (delivered a speech from a
        ship off the coast of Florida. No dinner was held
        in Washington because of his absence, but many
        were held throughout the country.)

1942—FRANKLIN D. ROOSEVELT (delivered the speech from
        the White House)
    EDWARD J. FLYNN, Democratic National Committee
        Chairman, presided.
    HENRY A. WALLACE, Vice President of the United
        States
    SAM RAYBURN, Speaker of the House of Representa-
        tives
    SERGEANT ALVIN YORK, hero of World War I
    MRS. FRANKLIN D. ROOSEVELT, wife of President
        Roosevelt
    CORDELL HULL, Secretary of State

1943—FRANKLIN D. ROOSEVELT
    HENRY A. WALLACE

MAJ. GEN. ALEXANDER VANDEGRIFT, leader of forces
at Guadalcanal
SAM RAYBURN
FRANK WALKER, Postmaster General and Democratic
National Committee Chairman

1944—SAM RAYBURN
HENRY A. WALLACE
FRANK WALKER
MRS. CHARLES W. TILLETT, Assistant Chairman of
the Democratic National Committee

1945—Note: No Dinner was held because of President
Roosevelt's death on the day prior to the proposed
dinner.
Those slated to be speakers were:
FRANKLIN D. ROOSEVELT
HARRY S. TRUMAN, Vice President of the United
States
JAMES V. FORRESTAL, Secretary of the Navy
ELLIS ARNALL, Governor of Georgia
MAURICE J. TOBIN, Governor of Massachusetts
FANNIE HURST, author and playwright
MILTON BERLE, stage, screen, and radio star

1946—HARRY S. TRUMAN, President of the United States
MRS. CHARLES W. TILLETT
ROBERT E. HANNEGAN, Postmaster General and
Democratic National Committee Chairman
JOSEPH E. DAVIES, Chairman of the Jackson Day
Committee, presided.

1947—HARRY S. TRUMAN
SAM RAYBURN
GAEL SULLIVAN, Executive Director of the Demo-
cratic National Committee
MRS. CHASE WOODHOUSE, Executive Director of the
Women's Division of the Democratic National
Committee

1948—HARRY S. TRUMAN

> Note: Since the dinner was divided into two groups, one at the Statler Hotel and the other at the Mayflower Hotel, the speakers at each place will be given. *Truman spoke at both places.*
>
> *Statler:*
>
> SAM RAYBURN, Minority Leader of the House of Representatives
>
> CLINTON P. ANDERSON, Secretary of Agriculture
>
> HELEN GAHAGAN DOUGLAS, Representative from California
>
> *Mayflower:*
>
> ALBEN S. BARKLEY, Minority Leader of the Senate
>
> WILSON WYATT, Dinner Chairman
>
> MARY T. NORTON, Representative from New Jersey

1949—HARRY S. TRUMAN

> ALBEN S. BARKLEY, Vice President of the United States (spoke by radio from San Francisco)
>
> Note: Two hotels were again used.
>
> *Statler:*
>
> SCOTT W. LUCAS, Senate Minority Leader
>
> MRS. INDIA EDWARDS, Executive Director of the Women's Division of the Democratic National Committee
>
> *Mayflower:*
>
> WILSON WYATT, Dinner Chairman
>
> MRS. PERLE MESTA, Socialite and Dinner Chairman
>
> J. HOWARD McGRATH, Democratic National Committee Chairman
>
> JOHN McCORMACK, House Majority Leader
>
> MAURICE J. TOBIN· Secretary of Labor

1950—HARRY S. TRUMAN

> ALBEN S. BARKLEY
>
> SAM RAYBURN, Speaker of the House of Representatives

WILLIAM M. BOYLE, JR., Democratic National Committee Chairman

MRS. O. MAX GARDNER, Cochairman of the Jackson Day Committee

1951—HARRY S. TRUMAN
ALBEN S. BARKLEY
SAM RAYBURN
MRS. INDIA EDWARDS
WILLIAM M. BOYLE, JR.
MRS. CHARLES BRANNAN, wife of the Secretary of Agriculture
JOHN L. SULLIVAN, Cochairman of the Dinner, presided.

1952—HARRY S. TRUMAN
ALBEN S. BARKLEY
SAM RAYBURN
FRANK E. MCKINNEY, Democratic National Committee Chairman
MRS. INDIA EDWARDS
WASH B. WILLIAMS, Chairman of the Jefferson-Jackson Day Dinner

1953—Note: No dinner was given in Washington this year, although many were held throughout the country.

1954—SAM RAYBURN, Minority Leader of the House of Representatives
LYNDON B. JOHNSON, Minority Leader of the Senate
DENNIS J. ROBERTS, Governor of Rhode Island
ROSALIND WEINER, member of the Los Angeles City Council
W. JOHN KENNEDY, Chairman of the Dinner
HARRY S. TRUMAN, former President of the United States (spoke extemporaneously)

1955—SAM RAYBURN, Speaker of the House of Representatives
HARRY S. TRUMAN

ADLAI STEVENSON, former Governor of Illinois and candidate for President

MRS. ELEANOR ROOSEVELT

1956—SAM RAYBURN

ALBEN S. BARKLEY, Senator from Kentucky

JOHN L. SULLIVAN, former Secretary of the Navy, Master of Ceremonies

ROBERT MEYNER, Governor of New Jersey

JOHN S. BATTLE, Governor of Virginia

EDNA F. KELLY, Representative from New York

1957—HARRY S. TRUMAN

ADLAI STEVENSON

DEAN ACHESON, former Secretary of State, Dinner Chairman

JOHN W. MCCORMACK, House Majority Leader

G. MENNEN WILLIAMS, Governor of Michigan

RUSSELL B. LONG, Senator from Louisiana

EDITH GREEN, Representative from Oregon

1958—HARRY S. TRUMAN

ADLAI STEVENSON

SAM RAYBURN

LYNDON B. JOHNSON, Majority Leader of the Senate

PAUL BUTLER, Democratic National Committee Chairman

1959—SAM RAYBURN

DAVID KING, Representative from Utah

ELLA GRASSO, Secretary of State in Connecticut

PHILIP HART, Senator from Michigan

LYNDON B. JOHNSON

J. MILLARD TAWES, Governor of Maryland

STEPHEN MCNICHOLS, Governor of Colorado

J. WILLIAM FULBRIGHT, Senator from Arkansas

SAMUEL STRATTON, Representative from New York

GENEVIEVE BLATT, Secretary for Internal Affairs in Pennsylvania

HARRISON A. WILLIAMS, JR., Senator from New Jersey

MIKE MANSFIELD, Senate Majority Whip

J. HOWARD EDMONDSON, Governor of Oklahoma

LeROY COLLINS, Governor of Florida

1960—HARRY S. TRUMAN

John F. KENNEDY, Senator from Massachusetts

HUBERT H. HUMPHREY, Senator from Minnesota

STUART SYMINGTON, Senator from Missouri

LYNDON B. JOHNSON

ROBERT B. MEYNER

EDMUND G. BROWN, Governor of California

G. MENNEN WILLIAMS

1961—JOHN F. KENNEDY, President of the United States

MRS. GEORGE WHEELER II, Cochairman of the Dinner

MRS. MARGARET PRICE, Vice Chairman of the Democratic National Committee

MATTHEW H. McCLOSKEY, Treasurer of the Democratic National Committee

HARRY S. TRUMAN

SAM RAYBURN

JOHN M. BAILEY, Chairman of the Democratic National Committee

LYNDON B. JOHNSON, Vice President of the United States

1962—JOHN F. KENNEDY

JOHN M. BAILEY

MRS. ORVILLE FREEMAN, Cochairman of the Dinner

MRS. MARGARET PRICE

HARRY S. TRUMAN

JOHN W. McCORMACK, Speaker of the House of Representatives

1963—JOHN F. KENNEDY (spoke for three minutes at the end of the gala in the National Guard Armory)

1964—LYNDON B. JOHNSON, President of the United States (spoke for several minutes at the end of the Salute to Johnson gala in the National Guard Armory)

1965—Lyndon B. Johnson (extemporaneous remarks at the Salute to Johnson gala in the National Guard Armory)

1966—Michael J. Kirwan, Chairman of the House Democratic Campaign Committee

Hubert H. Humphrey, Vice President of the United States

John W. McCormack

Mike Mansfield

Warren G. Magnuson, Chairman of the Senate Democratic Campaign Committee

Lyndon B. Johnson

Speakers at these affairs are usually the leaders of the Democratic Party who have authority by virtue of being elected or appointed by the party, or by being elected by the people of the United States under the party banner, or by being appointed by party leaders who are selected in one of the aforementioned ways. These men and women, because of their leadership qualities and positions, usually articulate the values and beliefs of the party in such a manner as to fulfill the purposes of the dinners.

Out of Jim Farley's acorn of Jefferson-Jackson Day Dinners has risen a forest of many trees which periodically shed their leaves of speeches and public pronouncements as a by-product for the fertilization and promotion of the party's growth. ★

Chapter 3

INCREDIBLE
VICTORY

THE MODERN-DAY Jefferson-Jackson Day celebration, resurrected as an annual affair in 1936 and continuing to the present, has a long and glorious history which can be directly traced to the dinners and celebrations held in honor of Andrew Jackson and his great victory over the British at New Orleans on January 8, 1815. On January 8, 1965, the United States celebrated the 150th anniversary of this famous battle.

It was in the waning months of 1814 that the British in the War of 1812 sought the conquest of the valley of the Mississippi because they believed that this area did not have strong ties with the Union. What a fatal mistake for the British!

The British Army of almost 10,000 men, under the leadership of the Duke of Wellington's brother-in-law, Sir Edward Pakenham, was selected from the veteran troops which had fought Napoleon's armies on the Spanish peninsula. They were dispatched to New Orleans for the purpose of gaining control of the western sections of the United States.

Major General Andrew Jackson, also a veteran fighter, found New Orleans almost defenseless when he arrived there on December 1, 1814. While the civilians prepared for the attack, Jackson sent urgent messages for reinforcements from Kentucky and Tennessee. With the help of his good friends and fellow fighters, Major General William Carroll and Brigadier General John Coffee, he was finally able to gather an army of 5,000. Most of his men were untrained volunteers and backwoodsmen who had not had very much military experience, but they did know how to handle guns.

In addition to Jackson's conglomeration of troops, he had the support of Jean Lafitte, a pirate captain who had offered his services. Pirates and backwoodsmen alike built fortifications of cotton bales in preparation for Pakenham's anticipated attack.

On January 8, 1815, the British made their historic attack on the city of New Orleans. The expert marksmanship of the pirates and frontiersmen was exhibited in the final results of the battle. The well-trained, disciplined British troops lost their commander and over 2,000 men in less than 20 minutes at the Battle of New Orleans. General Jackson lost only 13 men.

Ironically, had modern means of communication existed at that time, the Battle of New Orleans would never have taken place. The Treaty of Ghent, ending the War of 1812, had been signed on December 24, 1814, the very evening before Pakenham arrived off New Orleans. Since there were no cables or radios at that time, the news had to come by sailing ship and did not reach this country until February 14, 1815.

The Battle of New Orleans came at a time when fortune did not seem to be smiling on the United States. The Federalists referred to the war as "Mr. Madison's War" and condemned the acquisition of Louisiana, fought the Embargo and Nonintercourse Acts, and called a convention at Hartford, Connecticut, on December 15, 1814, to adopt resolutions which had the ring of secession in them and embodied their feelings about the war. When the ambassadors of the convention reached Baltimore on their way to complain to the government, they were met by the news of Jackson's victory at New Orleans. On the morning after their arrival in Washington on February 14, they learned of the Treaty of Ghent. With such events occurring, the ambassadors could do nothing but return home, completely dejected and destroyed. The Federalists had made the mistake of obstructing the war as a party measure when the nation itself was fighting for its very existence. The Hartford Convention, looked upon as unpatriotic and seditious, sounded the final death knell of the Federalist Party in the United States.

Major General Andrew Jackson wrote a letter to Secretary of War James Monroe, telling the particulars of the

victory. The heading on the letter was "Camp, 4 miles below Orleans, 9th January, 1815." It reads:

During the days of the 6th and 7th the enemy had been actively
employed in making preparations for an attack on my lines. With
infinite labor they had succeeded on the night of the 7th in getting
their boats across the lake to the river, by widening and deepening
the canal on which they had effected their disembarkation. It had
not been in my power to impede these operations by a general attack: added to other reasons, the nature of the troops under my
command, mostly militia, rendered it too hazardous to attempt ex-
tensive offensive movements in open country, against a numerous
and well disciplined army altho' my forces, as to number, had been
increased by the arrival of the Kentucky division, my strength had
received very little addition; a small portion only of that detachment being provided with arms. Compelled thus to await the attack
of the enemy, I took every measure to repel it when it should be
made, and to defeat the object he had in view. General Morgan
with the Orleans contingent, the Louisiana militia and a strong
detachment of Kentucky troops, occupied an entrenched camp on
the opposite side of the river, protected by strong batteries on the
bank, erected and superintended by Commodore Patterson.

In my encampment everything was ready for action, when
early in the morning of the 8th, the enemy after throwing a
heavy shower of bombs and congreve rockets, advanced their columns on my right and left, to storm my entrenchments. I cannot
speak sufficiently in praise of the firmness and deliberation with
which my whole line received their approach. . . . More could not
have been expected from veterans inured to war. For an hour, the
fire of the small arms was as incessant and severe as can be imagined.
The artillery, too, directed by officers who displayed equal skill and
courage, did great execution, yet the columns of the enemy continued to advance with a firmness which reflects upon them the greatest credit. Twice the column which approached me on my left was
repulsed by the troops of General Carroll, those of General Coffee,
and a division of the Kentucky militia, and twice they formed again
and renewed the assault. At length however, cut to pieces, they fled
in confusion from the field leaving it covered with their dead and
wounded. The loss which the enemy sustained on this occasion cannot be estimated at less than 1,500 in killed, wounded, and prisoners. Upwards of 300 have already been delivered for burial and my
men are still engaged in picking them up within my lines and carrying them to the point where the enemy are to receive them. This
is in addition to the dead and wounded whom the enemy have
been unable to carry from the field, during and since the action,
and to those who have since died from the wounds they received.

We have taken about 500 prisoners, upwards of 300 of whom are wounded, and a great part of them mortally. My loss has not exceeded, and I believe has not amounted to ten killed and as many wounded. The entire destruction of the enemy's army was now inevitable had it not been for an unfortunate occurrence which at this moment took place on the other side of the river. Simultaneously with this advance upon my lines, he had thrown over in his boats a considerable number to the other side of the river. These, having landed, were hardly enough to advance against the works of General Morgan; and, what is strange and difficult to account for, at the moment when their entire discomfiture was looked for with an assurance approaching certainty, the Kentucky reinforcements, in whom so much reliance had been placed, ingloriously fled, drawing after them, by their example, the remainder of the forces; and thus yielding to the enemy that most fortunate position. The batteries which had rendered me, for many days, the most important service tho' bravely defended, were of course now abandoned; not however until the guns had been spiked.

This unfortunate route [*sic*] had totally changed the aspect of affairs. The enemy now occupied a position from which they might annoy us without hazard, and by means of which they might have been unable to defeat in a great measure, the effects of this side of the river. It became therefore an object of the first consequence to dislodge him as soon as possible. For this object, all the means in my power, which I could with any safety use, were immediately put in preparation. However, it was owing somewhat to another cause that I succeeded even beyond my expectations. In negotiating a temporary suspension of hostilities to enable the enemy to bury their dead and provide for their wounded, I have required certain propositions to be acceded to as a basis; among which this was one . . . that although hostilities should cease from this side of the river until twelve o'clock of this day, yet it was not to be understood that they should cease on the other side; but that no reinforcements would be sent across by either army until the expiration of that day. His Excellency, Major General Lambert begged time to consider of those propositions until ten o'clock of today, and in the meantime recrossed his troops. I need not tell you with how much eagerness I immediately regained possession of the position he had just hastily quitted.

The enemy having concentrated his forces, may again attempt to drive me from my position by storm. Whenever he does, I have no doubt my men will act with their usual firmness, and sustain a character now becoming dear to them.

I have the honor to be, with great respect, your obedient servant,

ANDREW JACKSON
Major General, Commanding[2]

*The Battle of New Orleans as depicted in
an engraving by T. Phillibrown after a
painting by D. M. Carter. The subject was
a popular one for printmakers and
engravers of the period.*

The February 6, 1815, issue of the *Daily National Intelligencer,* heralded the victory:

ALMOST INCREDIBLE VICTORY!

FROM NEW-ORLEANS

Dates up to the 13th January —the enemy, attacking our entrenched army on the 8th, beaten and repulsed by Jackson and his brave associates, with great slaughter.

In this same edition of the *Intelligencer,* there was a description of the first celebration of what was to become Jackson Day, the predecessor to the Democratic National Committee Dinners. In a proclamation by Mayor James H. Blake of Washington, D.C., the celebration was to be a general illumination in the city on Saturday, February 4, 1815, when confirmation of the New Orleans battle was made. The houses were illuminated from 7 o'clock in the evening until 10 o'clock at night, and the police were enjoined to be "vigilant in preserving order and preventing mischief."

After receiving notice of the signing of the peace treaty ending the War of 1812, Major General Andrew Jackson sent the following letter to the Secretary of War, dated New Orleans, March 16, 1815, and written at "Headquarters, 7th Military District."

I have the honor to acknowledge the receipt of your letter of the 16th of ulto. advising me of the ratification of the treaty of peace between Great Britain and the United States.

In conformity with your directions I have forwarded to the officer commanding His Brittanic Majesty's Forces in this quarter information of that event.

The Tennessee and Kentucky militia will be immediately marched to their respective states and discharged, without receiving pay beforehand. The Louisiana and Mississippi militia will be discharged and receive their payment here. It is hoped that the necessary funds will be provided for the payment of the former in suitable time.

As soon as I get the troops mustered out of service here, it is my intention to remove my headquarters to Nashville; at which place I shall expect to receive the orders of my government. Major General Gaines will be left in the immediate command of this section of the district; and I am happy to commit it to one in whom the government has such high and deserved confidence.

I have the honor to be, sir, your obedient servant,

ANDREW JACKSON
Major General, Commanding[3]

In the years immediately following the victory at New Orleans, the usual type of celebration of the Eighth of January consisted of military balls, parties, parades, and sounding of cannon. The day was celebrated by the whole country, much as the Fourth of July is celebrated today.

IN 1816, on the first anniversary of the Battle of New Orleans, there was no celebration of Jackson Day reported in Washington. However, an "elegant supper" was held at the Bank Coffee House, "prepared in Mr. Niblo's best style,"[4] in New York City. ★

1816

A MILITARY BALL, given at the Marine barracks, was the mode of celebration on January 8, 1817, in Washington, D.C. The Ball was attended by a "large party of citizens, resident members of the government, members of Congress, foreign ministers, and visitors of the city."[5] ★

1817

FROM 1818 through 1822, no celebrations were reported in the newspapers although it might properly be assumed that balls, fireworks, and parades were held in each of these years since these were contemporary means for celebrating Jackson Day. ★

*1818-
1822*

1823-1824

PUBLIC and private balls were held in 1823 and 1824 in commemoration of the Eighth of January at the Washington Assembly Hall and also in Baltimore. On January 8, 1824, at General Andrew Jackson's Washington Home, Colonel Charles F. Mercer of the House of Representatives presented Jackson the pistols carried by General George Washington, stating that he was giving Washington's pistols to the successor of Washington "in the military character of America."

Newspaper reports in 1824 stated:

> From the manner in which the Eighth of January has been commemorated this year, it seems not likely to be soon forgotten. In this city, paradoxically, the "lady of the Secretary of State" [who at this time was Mrs. John Quincy Adams] gave "perhaps one of the most numerously attended private parties ever given in this city."[6]

Later in this year of 1824 John Quincy Adams ran against Andrew Jackson for the Presidency!

On January 8, 1824, a dinner was held at Annapolis celebrating the commemoration of the Battle of New Orleans, and there was a public ball in Baltimore. In Louisville, Kentucky, on the same day, a dinner was held. Major General Winfield Scott, on the occasion of his assuming the command of the western military department, gave the toast: "The Eighth of January . . . the second day in the calendar of the Republic."[7]

An immense ball was held in New York on the Eighth of January in 1824 for the purpose of raising funds to aid the Greeks. This is the first indication of a celebration of Jackson Day for the purpose of raising funds. The description of the affair in the *Daily National Intelligencer* of January 31, 1824, illustrates the importance of the event:

> Some objections were, at first, made of holding it in the theater; but as it was made to appear that it would accommodate more persons, and would, of course, increase the anticipated fund for the aid of the Greeks, and be susceptible of being got up in greater style, it was eventually agreed to; and the result actually surpassed all expectations. It was the admiration and delight of all who at-

tended it. Some of our papers have given a partial account of some of the decorations but the view of it alone could give a sufficient idea of the beauty and splendor of the whole scene. It was actually realizing the magic palaces which we read of, as razed by enchantment. There must have been upwards of 2,000 persons present, composed of all [respectable] classes of citizens; for the whole of the boxes were filled, the lobbies crowded with promenaders, and the floor, which extended from the front boxes to the end of the stage, occupied with 24 cotillions, and the lookers-on. Nothing occurred to disturb the pleasure of the scene; and the most perfect decorum having been observed on the floor, and throughout the house. Regulations for this purpose, extended even to the outside of the house, among the hackney carriages; which instead of creating that tumult and vociferation, common to all public entertainments, they were obliged to draw up as quietly and orderly as the platoons of a regiment. In short, the whole was conducted as we could have wished. ★

No specific celebrations were cited in Washington newspapers during 1825 and 1826, although mention was made of many celebrations taking place. ★

1825-1826

THE DAY was ushered in by a federal salute of 24 guns at sunrise which was repeated at noon. The year 1827 marked the first *public* dinner held in commemoration of the Battle of New Orleans.[8] It was held at Mr. Williamson's Hotel for a subscription price of $5.00. "The company consisted of citizens, members of Congress, gentlemen from the country together with Mr. Calhoun, the Vice President, and General John Coffee of Tennessee . . . the two latter as invited guests."[9] The report went on:

1827

> We can safely say, that in point of number and individual respectability we have never known anything of the kind in this country superior to it upon any similar occasion. The President of the United States, and the venerable Charles Carroll (of Carrollton) of Baltimore, the sole survivor of the signers of the Declaration of Independence, were also invited as guests, but both declined the invitation. The latter because of his age and infirmities, and the severity of the season.

Further evidence substantiating this 1827 dinner as the first of its kind is given in a letter from Sam Houston to Andrew Jackson:

> . . . before this letter reaches you, you will have seen an account of a dinner given here on the "eighth of January." The account given in the "Telegraph" is correct, but you cannot conceive the happy effect of our friend Judge White's speech and toast on that occasion. It was beyond all doubt the happiest effort of kind that I have ever witnessed. Its effect too, will be happy in the extreme, elsewhere.
>
> You will perceive that in all parts of the country, it was a day of joy, and rejoicing. It will increase every year, in a ratio not hitherto known in the country. New York has been where she ought to be, on the occasion, and I have no doubt but what she will be at her post on the presidential election.[10]

Judge Hugh White, to whom Houston refers, was a Tennessean and a close friend of Jackson. He was the only speaker at the dinner, although there were 25 regular toasts offered as well as 45 volunteer toasts. Rather than have several speakers formally addressing the group, as is the case today, most of the dinners throughout the 1800's featured regular and volunteer toasts. Occasionally, some of the toasts would become speeches, or some of the speakers would be appointed. Political speeches today seem long, but the speakers and toasters of the 19th century spent from five hours, as at this 1827 dinner, to as many as eight hours extolling the virtues and accomplishments of the Democratic Party and its various members.

In addition to the supper, a celebration ball was held by Lewis Carusi at his saloon. Even women were not omitted from such celebrations. For example, the *Daily National Intelligencer* reported that "Ladies, in the habit of attending these parties, who have not received cards of invitation, may obtain them on application."[11]

The *Boston Statesman* reported that the anniversary of the Battle of New Orleans was celebrated in several counties of Massachusetts by public dinners, military parades, and balls.   ★

THE *Daily National Intelligencer* reported that General
Jackson was at the battleground of New Orleans for the
Jackson Day celebration in 1828 at the invitation of the
Louisiana Legislature. He was to arrive in a steamboat
attended by nearly twenty other steamboats. Governor Sam
Houston of Tennessee and several other friends of Jackson
accompanied him on his visit to New Orleans.

      1828

On Tuesday, January 8, 1828, the second Jackson Day
Dinner was held at Mr. Williamson's Hotel in Washington.
With the 1828 election in prospect, when Jackson was to
oppose John Quincy Adams for the Presidency, tensions
and opposing camps were developing within the Democratic
Party. The *Daily National Intelligencer,* official organ of
the Adams Administration, printed the following article the
day after the 1828 Jackson Day Dinner:

> Yesterday, being the anniversary obtained at New Orleans by
> American arms in the year 1815, was celebrated by a portion of our
> citizens here, with a Public Dinner, and with salutes of artillery.
> Though the day is one which should not properly carry with it any
> party feeling, the celebration of it here, on this occasion, derived
> that character from the fact that no notice was given through the
> ordinary and established vehicles of information to the city. We
> hope that those of our fellow citizens, and Congressional Friends,
> who joined in the exclusive celebration of the day, enjoyed the
> good things set before them by Mr. Williamson, who we believe,
> provided the dinner; and we shall with pleasure publish all their
> proceedings as soon as we are furnished with a copy of them.[12]

In answer to the *Intelligencer* charge that the dinner
was a partisan affair, the *United States Telegraph* made this
statement:

> The *Intelligencer* reproaches those concerned in the celebration
> of yesterday, with giving it a party character! And why should they
> not give it such character. If ever parties in this country were clearly
> and distinctly divided, they are on the subject of General Jackson's
> merits. His friends who celebrated the memorable anniversary of
> that day when he saved the western country, maintained that he is
> not only fitted to defend the nation in war, but to fill its most im-
> portant office in peace. His opponents not only deny him all civil

qualifications, but have even endeavored to rob him of all claim to the merit of having achieved the victory at New Orleans. Among the latter are the editors of the *Intelligencer*. Why then should they object to party character of a celebration attended exclusively by those to whose cause and principles they are hostile. If they and their coadjutors were disposed to render the celebration general, they might have attended it.[13]

One of the highlights of the 1828 Jackson Day supper celebration was a poem read by Representative Gulian Verplanck of New York:

Ode for the Eighth of January from the New York Committee

Not for a realm or throne bowed to receive the chain;
We raise a song of victory . . . a loud exalting strain;

But for a city saved, . . . its streets from slaughter free;
And those who rush to smite its sons, driven back into the sea:

Backward, with blood and death, driven from the rescued
   strand:
On that proud day whose memory gilds the records of our land.

Pure drops from woman's eye, and grateful tears of age,
And those of childhood's tender lids, shall consecrate the page.

Then drink to those who won that meed of deathless fame,
And let our festive halls this day re-echo Jackson's name.[14]

In addition to the poetry reading, there were speeches by Mr. Edward Livingston of Louisiana, Mr. John Weems, the representative of Baltimore, Senator Robert Hayne of South Carolina, and Mr. John Bell of Tennessee. Actually the speeches were extended toasts. Most of those influential in politics in Washington favored Andrew Jackson for President. Such men as Hayne, Polk, Calhoun, Van Buren, Desha, Eaton, Benton, and Bell were among the many Congressional leaders present.

The toasts given were mainly paeans heaped upon the leader of the party, specifically, Andrew Jackson. However, a closer analysis of the toasts reveals the *dramatis personae* whose expressed thoughts reflected the issues of the era and the opposing positions which would develop in the pre-

Civil War period. For example, the toast given by John C. Calhoun, Vice President of the United States under John Quincy Adams at this time, was: "The general government . . . created to advance the interest of the whole, it may last forever, by defining its action to its appropriate sphere, and diffusing its benefits equally to all of the parts."[15]

Of course Calhoun believed that the government's appropriate sphere was of a decentralized nature which should not encompass or encroach upon the area of states' rights. Substantiating and opposing views were expressed in the form of other toasts, which numbered 75 in all!

Though the public dinners celebrating the Battle of New Orleans started as nonpartisan events, they were now becoming characterized as political ceremonies. As early as this second public dinner in 1828, complaints were registered about the political character of the occasion. From the following report of the anti-Jackson newspaper in Washington, D.C., on the Jackson Day supper given in 1828, the bitterness of the coming campaign between John Quincy Adams and Andrew Jackson for the Presidency can be felt:

The Jackson paper of this city has furnished us with the records of the ebullitions of fancy which were exhibited in this city on the Eighth of January; and now that they have become public property, they are fit subjects for public commentary. Our readers are aware that it is customary on these public days to include in the regular toasts, the President of the United States. It is a tribute of respect to the office of President, and is usual among all parties, no matter by whom the chair is filled. Whoever sits there is by the Constitution our first citizen . . . whoever sits there is by courtesy and custom entitled to be remembered in the hour when festive feeling has, or ought to have laid political differences to rest. On this occasion, we understand this testimony was deliberately and advisedly omitted. At a previous meeting of the committee to regulate the said toasts, the President was suggested as one by a liberal friend of Jackson . . . for there are liberal men among his friends. . . . On a division it appeared that six were in favor of it, and five against it; it was then decided in the negative by the vote of General Van Ness, the president. We notice this to show the spirit of the party by whom this dinner was got up; for had it originated in any other than party feeling, had the celebration been national in its character, there would have been found as many friends of the administration to have joined in it, as there were friends of Jackson actually present. It may be well to contrast this exclusive, proscriptive spirit, with the liberality displayed by the Administration members of the House of Representatives, in the debate on the proposition of Mr. Hamilton to cause a picture of the Battle of New Orleans to be made and placed in the Rotunda in the Capitol. Let it be received as characteristic of the two parties, while General Van Ness and his coadjutors were refusing to toast the President of the United States, Messrs. Everett, Storrs, Stewart, Gurley, and all the friends of the Administration, were rendering their separate testimony to the merits of General Jackson. Let it be recollected that while intolerance is the motto and watchword of one party, a liberal gratitude qualifies the hostility of the other.

. . . the public will perceive that some of these toasts are of a bullying character. Such indirect ungentlemanly attacks always record upon those who make them, and are unworthy of the notice of any highminded and honorable man. There is but one course for gentlemen to pursue, who consider themselves aggressed by another. What that course is, no honorable man will ask. It certainly does not consist in low insinuations contained in "toasts" given under the influence of wine. We are pleased to think that the friends of General Jackson commonly are too highminded to approve of such a course. We are certain the friends of the Administration are not to be intimidated or bullied by this favorite plan of some of the friends of the "military chieftan." Highminded honorable men will never stoop to notice the low insinuations contained in a toast, or in a grog shop speech, nor will such men condescend to adopt that course of action. All who are acquainted with those against whom these toasts are directed, know full well that if the conduct ordinarily pursued by men of honor who consider themselves aggrieved, had been followed, every satisfactory explanation would have been given if called for, or "honorable amends" accorded. A contrary conduct is calculated to excite contempt, to be placed among the bickerings of the day is unworthy of the notice of any gentleman, who feels that he is such. The most certain way for men who wish to "vapour," and who fear the consequences is to shield themselves from notice by adopting a conduct at war with every high and gentlemanly feeling.

The American people will not fail to observe this course and to draw their conclusions from it. For if, now, every independent man who chooses to be opposed to General Jackson's elevation to the Presidency is to receive the drunken insults of some of his friends, what may be expected if General Jackson should be elected. The answer is direct . . . not only will every man be obliged to maintain his sentiments by a pair of pistols, but he will be obliged to go armed to defend himself from the attacks of bullies who will surround him. We are far from applying this observation to the friends of General Jackson generally, for we know that he has many friends of too high character and honor to approve of such a course . . . but they cannot restrain such men as have no merit of their own, and who, being destitute of both merit, and talents to entitle them to favor, will aim to obtain it by adopting the contemptible character of bullies and desperados.[16]

From this report of the 1828 Jackson Day celebration, it is readily observable that the Jackson Day celebrations were no longer nonpartisan events. The *United States Telegraph,* friendly to General Jackson, answered some of these charges:

> Last year, the citizens who celebrated the day, were desirous to give to the proceedings a national character . . . appointed some of Mr. Adams' political friends on the committee of arrangements . . . sent him a polite letter of invitation and waited upon the heads of departments with a subscription paper. Mr. Adams refused to accept the invitation, and Mr. Clay rudely refused, and the other members of the Cabinet declined to subscribe.
>
> How Mr. Adams could, under such circumstances, expect to be invited by a committee constituted by the friends of General Jackson, is not for us to explain.
>
> Why did Mr. Adams and his friends not celebrate the Eighth? Is there anything in the character of the times which brings to his mind on that day, other sensations than he felt on the Eighth of January, 1823?
>
> If so, what is it? Has Mr. Adams, or his friends discovered that they were mistaken in the character and quality of service he had rendered to his country by General Jackson on that day? If so, it is for Mr. Adams and his "established organs of communication" to explain to the public.
>
> But why did not the officers of the Army and Navy attend the celebration on the Eighth? Many of them are known to prefer the election of General Jackson. They cannot agree with Mr. Clay, that the elevation of a Military Chieftain would endanger the liberties of the people. Is not the answer to be found in the fact, that Mr. Adams, who can attend an Ebene dinner, in Baltimore, can drink an Ebene toast to his liege vassals, then refuse to celebrate the anniversary of the victory at New Orleans.
>
> Is not the fact, that many of the officers of the Army and Navy,

whose "hearts were with us," were restrained from attending a celebration, one of the most powerful comments on the character of Mr. Adams.

Then why is this? May we never again be cursed with an Administration towards whom it is an unpardonable offense to rejoice at our victories, and to court popular fame, impute drunkenness to our Army and piracy to our Navy.[17]

In the continuing battles between the Jackson and Adams newspapers in Washington, implications and insinuations were made that Henry Clay and Andrew Jackson have a duel. All of this was an outgrowth of the toasts at the Jackson Day celebration in 1828. After such "goings-on," there was little doubt that thereafter the Jackson Day celebrations would take on a more partisan attitude than ever before.

After the election of Jackson, conflicting newspaper interpretations continued between the *Daily National Intelligencer* and the *Globe,* Jackson's official newspaper, run by men hand-picked by Jackson himself. Jackson persuaded Francis P. Blair, a farmer, banker, and newspaper writer in Frankfort, Kentucky, to come to Washington in 1829 to establish a paper in the interest of the Administration. John C. Rives, a government worker, resigned to form a partnership with Blair and to establish the *Globe,* which received all the government printing jobs.[18]   ★

1829

IN 1829, the *Daily National Intelligencer* again reported on the Jackson Day celebrations of that year:

> We hear also that there was a public dinner given at Gadsby's Hotel, which from no general notice given of it, we suppose to have been exclusively limited to the supporters of General Jackson for the Presidency.[19]

Further opposition to the partisan nature the January the Eighth celebrations were taking was announced by the *Daily National Intelligencer:*

> It has been seen with regret, that too great a disposition has been evinced, by mere party people, to make it an exclusively party

concern; as if none had a right to celebrate a national anniversary but those who have just floated into a temporary eminence upon the tide of a majority which the most noisy among them deceive themselves in supposing they led, instead of following, as they have done, on the flood of it.[20]

The 1829 public dinner was held at the National Hotel with Vice President John C. Calhoun, Speaker Andrew Stevenson, and Senator Richard M. Johnson of Kentucky as invited guests. At least 85 toasts were given. Throughout the 19th century, toasts were the means of exhortation and dehortation. Toward the end of the century, toasts were gradually supplanted by impromptu and informal addresses.

As preparations were being made for festivity and mirth on January the Eighth, 1829, news reached Washington that Mrs. Rachel Jackson, wife of General Andrew Jackson, President-elect of the United States, had died on December 22 at the Hermitage. Jackson was still in the midst of making arrangements to leave his home in Tennessee to assume his responsibilities and duties as President of the nation.

But the anniversary of the Eighth of January was still celebrated throughout the United States by public dinners and other affairs.

Once again, the *Daily National Intelligencer* assailed the toasts and speeches made at the Jackson Day affair in Washington, D.C.

. . . as for the toasts, it appears to us that for every one having application to the ostensible occasion of the meeting, there were, at most of the meetings, ten of furious hate against their fellow men, or bitter denunciation of men every way as honest as themselves. This remark will be permitted to us, who are known ever to have set our face against political vindictiveness, and persecution for opinion's sake.[21]

From Andrew Jackson's incredible victory at the Battle of New Orleans on January 8, 1815, to his incredible victory in 1828 when he was elected President of the United States, Jackson Day celebrations had grown remarkably throughout the United States. Present-day Jefferson-Jackson Day celebrations had their origin in these early events. ★

Chapter 4

"OUR FEDERAL UNION: IT MUST BE PRESERVED"

A JACKSON DAY DINNER and a January the Eighth Ball were held in Washington in 1830, but probably the most memorable Jefferson-Jackson Day Dinner in the long history of such affairs was the first Jefferson Day Dinner, given at the Indian Queen Hotel in Washington, D.C., on April 13, 1830, in commemoration of the birthday of Thomas Jefferson.

This dinner, held only three years after the first of such national Jackson Day Dinners, epitomized the political dimension and the political importance of toasts and speeches given before the partisan party members. Matters of contemporary political significance became the order of the day. A newspaper reported those present:

> The President, Vice President, Secretaries of State, War, Treasury, Navy, and Postmaster General and more than 100 Republican members of the two houses of Congress, together with most of the distinguished officers of the government, visitors in the city, and citizens of the District, and neighboring cities.[1]

There were 24 regular toasts and many volunteer toasts. The character of the dinner was highlighted by the headline of the April 19, 1830, *Daily National Intelligencer* —A POLITICAL DINNER. The story read:

> The regular toasts, which, as well as the speeches, seem to have been carefully prepared, were of a strong anti-tariff, and rather of an anti-Federal complexion; so much so, indeed, that it is understood that after seeing them, all the Pennsylvania members who intended to have been present at the dinner, seceded and withdrew from it.[2]

After the regular toasts and speeches were completed, President Andrew Jackson gave the following famous toast, one of the most classic lines in the history of our nation: "Our federal union: it must be preserved."[3]

For more than two weeks, a running battle was fought between the *Daily National Intelligencer* and the *United States Telegraph* over the true meaning and political significance of President Jackson's toast. The rivalry between these newspapers of different political views substantiates the generalization that the toasts and speeches given at these dinners became less a celebration of an historical event and more a ceremonial of political importance.

The editors of the *Daily National Intelligencer* said of Jackson's toast:

> We copy the toast as we find it. The sentiment which it conveys is one which it would be very unnatural for the President of the United States not to entertain: but there is something emphatic in it, under the circumstances which preceded and attended it. It was as much as to say, in reply to the authors of some of the preceding sentiments, "you may complain of the tariff, and perhaps with reason; but so long as it is the law, it shall as certainly be maintained as that my name is Andrew Jackson."[4]

The Union, or at least their interpretation of its relative importance, indeed seems to have been the uppermost thought in the minds of most of the guests, as will be seen by the following toasts of the Vice President and heads of departments, which followed in succession that of the President:

By the Vice President of the United States, John C. Calhoun:

> Next to our liberty, the most dear; may we all remember, that it can only be preserved by respecting the rights of the states, and distributing equally the benefit and burden of the union.[5]

By Martin Van Buren, Secretary of State:

> Mutual forbearance and reciprocal concession: through their agency the union was established. The patriotic spirit from which they emanated will forever sustain it.[6]

This drawing in black chalk on paper of Thomas Jefferson was by Charles Fevret de Saint-Memin, a French artist who worked in America in the late 18th and early 19th centuries. (Courtesy of Worcester Art Museum)

Similar toasts were given by others and illustrate the changing nature of the toasts and addresses at these dinners. To a certain degree, attempts were made to tie in the commemoration of Jackson or Jefferson with the "message of the day."

The *United States Telegraph* answered the *Intelligencer* by denying that the 1830 dinner was "political." The editors of the *Intelligencer* countered:

> . . . the dinner of the 13th instant was a "political dinner"; or it was a dinner of no character at all. It was not in the memory of the merits of Mr. Jefferson: that the object was expressly disclaimed. It was not a mere merrymaking, for nothing could be less akin to gaiety than either the toasts or the speeches on the occasion. From the egg to the apples, the whole entertainment savored of politics, and strongly marked politics, too. A particular effect was obviously intended.[7]

Furthermore, the editors of the *Telegraph,* supposedly the "official" organ of the Jackson Administration at this time, remarked that Jackson's toast meant that the policy of the country, whatever it may be, must yield to partial discontent as a means of preserving the Union.

In rebuttal, the *Intelligencer* came out with the statement that a modification of the tariff was judicious but "its modification must not be assented to upon the entire Republican principle that the minority have a right to control the majority, which strange doctrine seems to be coming into vogue, and was plainly hinted at, if not distinctly recognized, in the regular toasts at the late dinner; nor yet from the dread of nullifying state laws, under a version of the doctrine of states' rights which Thomas Jefferson never dreamt of."[8]

Another version of Jackson's toast was enunciated by the *Telegraph* on April 23, 1830, pointing out that the toast was an echo of a sentiment expressed by Senator George Bibb of Kentucky in his speech occurring before the President's toast. Again, the *Intelligencer* would not accept such an origin and interpretation of Jackson's toast.

James Parton, in his *Life of Andrew Jackson,* remarked on the origin of the famous toast:

It was supposed, at the time, that the toast offered by the President was impromptu. On the contrary, the toast was prepared with singular deliberation, and was designed to produce the precise effect that it did produce. Major Lewis favors the reader with the following interesting reminiscence: "This celebrated toast, 'The federal union: it must be preserved,' was a cool deliberate act. The *United States Telegraph,* General Duff Green's paper, published a programme of the proceedings for the celebration the day before, to which the General's attention had been drawn by a friend, with the suggestion that he had better read it. This he did in the course of the evening, and came to the conclusion that the celebration was to be a nullification affair altogether. With this impression on his mind, he prepared early the next morning (the day of the celebration) three toasts which he brought with him when he came into his office, where he found Major Donelson and myself reading the morning papers. After taking his seat he handed them to me and asked me to read them and then handed him the one I like best. He handed them to Major Donelson also with the same request, who, on reading them, agreed with me. He said he preferred that one himself for the reason that it was shorter and more expressive. He then put that one into his pocket and threw the others into the fire. That is the true story of the toast the General gave on the Jefferson Birthday celebration in 1830, which fell among the nullifiers like an exploded bomb!"[9]

Since the Jefferson Day Dinner of 1830, there has been very little doubt about the "political" nature of the affair and the use of the occasion for espousing contemporary postures on the problems of the day. The toasts at this dinner savored of nullification and spread the feeling that the dinner was originated to inaugurate the doctrine of nullification with Mr. Jefferson as its father. However, Jackson's toast very aptly summarized his feelings on the situation. The dinner revealed to the public mind the presence of an actual design tending to dissolve the Union with Mr. Calhoun as its apostle.

This dinner came a few months after the famous Webster-Hayne debate on the floor of the Senate. For Jackson and Webster, the Union was superior to the states and was

Andrew Jackson, Daniel Webster, and Henry Clay, three of the most powerful men in government of their era, as they appeared at the time of the famous 1830 Jefferson Day Dinner.

the only guarantee of liberty; whereas Calhoun and Hayne, although loving the Union, felt that the states' liberties should not be jeopardized.

Senator Isaac Hill of New Hampshire remarked that "a proclamation of martial law in South Carolina and an order to arrest Calhoun where he sat could not have come with more blinding, staggering force" than the toast which President Jackson offered at this 1830 dinner.

President Andrew Jackson had given warning to those who would divide the nation and defy the Constitution. He later stated: "I will meet treason at the threshold."　★

Chapter 5

IN THE DAYS OF JACKSON

DURING the three years from 1831 through 1833, the Jackson Day celebrations consisted of balls. A small party celebrated the occasion in 1831 with a dinner, but Jackson was not present; and there was no report of a supper being held in 1832.

A ball and a supper were given in 1833, although no detailed account can be found. ★

1831-1833

THE ANNIVERSARY of the victory of New Orleans was celebrated in Washington in 1834 by a public dinner, given by the "Democratic Citizens of Washington," at the Masonic Hall where Mr. Joseph Letourno served the dinner. The price of each ticket to this dinner was $2.50.

1834

> The utmost harmony and union prevailed on the occasion. There were no neutral politicians, no nullifiers, no apostate Jacksonians, no false friends, nor any equivocal Democrats present. It was a scene of unanimity and harmonious social intercourse, worthy of the occasion, and the illustrious hero and patriot who had created it.[1]

There were 13 regular toasts and at least 62 volunteer toasts. President Jackson did not attend the dinner. ★

JACKSON DAY, 1835, was most enthusiastically celebrated with a twofold purpose—celebration of the extinguishment of the national debt and celebration of the twentieth anniversary of the victory of New Orleans. "The Vice President and the Democratic members of the Senate . . . the Speaker of the House and the Representatives of that body . . . and all the members of the President's Cabinet were present. There were, besides, a great number of citizens from various quarters of the Union, who joined in the festivities."[2]

Although the extinguishment of the national debt

1835

could have been a celebration for all the people, it was made a highly partisan Republican affair. The *Globe* headline on January 14, 1835, labeled the affair "A Republican Celebration." The newspaper battle between the *Telegraph* and the *Intelligencer* over the partisan celebrations of the victory of New Orleans shifted to a running controversy between the *Globe* and the *Intelligencer* when the *Globe* became the "official" paper of the Jackson Administration. The editors of the *Intelligencer* commented on the Jackson Day celebration of 1835:

> The intention to hold such a festival was confined to that class of politicians [friends of the Administration]. No intimation of the purpose of holding such a festival was given in any journal but the *Globe*; no invitation was extended to any but to friends of the Administration; nor was it expected, we presume (unless among the invited guests there might accidentally be such), that there should be any general attendance of persons not belonging to the party of the Administration. If there were among the company an exception or two, the fact only confirms the view of the case.[3]

This example simply illustrates once more the partisan nature which Jackson Day Dinners took and have taken ever since. In 1940, when several top Republican leaders were invited by President Roosevelt to attend the Jackson Day Banquet, all declined the invitation with remarks to the effect that such affairs were purely partisan and were fund-raising devices for the Democratic Party.

Senator Arthur Vandenberg of Michigan, a leading contender for the Republican nomination for President at that time, offered to attend a "Jackson Day Dinner which is historically faithful to the original Jackson Day Dinner held to celebrate the extinguishment of the national debt on January 8, 1835."[4] Obviously Senator Vandenberg was teasing the Democrats because of the ever-rising national debt under the Roosevelt Administration.

But the partisan spirit of the Jackson Day celebration

during this early period in the 1800's is well illustrated by
the following anecdote:

From a private letter we learn that the Clay majority in the
Kentucky legislature refused (as usual with them) to fire a salute in
honor of the victory of the Eighth of January. It seems that Dr.
Cloud, of Lexington, and a number of Mr. Clay's neighbors, antici-
pating the rejection of the resolution for the salute, stole a march,
brought their cannon from Lexington before daybreak to the
heights above Frankfort, and at the dawn of the eighth, awakened
the malcontent nationals of the legislature with that sound, which
so frightened the foreign enemies of our country's institutions on
the famous 23rd of December, when Commodore Patterson opened
his first broadside from his ship, with the memorable words . . .
"We give them this, for the honor of America." The majority of
the General Assembly, we learn, were disposed to treat the pro-
ceeding of Dr. Cloud as a contempt and certainly, as it is now considered in Kentucky, "unbecoming a moral and religious people
to rejoice in the victories achieved by our arms," it must be held
as contempt of the present conservators of the morals and religion
of the people, to keep up the old custom of firing cannon on the
Eighth of January. Dr. Cloud, after giving his federal salute to the
legislature in the morning, returned in time to salute the corporate
authorities of the city of Lexington in the evening. Whether the
transgression will be punished by the city or state authorities remains to be seen.[5]

The Jackson Day Dinner in 1835 was served at Brown's
Hotel with nearly 250 gentlemen taking part. As was the
custom at these dinners, a full-length portrait of Washington was displayed at one end of the hall and on the opposite
wall was a portrait of President Jackson. Usually a band
was in attendance to provide entertainment between the
toasts and during the dining. The band also played "Hail
to the Chief" when the President strode into the hall. ★

1836

THE highlight of the 1836 celebration of Jackson Day was
the laying of the cornerstone of Jackson City by President
Jackson himself. An elaborate parade of bands, Congressional members, department heads, military officers, and
others started at Brown's Hotel in Washington, marched to

the east end of the Potomac Bridge where President Jackson and his suite joined the parade, and proceeded to the site of the new city. Refreshments were presented after the ceremonies. ★

No celebrations in Washington, D.C., were cited in the newspapers for 1837 and 1838. However, the *Daily National Intelligencer* in 1838 presented its sentiments concerning Jackson Day:

1837-1838

> The lesson furnished by the following brief paragraph ought not to be lost on those who court the applause of the multitudes, and prefer its climate to the impartial judgment of posterity. "Eighth of January in New York—the day was forgotten by the partisans of the Old Hero. Not a gun—not a drum—not a solitary sound of joy! General Jackson, in his Hermitage, can now see what all the adoration of the office holders was worth!"[6] ★

A PARADE by the Washington Guards, the Georgetown Invincibles, and the Potomac Dragoons (all local marching units and bands) was the mode of celebration in 1839. ★

1839

THE twenty-fifth anniversary of the Battle of New Orleans was marked by the return of Andrew Jackson to the battlefield where a celebration was held. In a letter from Andrew Jackson to Andrew J. Donelson on December 10, 1839, Jackson wrote of his invitation to be present:

1840

> My own opinion is that, in this inclement season, my health would fail me in reaching Memphis overland. Again I am out of funds, and the water is too low to take down our cotton, and I cannot bear to borrow or travel as a pauper. Van Buren and Armstrong urge me to go. I have no doubt but it will politically, have a good effect, but I have sacrificed both property and health in the salvation of New Orleans, paid $1,000 fine and costs, and the Legislature

thereof has never attempted to have that unjust sentence removed by resolutions and memorial to Congress to have the fine and costs restored to me with interest.[7]

Although hinting in this letter that he might not attend the New Orleans celebration, he did finally attend it. Conflicting reports about the detail and success of the 1840 celebration in New Orleans were printed by the *Globe* and the *Daily National Intelligencer*.

One description of the 1840 celebration at New Orleans indicated that more than 30,000 people had witnessed the affair. This source, a letter from New Orleans printed in the *Globe*, indicated that between 20 and 30 uniformed companies on horse and on foot and of almost all nationalities participated in the affair. Further, it noted that there were fire companies, charitable institutions, and every description of association present at the event. "The shipping of many nations, as far as the eye could see, had their flags hoisted, and their colors streaming in the breeze, while their small artillery kept up an almost constant roar."[8]

The *Daily National Intelligencer* gave a divergent report, which was from the *New Orleans Sun*, to the effect that the day had been a most "miserable business." It could be expected in those days that these two Washington newspapers would have such contrasting reports on the affair, since their political views were so different.   ★

1841-1844

AFTER this celebration, there was none in Washington, D.C., until 1844. Andrew Jackson wrote in this year that he could not be present at the supper at Apollo Hall because of "feeble health." More than 200 gentlemen, chiefly the Democratic members of Congress, participated in the repast. Thirteen regular toasts, at least 41 volunteer toasts, and many speeches were given.

The 1844 dinner was an extraordinary affair because it erased a blot on Jackson's record. When Jackson went to

defend New Orleans in December of 1814, he proclaimed martial law in the city, quelled a threatened mutiny, executed six of the mutineers, and arrested a judge who attempted to resist martial law. Once civil law was reestablished, Jackson was fined $1,000 by a court. Thirty years later, in 1844, Congress refunded his $1,000 fine with interest.

In a letter from Francis P. Blair to Andrew Jackson on January 9, 1844, Blair discusses how Jackson's fine was stricken from the records:

> I never saw a happier set of men than the passage of this Bill in the House by such a vote [passage of the Bill of reversal] made of the Democrats, who assembled at the celebration supper to greet each other on the moral victory achieved by them on the day of your great anniversary. Your letter was read and followed by shouts from the heart which showed with what joy the assurance that you lived to see the triumph of the Eighth in Congress was received. Wright, Benton, Allen, King, Dawson, Wilkins, Walker, Cave Johnson, and others made speeches. The President sent a very good letter which was much applauded. But you will have a skeleton of our affair in a day or two. I wish it could all have been literally reported.[9]

This was the last national Jackson Day Dinner held during the lifetime of Andrew Jackson. Jackson died in 1845, but his request that the celebrations of January the Eighth be continued has been completely fulfilled. In his letter to the 1844 Jackson Day diners, Jackson said:

> Methinks I now hear the glorious response to my order along the lines, when this force, displaying 10,000 bayonets, commenced their attack upon us. I directed my aide-de-camp, Major Reid, to pass along our lines and say that New Orleans must be here defended, and our wives and daughters shielded from pollution, or we must cheerfully fall in the ditch before us. This order was conveyed throughout the lines; and it was received with three cheers, which had not ceased to ring upon the ear when the battle began. History records the result. It is due to the brave men who so nobly performed their duty; that they should be remembered at each anniversary of the day which they rendered so memorable. Such remembrance may keep bright for other times an example that will teach our posterity what to do in a similar case. May it forever keep alive that spirit of holy patriotism which prefers death to the dismemberment of our union, and regards every sacrifice as desirable which is made to repel foreign invasion.[10] ★

Andrew Jackson appearing in court where he was fined $1,000 for arresting a judge who attempted to resist martial law imposed by Jackson in New Orleans. The money was finally refunded almost 30 years later, one year before his death in 1845.

Chapter 6

"INTERVENTION FOR NONINTERVENTION"

PEACE AND QUIET and perfect decorum have not always been the tenor of things at these Jackson Day celebrations. In 1847 the Jackson Day ball was held in the Jackson Hall in Washington, "the first occasion on which the ample and beautiful saloons of this building" were open to the public. The dance was interrupted by a fire in the building. Interesting comment and outlook on the fire was printed in the *Daily National Intelligencer:*

> Considerable damage has been done to Mr. Caton's store and goods, but this we understand will be the loss of the Fireman's Insurance Company. It was a fortunate event that this fire broke out early in the night, and while there were so many persons at the ball, and in the immediate vicinity, ready and willing to give assistance.
>
> We learn some rascal, taking advantage of the general alarm and confusion, walked into the refectory kept that night by Mr. John Miller, who provided the ball supper, and stole from him a basket of champagne.[1]

Balls represented the main type of celebration of Jackson Day from 1846 through 1849. There were no celebrations reported in 1850 and 1851. ★

THE ONLY Jackson Day Dinner at which a foreigner was the main speaker was the 1852 banquet given by the Jackson Democratic Association at Jackson Hall. Lewis Kossuth, a leader and champion of liberty in Hungary, spoke to more than 400 gentlemen and ladies. Among the invited guests were Hon. Lewis Cass, Hon. Stephen A. Douglas, Hon. Henry Dodge, Gen. Joseph Lane, Hon. J. D. Bright, Hon. A. C. Dodge, Francis P. Blair, Esq., Hon. Sam Houston, Major Donelson, and Mr. Thomas Ritchie.

As might be expected, the toasts and speeches resounded with comparisons between America's fight for liberty and Hungary's battles for freedom.

Francis P. Blair, a close friend of Andrew Jackson's, delivered an address and gave an introduction prior to the inspiring speech of Lewis Kossuth, who gave a testimony to the great influence of the United States upon himself and upon his country. Probably a more succinct and inspiring summary of the growth of the United States to that time cannot be found. The conclusion of Kossuth's speech gives some of the flavor of the main purpose of the speech.

> Gentlemen, how far this supreme duty for your own interest will allow you to go in giving life and effect to the principle which you so generously proclaim, and your party, as I have understood have so generously proclaimed in different parts . . . that you will in your wisdom decide, remaining always the masters of your action and of your fate. But that principle will rest; that principle is true; that principle is just; and you are just, because you are free. I hope, therefore, to see you cordially unite with me once more in the sentiment—intervention for nonintervention.[2]

Following Kossuth's speech, 13 regular toasts were made. Then volunteer toasts and speeches were entertained until midnight when the meeting adjourned.

Jackson Hall was decorated with the flags of the United States and of Hungary. Over each window was a small flag with stars and stripes and bearing the words "Welcome Kossuth, to the Land of Freedom."

Because Lewis Kossuth symbolized a man fighting for recognition of his country, and because his speech at this Jackson Day Dinner represented an outsider's views, a portion of his speech is given below:

> Just as man has to pass through several periods of age, each of them marked with its own peculiarities, before he comes to a settled position in life, even so a nation. A nation has first to be born, then to grow; then it has to prove its passive vitality by undergoing a trial of life. Afterwards it has to prove its active force in gaining ascendancy in its own immediate horizon. At last, it must take its confident seat amongst the nations of the world as a power on earth. Every one of these periods of national life must be gone through. There is no help against it. It is a necessary process of life and every one of these life periods has its own natural condition, which must be accepted as a necessity, even if we should not be pleased with it. As there is no jumping in nature, equally there is not a

stop to it. A man must be a child before he becomes a youth, and he must have been a youth before he becomes a man. But, then, it would be ridiculous to desire from the child to act as a youth, or from the youth to be a man, it is indeed impossible for a youth to be still a child, or for the man not to become a man. He must, because he is; and if, being a man, he does not act as it becomes a man to act, well, then, he loses the position of a man. It is quite the same with nations. . . .

The Victory of New Orleans was a proof of it . . . was the period of demonstrative passive vitality and the process of life went on. The natural period was to demonstrate your vitality. That was demonstrated by the war against Mexico.

If the history of New Orleans was the period demonstrating the security of your national existence, the victorious war against Mexico was the period demonstrating not only that nobody can dare to attack your existence, but that also your national interest must be respected, and nobody can dare to oppose them.

The period of active vitality is accomplished. Now one period then remains to achieve . . . that to take your seat, not amongst nations of the earth, because that you have since the day of New Orleans, but amongst the powers on earth. What is the meaning of that word "power on earth"? The meaning of it is to have not only the power to guard your own particular interest, but also to have a vote in the regulation of the common interests of humanity, of which you are an independent member . . . in a word, to become a tribunal controlling the maintenance of the law of nations, precisely as your supreme court controls the maintenance of your own constitution and laws and, indeed all logic of statesmanship, all philosophy of history, would be vain, if I were mistaken that your great nation is arrived at this unavoidable period of the natural process of your national life.

Your history was so much a book of life to me, that I was aware of this operation in the public mind of the United States. I knew before my coming hither that the question of what shall be the law amongst nations vitally interested public opinion here. I knew that the opinion was not only advanced by individuals, but agitated as a political doctrine appropriate to the broad principles upon which a republic stands. I mean that doctrine that every nation of the world has a right to stand by itself and regulate its own government—its own domestic concerns—and that individuals are not bound to the despot under whose flag they may have had the misfortune to have been born. I knew that the second part of the question—what is international law—went even so far as to enter into the causes of that war already which was decided by the Victory of New Orleans; and I knew that the former part of the question —the national, as I recall it—is brought home to public decision in the United States by being arrived in the process to national life to the very period of a power on earth, besides the urgency of many particular concerns.

The cause of Hungary, so intimately connected with doctrines of Europe, in which your country in so many respects is concerned . . . that cause of Hungary happened to lay [*sic*] within the scope of principles of international law, occupying not only the instinct of the people, but also the calm reflection of your statesmen, conspicuous by mature wisdom and patriotism; and herein is the key, besides the generosity congenial to free men, that the cause which I plead, is honored with so rapid a progress of public sentiment.

Now, as to these principles: Gentlemen, I of course can have nothing to do with whatever interior question or party movements in the United States; and even should anyone (of which I am not aware) have the desire to make a political capital, as it is termed here, out of myself, I trust it will not be laid to my charge, my having nothing to do with it. I indeed must humbly entreat not to be identified with a certain foreign gentleman now in the United States as well as myself. My position, gentlemen, is humbly and thankfully to acknowledge sympathy and support, whenever I am honored with it, without identifying with whatever question which is not my business at all. And I must be permitted to express my particular gratitude to you, though a political association, bearing the character of a distinct party in relation to your own domestic concerns, [in that you] were pleased to have the generous delicacy of offering me the benefit of your principal support in the consolation of your sympathy, without placing me in any difficulty inconsistent with my position. I, indeed, most warmly thank you for it. . . .

However, when I have on the one side nothing to meddle with interior party questions, and on the other side no equitable man can charge me with any fault when I declare that I feel infinitely obliged and gratified when I see that those principles of the law of nations which I humbly advocate have found a permanent place upon the platform of great political parties also: and they have found a place there before anybody could have imagined what I considered my humble mission to be. That is a fact, gentlemen, which is so consolatory, so bright with hope to me, that even my sad mind cannot fail to be highly cheered by it. . . .

Yes, indeed, sir, you were right to say that the justice of your struggle, which took out of England's hand a mighty continent, is openly acknowledged by the English people itself. The memory of the glorious day at New Orleans must of course recall to your mind the memory of wrongs against which you so gloriously fought. Oh, let me entreat you, bury the past hatred in the graves for all the crimes of the past lie buried with the mouldering ashes of those who sinned, and take the glorious opportunity to benefit the great cause of humanity. . . .   ★

Chapter 7

REMEMBERED
FOREVER

CLARK MILLS, the American artist and sculptor, finished work on the equestrian statue of Andrew Jackson in Lafayette Square, directly opposite the White House, in time for a double celebration on Jackson Day in 1853. The dedication of Mills's statue and the celebration of the Battle of New Orleans filled the day with pride and gaiety.

After a long parade from City Hall to the Executive Mansion to Lafayette Square, the Reverend Clement C. Butler, Chaplain of the Senate, opened the cermonies with a prayer. Hon. Stephen A. Douglas, the Senator from Illinois, was the orator of the occasion and delivered a speech "which cannot fail to command the attention and applause of every reader by the happy spirit in which it was conceived, by his admirable sketch of the civil and military services of Andrew Jackson, by its freedom from party allusions, by the patriotic sentiments it contains, and by the stirring language in which it was announced."[1]

More than 20,000 people occupied the Square and the neighboring housetops. The speaker's stand was crowded with eminent men—the President and his Cabinet, General Scott and his staff, Senators and Representatives. When Clark Mills was introduced after Douglas' speech, he could not express his feelings except to signal the withdrawl of the veil from the statue which showed Jackson in action on his steed.

On the evening of January 8, 1853, the Jackson Democratic Association held a banquet in honor of the anniversary of the Battle of New Orleans and of the dedication of the equestrian statue of Jackson. After the 13 regular toasts, Clark Mills simply remarked that he would allow his hero and his charge to speak for him. Those who answered toasts with short speeches were General Lewis Cass, General Sam Houston, Hon. James Buchanan, Hon. Stephen A. Douglas, General Robert Armstrong (a key officer to Jackson in the Battle of New Orleans and the man to whom Jackson bequeathed his sword), William M. Overton

of the *Washington Union,* Colonel George W. Hughes (a hero in the Mexican War), Mr. Thomas Ritchie, and Mr. Robert Ould, Esq. More than 42 volunteer sentiments were given.

With the growth of the Jackson Day Dinners, the struggle for the privilege to speak to the ingroup became more evident. Political ambitions exerted pressures on the politicians to become leaders of their party; position and influence were sought because of the increasing desire of politicians to speak before their own kind. The group of speakers listed above, for the most part, illustrates this point. As the other Jefferson-Jackson Day celebrations are described, this struggle for a speaking assignment is interesting to perceive.

The records of the Columbia Historical Society noted that "the first equestrian statue to be executed and set up in the United States (after George III) was the bronze group of General Jackson, the hero of the War of 1812, which stands in Lafayette Square, in this city."[2] The statue was modeled and cast from cannon captured in Jackson's campaigns. The Jackson Democratic Association of Washington, D.C., awarded Clark Mills $12,000 for the statue. However, the stipulated amount which was paid him did not begin to cover the artist's outlays in money, not to mention his time and skill devoted to the work. Therefore, Congress later appropriated an additional sum of $20,000 to be paid to Clark Mills for his statue of Jackson. "One-half of this latter amount was paid directly to Mr. Mills, and the other money was to be invested for the benefit of his family; whether that intention was carried out or not appears to be a matter of some doubt."[3]

This was another way in which Jackson Day was uniquely celebrated during the past 150 years. This monument of Andrew Jackson, created by Clark Mills, is a constant reminder that Jackson will be remembered by patriots of America and, especially, by Democrats.   ★

Clark Mills's equestrian statue of Andrew Jackson in LaFayette Square was dedicated at the 1853 Jackson Day celebration.

Chapter 8

THE END
OF AN ERA

IN THE PERIOD immediately preceding the Civil War, Jackson Day celebrations were infrequent. It was in this period that control of the government by the Democrats was interrupted, and enthusiastic celebrations were becoming more difficult to organize.

IN 1854, the following simple statement was all that could be found on the Jackson Day Dinner held that year:

1854

We are requested to state that a supper to be given this evening in honor of the anniversary of the battle of New Orleans will take place at 7 o'clock at Fuller's, corner of 6th Street and Pennsylvania Avenue.[1]

★

A NATIONAL convention of the veterans of the War of 1812 met in 1855 in Washington on this 40th anniversary of the Battle of New Orleans. They paraded during the day and were guests in the evening at a grand ball at Niblo's, the "proceeds of which will go to the relief of such of the corps as are in destitute circumstances."[2]

1855

The Washington Sentinel's report on the anniversary gave a touching description of the Jackson Day affairs of 1855 when the veterans of the War of 1812 gathered in the city:

Today has been generally celebrated in Washington as the anniversary of the victory at New Orleans. The convention of the gallant soldiers of the War of 1812 has given more interest than usual to the anniversary. No one who witnessed that long procession of brave men who now in the twilight of life met to celebrate the meridian glory of their existence, could fail to be impressed with the solemn interest of the occasion. There were those who had stood as the firm and valiant defenders of their country in the hour of her greatest trial and her greatest need. There was a mutual greeting of those who had long been separated in the different spheres of life in which they were engaged, and who now, for the first time, during 40 years, renewed associations made sacred by the sound dedication of the services and of lives to the defense of a common country. Forms, then straight and athletic, are now bent with years . . . eyes, which then brightened with the flash of martial valor, are now dimmed with care and time. But through the waste of years one and only one thought engrossed the minds of all, and that was the trying period through which all alike had passed.

But not only was the celebration of the anniversary of a day, which secured to the country a peaceful settlement of the principles involved in the contest of 1812–1815, the object of this meeting. These gallant defenders of our rights, so long contented with the mere voice of gratitude from their countrymen, now claimed from their government a higher reward than empty praise. A bill, even now before Congress, making provision for their wants should not only be advocated as a benefice, but urged as a right belonging to these brave supporters of our liberties in the War of 1812. It is a well established policy, as well as a well understood matter of justice in almost all civilized governments, that those who have engaged in the battles of their country should be entitled to the benefit of a pension. More particularly is this the case in a government like our own, where, in a peculiar sense, the soldier may be regarded as the self-devoted defender of his country, when the Army offers but little inducement, except that lofty sense of patriotism, which inspires us all with a desire to devote life, fortune, and all to the defense of our institutions—where war is not a profession but a personal sacrifice.

Let us trust that this celebration may not be without its effect on the minds of our statesmen, in urging the passage of a law providing some reasonable compensation for these gallant defenders of our country during the last war.[3]   ★

1856-1866

BETWEEN 1856 and 1866, the only Jackson Day celebrations were in 1858 and 1859 when balls were given by the Union Guards. During the War Between the States, the celebrations were suspended. The semicentennial anniversary of the Battle of New Orleans in 1865 was reported as a day which "will not be much remembered in the stupendous national tempests which are on this day so augmenting the anxieties of all thoughtful men for our very existence as a people."[4]   ★

1867

AMIDST the postwar tensions between the North and South, in 1867, the National Democratic Resident Executive Com-

Andrew Johnson, a Democrat, occupied a unique position. He had been nominated Vice President by Republicans and elected with Abraham Lincoln. He assumed the Presidency on Lincoln's assassination on April 15, 1865. Violent controversy with Congress, chiefly over post-Civil War policy, led to his impeachment. The trial was an international sensation. Tickets to the proceedings were issued (a facsimile is reproduced at right), different colors being used for different days. The trial, illustrated below by an artist of the period, lasted from March 30 to May 26, 1868, and ended in acquittal.

No. U.S. SENATE

To be taken up at MAIN ENTRANCE

U.S. SENATE

U.S. SENATE

Impeachment of the President

ADMIT THE BEARER

MARCH 13. 1868

Geo. T. Brown
Sergeant-at-Arms.

Philp & Solomons, Wash. D.C.

mittee gave a banquet at the National Hotel to commemorate Jackson Day. Those present and responding to
toasts included President Andrew Johnson, Honorable
Francis P. Blair, Sr., Senator Thomas Hendricks of Indiana,
and Senator James Doolittle of Wisconsin.

The general nature of the speech acts at these Jackson
Day Dinners became increasingly clear with each dinner—
praise of the Democratic Party, blame for the opponents,
and an effort to enunciate the topics of the party on matters
of contemporary political significance.

This latter aspect is well demonstrated in the speeches
and toasts at this 1867 dinner. For example, President
Johnson, replying to a toast, expressed his feelings on the
burning issue of his time when he said:

> No state of its own will has the right under the Constitution to
> renounce its place on or to withdraw from the Union. (cheers) Nor
> has the Congress of the United States under the Constitution the
> power to degrade the people of any state by reducing them to the
> condition of a mere territorial dependency upon the federal head.
> The one is a disruption and a dissolution of the government; the
> other is consolidation and the exercise of despotic power. The ad-
> vocates of either are alike the enemies of the Union and of our fed-
> eral form of government.[5]

Andrew Johnson's big task was to unite the North and
the South while retaining pride and respect in both camps.
His was the job of continuing the policies of assassinated
President Abraham Lincoln, of trying to bring the country
together. This was no easy job in the face of a Congress
hostile to Johnson and friendly to the idea of reconstructing
the South in a harsh manner.   ★

1868   At the Jackson Day celebration under the auspices of the
Resident Democratic National Committee in 1868 at the
Metropolitan Hotel, President Andrew Johnson replied to
a toast with the same words he uttered in 1867. Lasting six
hours, from 7 P.M. until 1 A.M., the celebration bore the

air of hope and expectancy for the coming Presidential campaign.

In addition to the President's response, others speaking briefly along similar lines were Judge Dunlop, Judge Black, Judge Marshall, Hon. Benjamin M. Boyer of Pennsylvania, Hon. Reverdy Johnson, Senator Doolittle, Attorney General Henry Stansberry, Judge Marvin of Florida, Colonel J. A. Babcock of Connecticut, and General Thomas Ewing.

Papers opposing President Johnson during the late 1860's called the Jackson Day celebrations "copperhead celebrations." The *Daily National Intelligencer*, which at this period in history was more favorable to the Democratic Party than previously, summarized the situation in 1868 in its extra edition describing the Eighth of January celebration:

> Never since the Battle of New Orleans to now has there been so much occasion for the celebration of that victory. Never 'til now has there been so great a reason to laud the virtues of Andrew Jackson and stimulate among the public men of the nation an emulation of his patriotism, his heroic daring and his unyielding firmness in the maintenance of what he believed to be the right. When the nation itself, through the unscrupulous assumptions of the Legislative branch of the government, has been driven to the very verge of anarchy; when the President, the people and the Judiciary are the only powers left to restore peace and unity and prosperity to a distracted and impoverished and famishing republic; when the President himself is dependent entirely upon the voice of the people to be able to right the wrongs that have been perpetrated in their name; and when the whole country is groaning under oppressions and outrages inflicted by a merciless and unscrupulous political faction, it is time that patriots, that good men, honest and true lovers of their country and of their country's welfare, should come together in the name of one whose patriotism was never doubted to exchange views, even in a social gathering, upon what has been, what is, and what must be.[6]   ★

FOLLOWING this climactic dinner of hope, the Democrats were crushed in succeeding attempts to attain the Presidency and to achieve amelioration of the measures imposed on the South. Accompanying this nadir of Democratic strength

1869-1879

immediately after the War Between the States was the absence of Jackson Day celebrations from 1869 to 1879. This period can be said to be a dark age in American history not only from a political standpoint but from a social standpoint as well. ★

Chapter 9

REVIVAL AND REMEMBRANCE

WITH THE ELECTION of some Democratic Presidents in the latter part of the 19th century, Jackson Day was revived and celebrated throughout the country. Gradually the South was emerging from the strong arm of the reconstruction imposed by such men as Representative Thaddeus Stevens.

THE Jackson Democratic Association celebrated the Eighth of January in 1880 in the Odd Fellows Hall where "a number of speakers" were invited. No detailed account of the event is available. ★

1880

AFTER another drought of Jackson Day celebrations during the next four years, a public meeting and a banquet of the Jackson Democratic Association in 1885 represented the mode of celebrating the anniversary of the Battle of New Orleans. The public meeting was held at the Masonic Temple at 7 P.M. with the following speakers: Mr. John E. Norris, President of the Jackson Democratic Association; Senator Eli Saulsbury of Delaware; Senator John Morgan of Alabama; Representative E. John Ellis of Louisiana; Senator Thomas Bayard, Sr., of Delaware; Hon. Barclay Henley of California; Senator Zebulon Vance of North Carolina.

At the end of the public celebration, the Association went to the National Hotel where a banquet was served. For the first time since the War Between the States, the national government was about to be transferred to the party of Andrew Jackson, under the leadership of Grover Cleveland. ★

1881- 1885

AFTER another lapse of eight years, from 1886 to 1893, the Jackson Democratic Association in Washington, D.C., revived its custom of celebrating Jackson Day with a banquet,

1886- 1893

President Grover Cleveland helped revive
the Democratic Party and the Jackson
Day celebrations after the long drought
of the Reconstruction period.

held in the Arlington Hotel in 1893. Hon. Benton McMillan of Tennessee spoke to the principal toast of the evening. Other speakers were Senator Zebulon Vance of North Carolina, Senator John W. Daniel of Virginia, Hon. Sherman Hoar of Massachusetts, Hon. J. J. Hemphill of South Carolina, Hon. W. L. Wilson of West Virginia, and Senator George Gray of Delaware.

During this time, a very active Businessmen's Democratic Association of New York held annual Jackson Day affairs. President Cleveland himself spoke at the one held in 1892. Guests from all over the country gathered there to eulogize Jackson and democracy.   ★

IT was during these last years of the 19th century that
toasts gave way to formal public addresses as the main means
of exhibiting ideas and arguments. Though there was no
dinner held in 1894, this interesting commentary on Jackson Day oratory appeared in an editorial in the *Washington
Post* in 1894:

1894

It is entirely mete and proper that such an anniversary should
be celebrated, although we could never clearly understand why
this function should be monopolized by any one party over another.
It has made the occasion, however, not so much of Jackson's glori-
fication as a soldier as of the Democratic principles which in after-
life he so valorously expounded and exemplified. It has become a
day on which the "Jacksonian Democracy" are particularly expected to magnify the virtues of their illustrious chieftain and pay
him effusive tribute. This also is well. It was better if his panegy-
rists were in a habit of more consistently following an example to
which they give such rhetorical exaltation.

It was during Jackson's administration that parties were di-
vided on new lines, or rather upon new names. The strict con-
structionists of the Constitution became Democrats. The high
tariff, internal improvements, national bank men of the time chris-
tened themselves Whigs, and the fight that then ensued was bitter
and protracted. It was thereabouts that the "Spoils System" was
inaugurated which has since been upheld with more or less per-
tinacity by both of the great parties of the country, even in the face
of the Civil Service Reform of a later period. Human nature has
not materially changed in the last sixty years.

But in celebrating the memory of Andrew Jackson it must be
borne in mind that his distinguishing characteristics were of a com-
bative and aggressive sort. His war against the United States Bank
is a case in point. In this matter his personal will asserted its su-
premacy. It called down upon his devoted head the censure of the
Senate, which Mr. Benton only succeeded in having expunged from
the records before General Jackson's retirement in 1837. He was
always in hot water with the Senate concerning his official appoint-
ments. He was stubborn, unyielding, and on many occasions dic-
tatorial, and hundreds of Democratic orators, it may be, will sound
his praises today in high-flown rhetoric for the self-same assump-
tions of executive authority, if in less degree, which in another
breath and aside from the banquet table they are charging against
President Cleveland as faults worthy of approbation.

We do not expect entire consistency of the orators of St. Jackson's Day, but it will be well for them and well for the country perhaps if in extolling the courage, the integrity, the unquestioned

patriotism of President Jackson they succeed in extracting some envigorating inspiration for the present benefit of the party.

Let it be duly remembered that he was true to his convictions, that he was positive in his declarations, that his policies were always clearly defined, that he haughted [*sic*] not upon expediency in the order of their execution, but he illustrated in numberless ways the qualities which too many politicians now prominently at the front, while reverencing in him, are not alert or brave in exemplifying themselves.[1]   ★

1895

In 1895 the Interstate Democratic Association decided to celebrate Jackson Day at the National Rifles Armory with a program which included "speechmaking and musical selections by talented vocal artists." Colonel B. F. Clayton of New York and Senator A. J. McLaurin of Mississippi were the speakers.

During the period of 1880 to 1895 the Philadelphia Young Men's Democratic Association had been very active and had held Jackson Day celebrations yearly. This was typical of some of the more active organizations throughout the country.   ★

1896

A further indication of the changing character of the Jackson Day Dinners was the celebration of 1896. The Washington celebration was organized that year by the Interstate Democratic Association and was held at the Odd Fellows Hall on Seventh Street. The program consisted of three parts: vocal and instrumental music and literary numbers; an address by Representative James D. Richardson of Tennessee; a reception and buffet luncheon at the rooms of the Association on New York Avenue.

Richardson, paying tribute to Tennessee's greatest patriot, made some comparisons between Jackson and President Grover Cleveland. This technique of comparing certain qualities and situations of Jackson in his time with

*William Jennings Bryan
was a powerful force in
the Democratic Party
for almost a third of a
century and was the
most sought-after speaker
of his time.*

those of a person in the period of the speech is recurrent
throughout the history of this type of speech.

Richardson compared Jefferson and Jackson, saying
that they were the Peter and the Paul of democracy and
that, while Jefferson was the planner, the adviser, the theoretical Democrat, Jackson was the man who carried out
the ideas and plans, the practical Democrat.

He closed his address in a very stirring manner:

By far the great majority of us must be content to be as though
we had not been, and trust to find our names in the register of God,
though they be not found in the record of man. Surely among
the few things that time and oblivion will spare will be the wonderful and marvelous story of Tennessee's greatest patriot, statesman
and soldier, the hero of the Hermitage.[2]   ★

In Chicago in 1897, William Jennings Bryan, defeated
Presidential candidate, was the major speaker at the Jackson
Day banquet held there under the auspices of the William
Jennings Bryan League. This is an example of the begin-
ning of the trend to send major speakers throughout the
country to speak to various groups on Jackson Day.

In Washington, D.C., in 1897, the Jackson Democratic Association held a banquet at the Masonic Temple
with Hon. A. S. Colyar, a Nashville newspaperman, as the
principal speaker. Bearing a "strong resemblance to Old

1897

Hickory," Colyar was chosen to be the speaker because he represented Jackson's home state of Tennessee. Up to this time, the custom of these dinners was to have Tennessee represented either by a speaker or by someone giving a toast. The speakers and toasters at Jackson Day banquets had generally been members of Congress, judges, federal officials, and residents of Washington.

With improved and increased transportation and communication at the turn of the century came increased participation in the Jackson Day affairs. Greater geographical distribution of those attending the dinners became more apparent. In addition to the public display of the Democratic ingroup, there was an increased struggle for position and influence within the party, which is less unified in reality than it pretends at such moments of public display.

Throughout the 19th century the Jackson Democratic Association had worked hard and continuously to promote the ideas of Andrew Jackson throughout the country. The Association was formed just before Jackson was inaugurated President of the United States on March 4, 1829. It did herculean work during the period Jackson was in office and adhered to him and his Administration with unswerving devotion. After Jackson's retirement to the Hermitage, the Jackson Democratic Association held him in final reverence as one of the noblest men America had ever produced, and it held the annual banquets as an indication of that devotion.

Typical of Jackson Day orators, Mr. Colyar wound up his 1897 speech by saying:

> Gentlemen, around this board who are high in office, are you here to renew your faith in Jackson Day Democracy? Then let the country know that in the great issue between corporate greed and the people, you are for the people. Gentlemen, the one thing I am sure of: If the people of this country become satisfied by a second . . . certainly by a third test . . . that corporation money can take the election of the President out of their hands and that corporation rule is a fixed system, it will rend the public as an earthquake rends the rocks.[3] ★

Chapter 10

A CHANGING
CELEBRATION

FROM 1898 through 1912, William Jennings Bryan was a major speaker at Jackson Day celebrations held throughout the United States. His favorite speaking place was at the annual Jackson Day affair in Chicago where approximately 2,000 to 3,000 people gathered. Practically all major cities in the country held annual Jackson Day events during this period, but no Jackson Day celebrations were cited in the Washington press during the period from 1898 through 1911.

The days of Reconstruction were past, and the chances of electing a Democratic President were much greater. With a more favorable political climate and with the Democratic National Committee sponsoring Jackson Day banquets, the struggle of politicians to lead and to speak before their party became more obvious at each succeeding banquet.

A Jackson Day celebration which substituted for a dinner in Washington was held on January 17, 1911, in Baltimore. A special train from Washington took almost every Democratic member of the Senate and House of Representatives to Baltimore for the affair. More than 1,000 faithful Democrats attended the dinner at the Fifth Regiment Armory. Judge Ferdinand Williams of Maryland served as toastmaster at the dinner, which was billed as the most elaborate in the history of Baltimore up to that time. People throughout the country were invited to the conference, which was designed to bring about harmony in the Democratic ranks in order to get ready for the 1912 Presidential election.

There were 53 seats at the speakers' table, although not all sitting there gave a speech.

The *Washington Post* of January 17, 1911, prefaced its report of the affair with:

Content during the lean years of defeat to dine at "dollar dinners," with "hog and hominy" as the central theme, and springwater on the side, the militant Democracy of 1911 will sit at a feast in the city tomorrow night where the exclusive diamond-back terrapin will vie with the aristocratic canvasback duck and the epicurean Smithfield ham, in the courses of a banquet that is fittingly to celebrate the Democratic victories of 1910.[1]

The banquet was so thronged with people anxious to discuss party issues with each other that it was 10:30 P.M. before order was established. By this time the diners were in no mood to listen to long political harangues. These Jackson Day celebrations had grown so large in size that they were forced to undergo some changes. The transportation advances that enabled such a crowd to assemble merely emphasized the communications lag that prevented them from hearing the speeches. At this Baltimore dinner, the description of the affair was a portent of Jackson Day affairs for the next twenty years:

> The gentlemen who sat at the speakers' table did their best to deliver the messages they had prepared for the occasion, but the confusion was so great that a foghorn would have been ineffective, and the megaphone of Toastmaster Williams was lost to everyone more than 50 feet away.
>
> Mr. Williams went through his speech without the audience being able to grasp more than his gestures which aroused applause, but his usual eloquence failed utterly to still the crowd. Occasionally the words "Democratic Party" could be caught above the din, and these were all the audience needed as a signal for the renewed outbursts of hand-clapping and cheering, interspersed with "rebel yells." Too much was attempted.
>
> It was apparent that too much had been attempted in the way of banquet speaking. The Armory was too large, the diners too numerous, and the acoustics too bad to permit any semblance of order. Champ Clark was asked to speak at the night gathering but said that he was unwilling to burst his throat talking against such a throng, as he expected to have use for it later in Congress.[2]

1912

On January 8, 1912, the Democratic National Committee met at the Shoreham Hotel to fix the national convention date and select a site for the convention. The Jackson Day banquet was scheduled for 8 P.M. at the Raleigh Hotel where a host of Democratic leaders would hold forth.

The Democrats smelled victory in 1912, and prospective candidates were anxious to get on the inside rail at the very important Jackson Day banquet of this year. In this jockeying for a power position at the dinner, several points are very interesting. A summary of the 1912 dinner and this struggle for power can be observed from the headlines of the day:[3]

DEMOCRATS UNITE FOR PARTY'S GOOD

PEACE AND HARMONY
KEYNOTE OF LEADERS
AT JACKSON DAY BANQUET

PLEDGE LOYAL SUPPORT TO NOMINATED CANDIDATE

RECEPTION ACCORDED
GOV. WILSON REGARDED
AS SIGNIFICANT

JERSEY MAN LAUDS BRYAN

MORE THAN 770 DISCIPLES
OF OLD HICKORY ATTEND
ONE OF THE MOST REMARKABLE
DINNERS IN RECENT YEARS

DEMOCRATS END FEUDS AT JACKSON BANQUET

BRYAN CHEERS WILSON
AND CLARK WELCOMES FOLD
AT HARMONY FEAST

APPLAUSE FOR MR. HEARST

VARIOUS PRESIDENTIAL BOOMS RESOUND IN HALL

SEN. POMERENE SPEAKS FOR GOV. HARMON

PARKER AND KERN ASSAIL ROOSEVELT

MR. HEARST SAYS LAFOLLETTE REALLY IS A DEMOCRAT

In this scramble for the Democratic nomination for President, the front runners at this time were Governor Woodrow Wilson of New Jersey, William Randolph Hearst of New York, Speaker Champ Clark of Missouri, former Governor Joseph W. Folk of Missouri; Governor L. Harmon of Ohio, Senator Charles Johnson of Maine, Governor Thomas R. Marshall of Indiana, and William Jennings Bryan of Nebraska.

> Presidential candidates, who for months have given the Democratic nomination a careful consideration, proclaimed, one and all, that whoever might be the selection for the Democratic standard-bearer, he would have their undivided support, that personal ambitions were to be forgotten for the party good.[4]

Senator James O'Gorman of New York served as toastmaster. Those who spoke to the assembled Democrats were Norman E. Mack, Chairman of the Democratic National Committee; Representative James Lloyd of Missouri, Chairman of the Democratic Congressional Committee; Judge Alton B. Parker, Democratic candidate for President against Theodore Roosevelt; Governor Joseph W. Folk of Missouri; Woodrow Wilson; Senator John W. Kern of Indiana; Hearst; Champ Clark; Senator Francis G. Newlands of Nevada; Senator Robert Taylor of Tennessee; Senator Atlee Pomerene of Ohio; Johnson; and Bryan. Thirteen speakers visited the podium at this dinner for a total speaking time of 7½ hours—8 P.M. to 3:30 A.M. The crowd was eagerly awaiting William Jennings Bryan's speech (which was last) to see if he would make a statement about his candidacy. Bryan stated he would support the Democratic nominee for President with more vigor than he had given to his own three campaigns.

> *On the centennial of the Battle of New Orleans, the last big battle of the War of 1812, Woodrow Wilson was trying to keep the United States out of another war which was raging in Europe.*

The topics of the speakers were:

Senator O'Gorman—Introduction
Representative Lloyd—"The Democratic National Committee"
Chairman Mack—"A Word From the Chairman"
Judge Parker—"Some Conditions of Success"
Governor Folk—"Trans-Mississippi Democracy"
Governor Wilson—"Democracy, Past and Future"
Senator Kern—"Jacksonian Democracy"
Champ Clark—"Democratic Success and How To Achieve It"
William R. Hearst—"The Beauty of a Democrat"
Senator Johnson—"New England Democracy"
Senator Pomerene—"Buckeye Democracy"
Senator Taylor—"Old Hickory"
Senator Newlands—"Constructive Democracy"
William J. Bryan—"The Passing of Plutocracy"[5]

The longest and loudest applause was given to Woodrow Wilson and William Jennings Bryan. The files at the Democratic National Committee Library indicate that "it was Wilson's speech that night which really put him on the way to the nomination at the Democratic convention in Baltimore in June, 1912, about five months later." Both Bryan and Wilson had to wait several minutes before beginning to speak.

> Significant was the reception accorded Governor Wilson when he entered the banquet hall and when he made his address. More significant still, believed many Democrats, was the laudation of Col. Bryan pronounced by Governor Wilson and the evident pleasure with which his remarks were received.[6]

Throughout the evening, there was an accumulation of evidence which indicated that Bryan was looking with favor upon the candidacy of Governor Wilson. Contemporary issues formed the core of each speech—Supreme Court decisions on trust cases, initiative and referendum, direct election of Senators, and the income tax.

The maneuvering for position at this dinner most vividly illustrates the internal struggles for power within the party. Although the outward appearance was one of unity and harmony, fierce battles and machinations for position in the party rumbled under the surface. A *Washington Post* editorial comment on the day after the banquet said:

> Jackson Day passed without any fatalities among the Democrats of high degree, either as to persons or as to reputation. The avowed candidates are in possession of their booms and dark horses are still chomping at their bits.[7]

Tickets to the 1912 banquet were in such great demand that scalpers were not only selling the tickets at extremely high prices but were also forging them. The regular price for a ticket was $5; scalpers were getting better than $20 per ticket.

> The regular tickets are signed across the front with the name of Mr. Clayton in red ink, and bear a secret sign, known only to him. It is through these identifying marks that the members of the committee hope to detect all forgeries. It is said that the bogus tickets have been signed with Mr. Clayton's name in black ink.[8]

William Jennings Bryan, the three-time Democratic candidate for President, felt very happy about the unity displayed in the party at the Jackson Day Dinner. At the dinner he stated:

> I have been accused of overweening ambition. For three times I have been the Democratic candidate for President but do not think that to be the Democratic candidate or to fill that office is the object of my life. I am reminded of the fat woman on the train who asked a gentleman to assist her to get off at the next station. She said that she was so fat that she had to get off backwards.
> Three times, she said, she had tried to get off the train, and each time the conductor, thinking that she was boarding the train, had pulled her up the steps. I have been trying to avoid nominations in the past but I have been too awkward about it. For the last three years, however, I have been learning and this time I will get off the train without doubt.[9]

This statement by Bryan seemed to clear the way for the nomination of Woodrow Wilson by the Democrats. The "Boy Orator of the Platte" attacked the decisions of the Supreme Court in trust cases; commended the initiative and referendum, but said that they were not national issues; advocated direct election of Senators; and rejoiced that an income tax would soon be a fact in the United States.

Woodrow Wilson talked about the tariff and similar issues but his reference to the currency question aroused the greatest interest.

> The country will not brook any plan which concentrates control in the hands of the bankers, because it knows that the bankers themselves are not isolated, and that the banks are tied in by a thousand enterprises, by community holdings, and by interests in many intricate ways. The outside public must in some thorough and effective way be put in a position to keep its credits and financial opportunities free and undicated. The bankers of the country may have the highest and purest intentions, but no one class can comprehend the country; no one set of interests can safely be suffered to dominate it.[10] ★

1915

AT the Jackson Day celebration in Washington D.C., in 1915, William Jennings Bryan spoke at the Women's National Democratic League convention at the Willard Hotel. He advised the women to rear their children according to Jacksonian principles. He also reiterated his conviction that women should have the right of suffrage:

> The right of voting requires the expression of two qualities, intelligence and morality. Until it can be proved that women have not these qualifications, they should never be denied the ballot.[11]

President Woodrow Wilson celebrated the centennial celebration of the Battle of New Orleans by giving a speech at Indianapolis where he hinted that he might run again in 1916 and where he advocated a Federal Employment Bureau. Comment on the President's speech and the announcement of his intention to run in 1916 was summarized succinctly by the *Washington Post:*

The political speech of President Wilson at Indianapolis Friday was the topic of conversation among men of all parties at the capital yesterday. The speech was accepted as an official announcement by the President of his candidacy in 1916 for a renomination to reseat himself, and as an appeal to the people to give careful heed to the policies he has advocated and prepare to voice their approval by supporting him in the next Presidential election.[12]

An editorial in the *Post* on January 8, 1915, raised a very interesting point when it posed the question of why Wilson was not speaking at New Orleans instead of 1,000 miles away from Jackson's battlefield. It was suggested that it might be because the Democrats of Louisiana were not in sympathy with the Democratic Party of 1915. In March of 1914 a reduction of the duty on sugar was made, and a provision in the law stated that all the duties should be removed by May 1, 1916. It was claimed that this tariff law, enacted under Woodrow Wilson's Administration, had destroyed the sugar business of thousands of Democrats in Louisiana, "without profiting the consumers of the United States by one cent." Whether this was the real reason President Wilson did not go to New Orleans is unknown, but there was probably some element of truth in it.

Speaking to more than 4,000 people in Indianapolis, Wilson rapped the Republican Party for not having a new idea in thirty years, stating, "The Republicans do not know how to do anything but sit on the lid." This he said in reference to the ship purchase bill which was pending at that time.

Wilson weakly referred to the war which was being waged in Europe at the time. He said that the citizens of America should not pay too much attention to it, but should attend to domestic affairs so that they might be of the most help in bringing about peace. In this century, Americans have not been able to avoid being aware and alert to conflict which may be raging abroad. As Wilson was to discover, the American people could not sit idly by and ignore the events of the modern world. ★

1916-1919

BETWEEN 1916 and 1919, there were no national Jackson Day celebrations reported. A possible reason for no dinner in 1919 was the fact that President Wilson was overseas participating in the solution of peace problems, and ex-President Theodore Roosevelt died on January 6, 1919. These two significant factors probably had some bearing on the absence of a Jackson Day celebration on January 8. Although Theodore Roosevelt was a Republican, he still was very highly respected among people of all parties throughout the country.

What had started out in the early 1800's as celebrations of the anniversary of the Battle of New Orleans had mushroomed to significant political events where formal speeches, rather than toasts, were given. Whereas approximately 200 or 300 people had participated in the earlier Jackson Day affairs, now the celebrations are carried on by 6,000 or more people at one time and in one place.

As Ralph Waldo Emerson once wrote in his essay on heroism, "The characteristic of heroism is its persistency." Andrew Jackson and Thomas Jefferson have been remembered down through the ages for the persistent manner in which they pursued their principles of Democracy for all the people of America. ★

Chapter 11

TALKATHON TIMES
OF THE TWENTIES

THE 1920's were times of temperance. They have also gone down in history as being roaring, tempestuous, turbulent, and tumultuous. With tension released after World War I, the twenties took on the tone of affluence and recklessness. All that glittered seemed like gold.

The Jackson Day events of that era are evidence of these traits of the twenties. The trademark of the many speakers at the Jackson Day affairs during this period was the giving of testimony and tribute to the Founding Fathers of the Democratic Party. The eulogizers spoke at length, as if in a contest to see who could win the favor of their contemporaries, as the listeners sat tired and tortured but pleased to be part of the affair.

1920

IN 1920, the Jackson Day banquet was sponsored by the Democratic National Committee and, for the first time, was held in two hotels, the Willard and the Washington. The response to the dinner was overwhelming. Later, in President Truman's time, the practice of holding the Jackson Day Dinner in two different places was revived because of increased attendance.

In 1920, each speaker addressed both groups, those at the Willard Hotel and those at the Washington Hotel, by a system of rotation. President Wilson sent a message to the diners, and addresses were given by Presidential aspirants— William Jennings Bryan; Secretary of the Navy Josephus Daniels; Attorney General A. Mitchell Palmer (who made the greatest impact on the audience); Governor James M. Cox of Ohio; Hon. James W. Gerard, former Speaker of the House of Representatives; Governor John J. Cornwell of West Virginia; Senator Gilbert M. Hitchcock of Nebraska; Senator Atlee Pomerene of Ohio; Senator Oscar Underwood of Alabama; Senator Robert L. Owen of Oklahoma; and Mrs. Peter Olesen of Minnesota, the first woman ever to address a national Jackson Day Dinner.

*Presidential aspirants and speakers at the
1920 Jackson Day banquet were Governor
James M. Cox of Ohio, who won the
Democratic nomination a few months later,
and William Jennings Bryan, who had
already run unsuccessfully for the Presidency
three times. (Courtesy of Underwood
and Underwood)*

In the context of history, it should be noted that the
Nineteenth Amendment to the United States Constitution giving women the right to vote was ratified in this
year. Up to this time, no woman had made a formal address
or toast at any of the national Jackson Day Dinners.

In the January 9, 1920, issue of the *Washington Post,*
five solid pages were used to describe the Jackson Day banquet and the speeches of the twelve orators. According to the

Post, the dinner was the "largest political gathering of its kind in the history of American politics." Approximately 1,500 attended the dinner, which lasted from 6 P.M. until 3 A.M.

The Democratic National Committee took over the arrangements for the banquet since it "is representative of the whole Democratic Party and not the instrument of any man or faction." Some Democrats in Washington thought that the "significance of the Jackson Day Dinner with respect to its bearing on the fortunes of candidates has been overplayed; that, in fact, the object of the National Committee in taking over the arrangements was to put the soft pedal on personal ambition."[1] Obviously, from the dozen speakers chosen to speak to the party, nonpartisanship became partisanship twelvefold. The Committee tried to be impartial and wound up with twelve speakers who held forth for nine hours. Only brave, devoted, dedicated Democrats would be willing to sit so long listening to so many.

There was a high intensity of expectation of important developments at the dinner. Unusual interest in the speeches was suggested by those expectations and possibilities—a conflict between President Wilson's message and William Jennings Bryan's, a declaration of a third term by Wilson, Wilson's making a last-ditch stand on the League of Nations, Wilson's coming out for unqualified ratification of the treaty, and a "comeback" by William Jennings Bryan.

No mention was made of a third term by Wilson, but a definite split in the Democratic Party came from the plea by President Wilson for the party to stand firm for the peace treaty and the League of Nations, while William Jennings Bryan demanded the ratification of the treaty with such compromise reservations as were obtainable. Because Bryan's utterances were in great variance with Wilson's suggestions, cries of "Stand by the President," and even "Put him out," caused so much confusion that Bryan had to halt his speech. Chairman Homer S. Cummings was forced to rap vigorously for order before the Nebraskan could continue.

In writing about the struggle for power within the in-group of the Democratic Party, Robert T. Small of the *Washington Post* commented on January 10, 1920, after the Jackson Day banquet:

> The great elimination derby of the Democracy ended about three o'clock yesterday morning . . . with a number of Presidential booms deflated and derelict along the trial course. The field was narrowed from an entry of 11 starters to a select 4 or 5 in whom campaign interest will center from this time forward.

Some of William Jennings Bryan's lieutenants had been spreading the report prior to the dinner that the Democratic National Committee had sought to pack the dinner with Wilson supporters and to prevent prominent Bryan supporters from attending.

> It is thought not likely that Mr. Bryan will find it expedient and in the interest of fair play to make an announcement repudiating this suggestion that he has been the victim of attempted discrimination upon an occasion so notably Democratic as the Jackson Day dinner, made more conspicuous this year by the fact that it is being held under the auspices of the Democratic National Committee, which during the interim of campaigns is representative of the whole Democratic party and not the instrument of any man or faction.[2]

In addition to displaying would-be candidates for the Presidency, the Jackson Day Dinners also provided an appropriate kickoff for the campaign of a given year since the dinners were usually held in late winter or early spring. This additional purpose for holding the dinners was another 20th-century innovation.

The Democratic National Committee had set up a women's division at this time known as the Associate Democratic National Committee. Mrs. Peter Olesen of Minnesota, who spoke at the dinner, was accompanied by about thirty other women of the Associate Democratic National Committee.

The 1920 affair was billed as a dinner where Bryan and Wilson might "start something." President Wilson and his followers wanted the treaty to be submitted by a referendum to the voters while the Bryan faction resisted such an idea. Bryan's followers wanted to draw up reservations which would be agreeable to two-thirds of the Senate and assure ratification.

After the dinner, it was evident that a continual clash would resound from that time until the National Convention met when delegates would draw up the platform. The headlines in the *Washington Star* on January 9, 1920, gave evidence of an impending battle:

DEMOCRATS SCENT WILSON VS. BRYAN TO CONTROL

SEE TWO MASTERFUL MEN
IN STRUGGLE TO DOMINATE
IN COMING CAMPAIGN

SPLIT AS TO PACT HELD MORE IMMINENT PERIL

The *Star* continued its analysis of the situation:

Looming large upon the horizon of the future, people see outlined there the figures of two masterful men struggling for the domination of the policies of the Democratic Party in the coming campaign. Realizing as do these politicians in Congress and others in the national management of the party that success at the polls in November, 1920, about which so many thousand political fortunes are staked, is involved, they visualize a titanic struggle at the next national convention June 28 at San Francisco over the framing of the platform and the writing of principles on which the party will appeal to the voter in November.

Some of the headlines of the January 9, 1920, *Washington Post* provide a succinct summary of the events at the Jackson Day Dinner:

DEMOCRATIC CHIEFS DOUBLE AT DINNERS

UNIQUE JACKSON DAY FEAST MAKES PARTY HISTORY

DRY TALK CHILLS CROWD

BRYAN THREATENS APPEAL
TO PEOPLE ON
PROHIBITION QUESTION

TUMULTY BESIDE COMMONER

REFERENCES TO "GREAT SECRETARIES"
DANIELS AND BAKER LEAVE CROWD UNMOVED

PALMER WINS LOUD APPLAUSE
AS HE ENDORSES PRESIDENT'S POSITION

GERARD SAYS BRYAN'S
PEACE TREATIES WOULD
HAVE PREVENTED WAR

DISCRETIONS ENLIVEN BANQUETS

BRYAN PROCLAIMS HIMSELF FOE
OF WILSON'S LEAGUE POLICY
*President's Silence
on Third Term
Causes Speculation*
Democratic Convention To Be
at San Francisco June 28

NEBRASKAN DISAVOWS ROLE OF ACTIVE CANDIDATE

GERARD IS WITH BRYAN

LEAGUE NOW BECOMES
STRICTLY PARTY QUESTION
FOR CAMPAIGN

ADMINISTRATION'S BANDWAGON IS
CROWDED WITH CHEERING SUPPORTERS

BRYAN AND GERARD
LONESOME AS THEY
STAND ALOOF

MANY SEE WILSON AS LOGICAL CANDIDATE
TO CARRY TREATY TO PEOPLE

CHAMP CLARK ELOQUENT IN
PRAISE OF DEMOCRATIC RECORD

Up to this point in history, this Jackson Day affair was
reported to have been the "greatest banquet, the greatest

outpouring of Democratic chieftains and workers and files and ranks known to the history of the party."[3] Those at the dinner heard the reading of President Wilson's letter which declared that he could not accept the action of the Senate on the peace treaty as the decision of the nation, and that he would take the matter before the people. Wilson, a very sick man at this time, insisted that the 1920 Presidential election be made a great and firm referendum. He attacked the Republican Senators for their "nullifying reservations." Of special concern was the reservation to Article 10, the reservation which Wilson felt was the most fatal to the covenant. Bryan thought that the reservation assured the Constitutional right of Congress to declare war and should not be vested in any other power. He insisted that the Democratic Party could not go to the people with an issue which involved transferring to a foreign nation the right to say "when our boys shall be conscripted."

Bryan approached the treaty problem from a pragmatic point of view when he indicated that the Democrats were in a minority in the Senate, that the election would not overturn the wide Republican margin in the fall elections, and that the "Democrats at once should seek a compromise." He stated that it would be very foolish to go to the country on the issue that the minority view in the Senate should prevail over the majority.

The activity at the $6-a-plate dinner was similar to a big rally where everyone scrambles for a ringside seat. About 800 people were accommodated at the Willard, and about 700 went to the Washington Hotel. "Standee" tickets were given out and caused a great influx of people after the speaking began, thus causing quite a bit of confusion in the hall and ultimately forcing all people standing to leave. Homer Cummings of Connecticut, Chairman of the Democratic National Committee, presided at the Willard Hotel while J. Bruce Kremer of Montana, Vice Chairman of the Democratic National Committee, presided at the Washington Hotel.

*The prohibition issue in the country and
in the Democratic Party became divisive
and emotional in the middle and late 1920's.
In this Berryman cartoon Miss Democracy
pretends not to hear the "drys" and
"wets" in discord.*

Although each of the twelve speakers was notified that
he could talk for only twenty minutes, Champ Clark was
the only one who kept within the allotted time. The talkathon had begun; their victory was yet to be won.   ★

1928   THE next Jackson Day banquet sponsored by the Democratic National Committee was held at the Mayflower Hotel
in 1928 with 2,000 people attending. More than 5,000
requests for tickets were left unfilled for this dinner.

Prior to the dinner, expectancy and suspense centered
around a possible fight between William G. McAdoo and

Alfred E. Smith, who had locked horns at the Democratic National Convention in 1924. Reports before the dinner indicated that the "drys" intended to "lay down the law" to Smith and his "wets." The issue of greatest interest to most people at this time was prohibition.

At previous dinners the party speakers had deliberately shied away from talking about the prohibition problem. When a few of the speakers happened to obliquely mention prohibition at former dinners, the remarks received a chilly reaction from the audience. At the 1920 dinner, Mrs. Peter Olesen of Minnesota, although reported as giving one of the best speeches at that dinner, did mention the prohibition problem. She gave the Democratic Party credit for putting through the Eighteenth Amendment, but there was not much applause. Instead, a gale of laughter swept through the Democratic audience. William Jennings Bryan smiled his familiar grin—a very tight, small smile—when she made her statement.

Year after year, the prohibition amendment and its supporters were being pressured by the "wets" on all sides. The nation, frustrated by the hit-and-run bootleggers who caused an increase in crime, was ready to explode over the dilemma of prohibition or nonprohibition.

The Democratic National Committee, to avoid any disharmony at the 1928 dinner, extracted a pledge from each speaker that he would not purposely cause disharmony. "It was learned from a reliable source that all of the 12 speakers have pledged themselves to refrain from touching upon any controversial subject."[4]

However, Governor Ritchie of Maryland, a believer in local option, "let the cat out of the bag when he said he had been warned to avoid controversial questions."[5]

Governor Alfred E. Smith of New York, fearing an anti-Smith campaign, chose not to attend the dinner and sent a message instead.

For some reason or another the friends of the New York governor have viewed, and still view, the dinner as unfriendly to them. One of the most prominent of Democratic chieftains said frankly yesterday that he thought the New York governor had been badly advised about the matter and that he was making a grave mistake by not attending. Certainly the list of speakers has more of a Smith complexion than an anti-[Smith] one.[6]

The speakers scheduled to address the party were John W. Davis, 1924 Presidential candidate, toastmaster; Claude C. Bowers, a party historian and formerly on the *New York World* editorial staff, and the real keynoter of the affair; William G. McAdoo; Senator James A. Reed of Missouri; Senator Joseph T. Robinson of Arkansas, the Senate floor leader; Governor Ritchie of Maryland; Senator Alben Barkley of Kentucky; Representative Finis J. Garret of Tennessee; Juston Thompson, former member of the Federal Trade Commission; Representative Mary T. Norton of New Jersey; former Governor Nellie Ross of Wyoming; Representative William Oldfield of Arkansas; Governor William Bulow of South Dakota; Governor Dan Moody of Texas; Evans Woolen, an Indiana banker; Clem Shaver, Democratic National Committee Chairman; and Will Rogers.

Although the dinner started at 7 P.M., at 2:30 A.M. five speakers still remained to be heard, but by common consent the meeting adjourned. Seventeen speakers were just too many even for the Democratic Party. Never before had such a number of speakers approached the podium at such affairs; never again have so many been put on the schedule at these events; many Democrats hope that the Democratic National Committee never again will even entertain such an idea.

The greatest attention and applause was given to the message sent by Governor Alfred E. Smith. Like the 1912 dinner and the Wilson boom, this dinner reinforced Al Smith's chances of gaining the 1928 Democratic Presidential nomination.

Will Rogers, speaking at 1 A.M., quipped:

We ought to be home by now, but if we go to anything given by the Democrats, we never get home.
I don't know when the Democratic Party started, but from all

I've heard tonight it started several hundred years before Jackson, for all they have dug up tonight couldn't have happened since his time.[7]

Many memorable sayings have been spoken by the sage Will Rogers. One of these was his remark about the Senate at this dinner:

It opens with a prayer and closes with an investigation. They investigate how much each paid to get in and if one paid more than they did, they throw him out. The House never minds how much a member paid to get in because it figures if he did pay he's a simp.[8]

Key figures at the 1928 dinner were John J. Raskob, Democratic Party National Chairman, Alfred E. Smith, a few months later to become the Democratic nominee for the Presidency, and Senator Joseph T. Robinson of Arkansas, a speaker at the dinner. Will Rogers (left), one of 17 speakers at the 1928 talkathon dinner, razzed the Democrats at 1 A.M. when it came his turn to speak. (Courtesy of Underwood and Underwood)

In the record-breaking Democratic National Convention of 1924, William G. McAdoo and Alfred E. Smith (right) were deadlocked for 102 ballots. On the 103rd ballot, John W. Davis (left) emerged from a dark-horse position to gain the nomination. (Courtesy of Underwood and Underwood)

The clincher put on the dinner was Will Rogers' statement that the "Democrats eat at least in harmony, even if they cannot drink in harmony."

Most of the publicity surrounding the 1928 dinner centered on William McAdoo, the former Secretary of the Treasury, who was the leader of the anti-Smith cause and a symbol of anti-Smith sentiment within the Democratic Party at this time. It was expected in some corners that McAdoo would denounce the "nullificationists," as he had done in a renunciatory statement a few months before the dinner.

At the 1924 Democratic National Convention in Madison Square Garden in New York on June 24, the delegates had wrestled for five days in the sweltering heat over whether the Democratic platform should advocate the entrance of the United States into the League of Nations and whether it should denounce the Ku Klux Klan. The party platform point which advocated entrance into the League of Nations was nullified by a vote of 742 to 353 while the Ku Klux Klan denouncement was defeated 546 to 541. At that time in Democratic Party history, there were a dozen candidates seeking the nomination for President, but this roster was soon reduced to ex-Secretary William G. McAdoo of California, the champion of the "drys" and of the rural sections of the South and the West, and Governor Alfred E.

The 1924 Presidential campaign produced more than a dozen Democratic aspirants, but no hopeful was able to pull out in front with enough support to overcome the prosperous Coolidge Administration.

Charles Bryan, shown here with his brother, William Jennings Bryan, was chosen as Vice Presidential candidate in 1924 in an attempt to appease party faction. (Courtesy of Underwood and Underwood)

Smith of New York, a "wet" and a Roman Catholic, who was supported by the Northeast with its large electoral vote. McAdoo and Smith fought fiercely and determinedly as the delegates cast 102 ballots in the record-making deadlock. On the 103rd ballot, the tired and beaten delegates broke the deadlock by going for a dark horse, John W. Davis of West Virginia, who had served as Ambassador to London during the Wilson Administration. To appease the radical elements of the party, Governor Charles W. Bryan of Nebraska, the brother of the Great Commoner, was selected as the candidate for Vice President.

During the four years after that historic Democratic convention, McAdoo formed the focal point of power for the "drys" and Alfred E. Smith served as the center for the "wets."

Pronouncements and predictions prior to the 1928 Jackson Day program indicated that McAdoo was planning to attack Governor Smith. Although these rumors had no solid base, they provided the Jackson Day Dinner with some excitement. The role of the Democratic National Committee was to keep the various factions from fighting each other openly to the embarrassment of the party.

The Democratic National Committee still had a $220,000 debt left from the 1924 campaign as this 1928 Jackson Day Dinner was approaching. Although the dinner was not a fund-raising affair, it was held in conjunction with the selection of a convention site by the National Committee. The meeting was held the day before the Jackson Day Dinner to select the site which would provide money to rid themselves of the 1924 campaign debt. It was more obvious year by year that campaigning nationwide was becoming an extremely expensive item for the political parties. Such pressure kept building until 1936 when James Farley and the Democratic National Committee had to invent some new ways of raising money for the party's campaigns.

But the 1928 dinner provided a great deal of activity and excitement in kicking off the campaign for the Presidency. The dinner proved to be very harmonious—seven and a half hours of harmony!

Senator James Reed of Missouri, a hopeful for the Democratic Presidential nomination, rose to the occasion with probably the most inspiring speech of the evening and urged that Democrats rally around a platform on which most of them could agree. He suggested that they use practical common sense in the campaign of 1928.

If every Democrat insists on his own way in everything, no Democrat will have his own way in anything. If everything is put into the platform that has been mentioned here tonight, we will get nowhere. . . .

We have had the wet and dry question thrust into the discussion. The wet Democrat who insists upon putting a wet plank into the party's platform will alienate 50% of the party, and the dry who insists upon putting into the platform a dry plank will alienate the other 50%. They will insure a Republican victory at the polls. Those who would thrust in a foreign policy which does not meet the common judgment of the party will cause party suicide.[9]

Senator Reed gave this speech on the same platform

where Governor Ritchie of Maryland, another hopeful for
the Democratic nomination, had stated that the Democratic
Party must face the prohibition issue and settle it with local
option. He gave the speech on the same platform where
Governor Dan Moody of Texas predicted that trying to
change the Eighteenth Amendment would get one about as
far as trying to change the Golden Rule or the Ten Com-
mandments. Others on the platform were William Gibbs
McAdoo, the "dry" leader and son-in-law of the late President Woodrow Wilson, who had fought Senator Reed on
the League of Nations issue, and Mrs. Woodrow Wilson,
widow of the late President.

Some headlines of newspaper articles describing the
dinner give a kaleidoscopic view of the affair:[10]

DEMOCRATS AVOID ALL
CONTROVERSIES
TO ATTAIN UNITY

LEADERS CONGRATULATE SELVES
ON SKIRTING DISPUTES AMONG FACTIONS

SEVEN-AND-A-HALF-HOUR DINNER HALTS
AFTER REED TALKS WITH FIVE UNHEARD

DEMOCRATS PICK HOUSTON: CHEER AL SMITH

NEW YORK GOVERNOR URGES
PARTY LEADERS AT DINNER
TO MEET PROHIBITION ISSUE

CANNOT CARRY "WATER" ON BOTH SHOULDERS, HE WRITES

BEGIN ON PLATFORM NOW, HE SUGGESTS

FAVORS "STRAIGHT" TALK
TO AMERICANS IN
THE PARTY'S PLANKS

HARMONY SPIRIT RULES AT THE BANQUET;
CROWD CHEERS WOODROW WILSON

SPEAKERS TAKE UP
ALL TOUCHY ISSUES

Nothing like the array of speakers at the 1928 dinner was to be seen again in the modern history of the Jefferson-Jackson Day celebrations. This dinner climaxed the attempts to give everybody interested in the Presidential nomination a chance to speak before the party faithful. Later Jefferson-Jackson Day celebrations had potential Presidential candidates speaking at the affairs, but never were there as many as there were at this historic 1928 dinner. ★

Three unsuccessful Democratic candidates for the Presidency in the 1920's, James Cox, John Davis, and Alfred Smith, were the major speakers at the 1932 Jackson Day Dinner. Franklin D. Roosevelt had run for the Vice Presidency on the 1920 ticket with James Cox.

1932 THE last Jackson Day celebration before the modern $100-a-plate dinners was held in 1932 at the Mayflower Hotel with approximately 2,000 attending and was sponsored by the Democratic National Committee. With the three unsuccessful Democratic Presidential nominees of 1920, 1924, and 1928—James M. Cox, John W. Davis, and Alfred E. Smith—doing the speaking, the oratorical program was much shorter than the 1928 talkathon. Claude Bowers repeated his role as toastmaster. For the first time in the history of the Jackson Day Dinners, the three speeches were broadcast over the radio and were heard by a vastly greater number of people than ever before.

Cox and Davis explicitly withdrew themselves from

Franklin D. Roosevelt's chances for winning the Presidency in 1932 were beclouded by the uncertainty of the actions of his own party in regard to the prohibition problem.

any possibility that they would be Presidential candidates again. Alfred E. Smith made no such statement and was regarded as a politician seeking the proper opportunity to announce himself as a seeker of the Presidency. The struggle for power within the party at this time was noted by the editors of the *Washington Post:*

> The Democrat most acceptable to the greatest number of Democrats in all sections is Franklin D. Roosevelt. It is not necessary for him to come to the Jackson Day dinner to impress himself upon the Democratic leaders. They know he is the first choice of the rank and file of the party. Some of these leaders have declared for him, others are inclined to do so, and others oppose him.[11]

Roosevelt had carried New York State in 1930 with 725,000 votes to spare in his race for the Governor's chair.

With the great depression under way throughout the country, Smith, Cox, and Davis spent most of their speaking time tearing apart the "prosperity" slogan of Hoover in 1928. Smith suggested a plan of selling bonds for the re-

Alfred E. Smith, "The Happy Warrior,"
still desiring the nomination for the
Presidency in 1932, flatly endorsed repealing
the prohibition amendment. He said that
"rum, gin, booze, and beer are running
all over the United States untaxed."

lief of the unemployed; Davis branded the Republican re-
gimes as "eras of betrayal, complacency, and wild dismay";
and Cox asked the South to show consideration for the
North in the prohibition controversy which was still the
issue getting most attention and interest from the public.
All three speakers attacked prohibition.

Al Smith, long an advocate of repealing the Eighteenth
Amendment, shouted:

Think of the billions we are kicking away from us that would
come in taxation. Why, rum, gin, booze and beer are running
all over the United States untaxed, and the only man that is going to
be safe during March, when you have to make all those income tax
figures up, is the bootlegger.[12]

When Smith concluded his speech, Mrs. Woodrow Wilson, who sat between Smith and Chairman John J. Raskob, grasped his hand and showed her enthusiasm for him.

Governor Albert Ritchie of Maryland, who had announced his candidacy for the Presidential nomination just the night before this banquet, was given a ringing ovation when he entered the dining hall. The same was true of the Speaker of the House of Representatives, John N. Garner of Texas, who was being boomed for the Presidency by the Hearst newspapers.

Sitting at the speakers' table in addition to those already mentioned were former Governor Harry Byrd of Virginia; Senator Joseph P. Robinson of Arkansas; Mrs. Nellie Ross, former Governor of Wyoming; James W.

John J. Raskob's main task at the 1932 dinner was to produce harmony between the warring "wets" and "drys" in the party. Prohibition by this time was second only to the depression as a political issue.

Gerard, Treasurer of the Democratic National Committee; Jouett Shouse, Executive Chairman of the National Committee; and Frank Hague, the Democratic boss of New Jersey.

The Democratic Party throughout its entire history has fought against the "special privilege" philosophy of government while concurrently promoting the philosophy of equal opportunities for all. Probably the only solution which could have eliminated the talkathon times of the twenties was the one offered by Will Rogers at the 1928 dinner: "I have one thing to offer—that's equal opportunities for none and special privileges for all. If that line had been cut out, we'd have been home hours ago."[13]   ★

Chapter 12

GENESIS OF THE $100-A-PLATE DINNER

FROM THE PRECEDING descriptions of the predecessors of the modern Democratic National Committee Dinners of the $100-a-plate variety, it is evident that such occasions had their beginning with the celebrations of the Battle of New Orleans, which was fought on January 8, 1815. The present form and character of the dinners also have their seeds in the earlier dinners.

Complaints that the suppers were partisan in nature originated as early as 1828, the second Jackson Day banquet held in Washington, D.C.

In addition to the partisan nature of these gatherings, other characteristics of the Democratic National Committee Dinner speeches can be traced to their predecessors. Near the turn of the century, regular public addresses began to replace the numerous regular and volunteer toasts which made up the mode of address prior to that time. At this same time, the Democratic National Committee began sponsoring the Jackson Day Dinners. The dinners began to be tied in with the quadrennial meeting of the Democratic National Committee when a site for the Presidential nominating convention would be selected.

The audience attending these dinners has always been composed mainly of Congressmen, party leaders, and party workers. During the first fifty years of these dinners, the people came almost entirely from within a small radius of Washington. However, with improved transportation and communication and westward expansion, people attending the dinners came from all sections of the United States. Although there is greater geographical distribution of the people attending the Jefferson-Jackson Day affairs today, the basic nature of those attending has not changed.

The main purposes for holding these dinners prior to 1936 were to celebrate the Battle of New Orleans and honor Andrew Jackson, to provide an opportunity for Democrats to harmonize their interests and unite for concerted action, and to serve as an occasion for socialization in an ingroup, the Democratic Party.

Another characteristic which emerges from these dinners is the desire of politicians to be one of the "chosen few" who are selected to give regular toasts or to speak to the group. Since the occasion is one of the very few times for the Democratic Party to meet as a national party, it is considered an honor and a political advantage to speak to the party. In more explicit terms, to be a speaker at these dinners gives the speaker a feeling that he is something more than a member of the party. In the eternal search for power in politics, being a speaker at these occasions enhances political stature within the group.

From the toasts and speeches given at the early dinners, several categories of topics may be found enunciated at almost every occasion. First, reference is usually made to the ideas and accomplishments of the Democratic Party and of the great Democratic leaders of the past and present. Second, an attack is usually made on the ideas and accomplishments of the opponents. Third, a discussion of current issues is held with suggestions as to the expediency or inexpediency of certain avenues of action.

The main toasters and speakers at the dinners have always been the leaders of the party, whether these leaders are in national, state, or local government. The one major exception to this was the dinner given in 1852 when Lewis Kossuth, a Hungarian patriot, was the featured speaker. This is the only dinner at which a foreign dignitary has been a principal speaker.

There seems to have been no regular schedule by any group for having these dinners, although the Jackson Democratic Association of Washington, D.C., was the organization which most consistently sponsored them from Jackson's era to the turn of the century. The only real consistency these dinners had was the date on which they were given, January 8, and even this consistency has disappeared during the past 15 years.

The price of the dinner did not change much from 1827 to 1935. It was $5 for the first one and most of them

In 1931 the Democrats faced a deficit from the 1928 campaign, a not too unusual predicament for the party. James Farley demanded that the deficit be eliminated. Later Farley was primarily responsible for raising large funds through the $100-a-plate dinners.

thereafter until 1936. The money was used to pay for the dinner, instead of the dinner being employed as a fund-raising device, as is the practice today.

Marie Chatham, in her doctoral dissertation on the role of the National Party Chairman from Hanna to Farley, wrote:

Under Farley's chairmanship, the Democratic Party was very inventive on the effective money making schemes. One of these schemes, the sale of an elaborate campaign book, nearly died abornin', for the passage of the Hatch Act made the life of this lucrative device very short, but Farley took an older propaganda device—the party dinner—and started it on its way to being one of the Democratic Party's most effective sources of income.

Political dinners are by no means new . . . however, the purpose of the chairman in gathering the clan in the old days was not that of immediate order of revenue returns. The pre-Farley dinners were simply devices by which the chairman incited the enthusiasm of the potential contributors to the degree that the men present were sufficiently impressed with the candidates and the party's chances that contributions would be forthcoming later. Apparently, the method was effective, too.[1]

As mentioned earlier, the $100-a-plate dinners came about as a result of the quest of James A. Farley, the Democratic National Committee Chairman in 1936, to find ways and means of reducing the large Democratic Party debt which resulted from the Presidential campaigns of Alfred E. Smith in 1928 and Franklin D. Roosevelt in 1932. The dinners since 1936 have been known by many names, but they have revolved around Jefferson-Jackson Day affairs.

1936

THE first annual Democratic National Committee Dinner held primarily for a fund-raising purpose, costing $50 a plate, was held in 1936 in the Mayflower Hotel with President Franklin D. Roosevelt as the only speaker. More than 2,000 attended this dinner and paid $100,000 for the privilege. During the deep depression, this was a great amount of money. Since this first dinner in 1936, the price of the "contribution" has been $100 a plate. After the great success of this experiment by Farley & Company in 1936 at $50 a plate, it was judged, and correctly so, that the party could receive $100 a plate for the privilege of attending the dinner. Thus, in 1937, the $100-a-plate tradition began.

Much planning and soliciting went into the 1936 dinner. Evidence of this came out in the open on the eve of the national dinner party when the American Liberty League, a foe of the New Deal, attacked Farley and the Democrats for the way they were soliciting funds.

The League charged that Postmaster General Farley had solicited Democratic campaign funds from other federal officeholders through the medium of Jefferson-Jackson Day Dinners. It emphasized that it was unlawful for any officer or employee of the United States government, directly or indirectly, to solicit or receive contributions for any political purpose from any other officer or employee of the government. The League continued its attack by pointing out that Farley had addressed the state presidents of the Young Democratic Clubs on December 6 over a nationwide telephone circuit from Democratic Headquarters in New York. The League quoted Farley as saying:

> In order that every Jackson Day participant may feel that he or she is indeed being of material assistance to the Democratic Party, the price of your dinner should be worked out on a basis which will permit forwarding a part of what every diner pays to the Democratic National Committee. . . .[2]

Farley had been trying to organize Jefferson-Jackson Day affairs throughout the country, as well as the $50-a-plate dinner in Washington, D.C. The cost of the Jackson Day affairs ranged from $50 a plate at the dinner attended by President Roosevelt down to $2 in other places in the country.

The device which would connect all of these Jackson Day Dinners was the radio. President Roosevelt's address was to be sent throughout the country, much as his fireside chats were. Little did the people know, even the participants themselves, that this nationwide Jackson Day celebration would become an annual affair and an annual broadcast to the people. It was estimated that approximately 250,000 people would attend the Jackson Day Dinners throughout the country, in Puerto Rico, and in Hawaii.

Just a few days before the January 8, 1936, Democratic National Committee Dinner, the Supreme Court of the United States declared the Agricultural Adjustment Act unconstitutional, feeling it was coercive federal regulation of farm production and prices that invaded the reserved powers of the states.

This Democratic National Committee Dinner address by President Roosevelt, broadcast to the more than 3,000 Jackson Day Dinners throughout the country, activated widespread anticipation that Roosevelt would discuss his feelings concerning the Supreme Court decsion on the AAA. During the first few years of Roosevelt's Administration, much social legislation was passed, and cases to determine the constitutionality of those bills were beginning to appear on the Supreme Court docket. The declaration of the un-constitutionality of the AAA gave immediate impetus to Roosevelt's belief that the Supreme Court needed revamp-ing. However, his plans for "packing" the Supreme Court had to await the Presidential campaign and election in the fall of 1936.

Though speculation ran high that Roosevelt would speak on the Supreme Court decision, he merely said that he desired more time to study "two of the most momentous opinions, the majority opinion and the minority opinion, that have ever been rendered in any case before the Supreme Court of the United States."[3] At the mention of the mi-nority opinion, there was great applause from the partisan crowd.

Even though Roosevelt did not say much directly about the AAA decision, the general tenor of his speech was an appeal to the people of America to support him in his en-deavors to promote the right of each man and woman in America "to lead a finer, a better, and a happier life."

Washington, D.C., had never seen the likes of the 1936 $50-a-plate dinner. An orchestra was present, played over and over "Happy Days Are Here Again," and rang out with "Home on the Range" (thought to be a Roosevelt favorite) when the President arrived.

The Mayflower Hotel was crammed from top to bot-tom; the ballroom floor was filled, balconies were crowded, and the lobby was overflowing with enthusiastic Democrats.

The arrival of President Roosevelt was very dramatic

and in keeping with a dinner which cost each participant $50. After the room was filled with diners, a curtain opened and President Roosevelt was seen standing beneath a large picture of Andrew Jackson. The President wore a tuxedo as did many others at the earlier Jackson Day affairs in the thirties. The orchestra played the familiar "Hail to the Chief" as the enthusiastic and dedicated Democrats yelled, cheered, and clapped.

Since the opening of the 1936 Presidential campaign had been sounded just a few days before this Jackson Day occasion, an attempt by Roosevelt to influence all types of people, not just Democrats, had the ultimate purpose of seeking favorable attitudes toward his program and votes for his election in the fall. Roosevelt likened the political struggles of his time to those which Jackson waged during his Adminstration. Throughout the praise of Jackson, Roosevelt inferentially drew the comparison that the forces which fought Jackson were the same ones now arrayed against himself. Roosevelt suggested that only a minority with "haughty and sterile intellectualism" opposed him. Although this statement referred to Jackson, many throughout the country apparently (according to the response he received) took this to be a thrust at the Supreme Court. The *Washington Star* hailed the speech as "a masterful appeal to the great mass of Americans."

The headlines in the *Washington Post* on January 9, 1936, highlighted the Jackson Day affair:

ROOSEVELT ASKS PARTY DRIVE
TO GET "THE TRUTH" TO PEOPLE;
HOUSE STARTS SALVAGE OF AAA

JACKSON DAY TALK HITS FOES'
STATEMENTS ON NEW DEAL

CALLS ON HEARERS
TO PRESENT ISSUES

PRESIDENT'S FIGHT
FOR SOCIAL JUSTICE
IS STRESSED.[4]

In Roosevelt's conclusion, he said, "The American People and we will not retreat." It was very clear that Roosevelt wanted his hearers to read into that statement that he and they would fight for the programs of the New Deal despite reversals by the Supreme Court.

Farley's fund-raising affair became an overnight financial success. He had hit upon a device for digging the Democrats out of their campaign debt. The $100-a-plate dinner, as an occasion both for raising funds and for promoting party policies, was born and would soon grow into a giant. ★

Chapter 13

REPRISE
BY ROOSEVELT

THE REFRAIN of the Jackson Day celebrations was repeated annually by President Roosevelt right up to his death in 1945. Actually, the last speech he prepared was for the 1945 Jefferson Day affair; he died on the day prior to the occasion.

JACKSON DAY celebrations were to become annual fund raisers, not even to be interfered with by World War II. The first $100-a-plate price was set in 1937 for the dinner which was held at the Mayflower Hotel with over 1,300 people attending.

1937

The dinner, called the Democratic Victory Dinner, was given on March 4 rather than the traditional Jackson Day, January 8. The affair was a combination celebration of Roosevelt's victory in the fall of 1936 and the completion of four years he had spent in office—Roosevelt having taken office on the old date for inauguration, March 4.

Beginning in January of 1935 with the nullification of a section of the National Industrial Recovery Act and continuing through the time of this speech, the Supreme Court had declared unconstitutional many of the important economic and social programs Roosevelt and the Congress had made law. For example, the National Industrial Recovery Act and the Agricultural Adjustment Act, the pillars of the New Deal program, were declared unconstitutional. The Supreme Court struck down a railroad retirement plan, the bituminous coal act, Congressional legislation to protect farm mortgages, and a municipal bankruptcy act. Because of these actions the Supreme Court came under close scrutiny and bitter criticism. Congress and Roosevelt defended the measures by saying that the laws were constitutional since they fell within the domain of the general welfare clause, the taxation powers, and the regulation of interstate commerce. Because of the frequent unfavorable decisions on New Deal legislation, Roosevelt was convinced that something had to be done to prevent the Supreme Court from wrecking his whole program and from tying his hands in his efforts to cope with the economic and social problems of the day.

After the tremendous landslide in the election of 1936, Roosevelt felt more confident than ever that the "mandate" the people had given him was a vote of confidence for his measures and program. In his speech at the 1937 Victory Dinner, he said:

> I speak at this Victory Dinner not only as the head of the Democratic Party but as the representative of all Americans who have faith in political and economic democracy.
> And, incidentally, our victory was not sectional. It did not come from compromises and bargains. It was the voice of 27 million voters—from every part of the land.[1]

Also, he believed that the people would be solidly behind him in his efforts to do something to bring the Supreme Court into line.

In a special message to Congress on January 5, 1937, Roosevelt submitted a bill which would empower the President to appoint a new federal judge when any judge failed to retire within six months after reaching the age of 70. The bill would have made it possible to increase the Supreme Court to fifteen members.

This message was an invitation for an attack and set off the bitterest nationwide debate in New Deal history. In Congress, New Deal Democrats supported the plan while many of the conservative Democrats joined the Republicans in opposing it. Since the debate raged for more than six months, the speech at the Democratic Victory Dinner came at a time when the battle was at its peak. This speech was to

President Franklin D. Roosevelt, swept into office in the record-breaking landslide election of 1936, made effective use of the Jefferson-Jackson Day Dinner speech to reach a nationwide audience via radio.

serve as the foundation for the fireside chat which followed in just a few days. Both addresses were on the topic of the reorganization of the federal judiciary, including the Supreme Court. Roosevelt explained that the subjects he had to discuss could not be covered in a single speech.

Roosevelt's main purpose in this speech, as might be surmised from his background, was to rally the support of Congress and the people in his battle to get the Court bill passed. He attempted to portray himself and the New Deal Democrats as sincere, inventive men who were trying to solve the economic and social problems of the people through ingenious corrective legislation which was being invalidated by a group of men who were not in stride with the times.

Roosevelt tried to show the achievements and attempts he and the Democratic Party had made on the people's behalf and to warn the people and the party that decisions by the Supreme Court were endangering democracy in the United States. Ultimate results show that Roosevelt was not successful in getting the Court bill passed.

The failure touched off the "Purge of 1938" in which Roosevelt tried to replace conservative Democrats who had sided with the Republicans in opposition to his Court bill. Even though Roosevelt did not win the battle, he won the war. In the same month as this Victory Dinner speech, Congress passed a bill permitting Supreme Court justices to retire on full pay at the age of 70, which made retirement financially possible. The Judicial Procedure Reform Act, passed in August of 1937, permitted the Attorney General to intervene in suits involving the constitutionality of acts of the Congress, making possible a more rapid and orderly settlement of issues.

More significantly, the unchanged Supreme Court began to approve New Deal legislation. In late March, 1937, the Supreme Court reversed itself on a decision by upholding a minimum wage law in Washington when a year prior to this it had invalidated a similar law in New York. The

THE INGENIOUS QUARTERBACK!

National Labor Relations Act was upheld, as were many other New Deal laws.

Once again President Roosevelt spoke to $100 contributors and others throughout the country in his usual thirty-minute radio address. The *Washington Star* of March 3, 1937, explained the financial aspects of this first $100-a-plate dinner:

> The $100-a-plate affair at the Mayflower is thought to set a record for high cost in political banquets. A down payment of $25 admits the diner to the dining room, and the remaining $75 is to be collected in three installments of $25 each.[2]

On the same night, March 4, 1937, approximately 1,500 Young Democrats dined at a Junior Victory Banquet at the Willard Hotel where Mrs. Eleanor Roosevelt was the guest of honor. This affair cost $10 a plate.

It was estimated that President Roosevelt's speech was carried by radio to 1,262 victory dinners held throughout the nation. It was reported that a total of 515,000 men and women attended these victory dinners.

The editorial in the March 6, 1937, edition of the *Washington Star* summed up President Roosevelt's address:

President Roosevelt has taken his fight to revamp the Supreme Court to the people in a radio broadcast to be followed by others. His purpose is to arouse public sentiment so that opposition in Congress to his Court Bill will subside. With the passage of that measure, the President will appoint a maximum of six new justices who will construe the Constitution on conformity with New Deal ideas. . . . What the President is now trying to do is to bring sufficient pressure upon Congress to enforce the enactment of his Court Bill into law. He is trying to accomplish his end through addresses calculated to enflame the people against the Supreme Court as it is now constituted. He tells the people that the Court, and the Court alone, stands in the way of laws to help them, laws calculated to solve the farmer's problem and to give the laborers less

hours and more wages, laws which will make it possible for the federal government to prevent floods and dust storms. . . .

The President's address at the Democratic Victory Dinner was a demand for party action to put through "now" his Court Bill, and so to give him in effect the right to interpret and construe the Constitution. The President, as always, spoke eloquently. He spoke militantly. He decried the "defeatist lawyers," the men who have urged that the Constitution, if it is to be amended, be amended in the orderly manner prescribed by reference to the states and the people. "Defeatist lawyers" becomes now a term of utmost approbrium in the New Dealer's lexicon.

Jackson Day celebrations, which had started out in the 1800's merely as social gatherings, had become in 1937 very important political meetings as well as social gatherings. The affair produced a legitimate excuse for the President of the United States to speak in a very partisan manner on the important subjects of the day. In the case of 1937, President Roosevelt was speaking on one of the most historic aspects of his four terms. In addition to raising huge sums for the party, the President struck a "body blow"— though not a fatal one—to the opposition of his Court plan.   ★

THE fighting Roosevelt fired again with a militant speech at the 1938 Jackson Day Dinner held in the Mayflower Hotel on January 8. More than 1,200 people were at this dinner when Franklin D. Roosevelt was introduced to the hotel audience and to a national radio audience by Democratic National Committee Chairman James A. Farley. William B. Bankhead, Speaker of the House of Representatives, followed Roosevelt with a second address of the evening.

With the big battle over the Court bill having ended during the summer of 1937, another crisis faced Roosevelt and America in the fall of 1937 and during 1938. Prevalent at the time of this 1938 Jackson Day celebration was the business recession into which the United States had plunged. Still trying to gather strength after the deep de-

1938

pression of the early 1930's, America did not welcome the onslaught of a new business recession.

During the months prior to this celebration, in November and December, Attorney General Robert Jackson and Secretary of the Interior Harold Ickes had made vitriolic attacks on big business and were charging that big business was the causal culprit behind the recession. President Roosevelt, in his annual message to Congress, had been conciliatory. He felt that he had to work with big business to solve the problems of the business recession, and he therefore did not want to alienate big business. In anticipation of Roosevelt's Jackson Day address in 1938, there was much speculation as to the manner in which New Deal adherents would attack the recession problem. Speculation settled on the posture Roosevelt would take in trying to pull the United States out of the recession. Business was especially anxious to see what attitude Roosevelt would take toward business itself and the recession.

Many people feared that the 1937–38 recession would be another major depression as the relief lines queued up and unemployment rose to ten million.[3] Jackson and Ickes accused the "economic royalists" of deliberately fomenting industrial and financial panic in order to discredit Roosevelt. Big business replied that excessive government regulations, a tax on the utility companies, new taxes on profits and capital gains, and the growing public debt had created an uncertainty in business circles and were making industry fearful of expanding.

In his annual message to Congress on January 3, 1938, just five days before this Jackson Day speech, Roosevelt disclaimed any animosity toward business, which, he thought, was sincerely trying to restore prosperity. But he did accuse a "minority" of big business of tax evasion, unfair competition, and the maintenance of excessive prices. This was the scene as Roosevelt began to speak to the party at the Jackson Day Dinner on January 8, 1938.

In this speech, Roosevelt took as his principal theme

the position that the 1937–38 recession was the product of evil practices by a minority of the business world, and that all of the American people, including the great majority of the businessmen, whom he distinguished from his enemies, should support the New Deal in its efforts to improve business conditions. He pictured himself as seeking greater cooperation between business and government in order to bring the United States out of the recession.

Roosevelt spoke to the diners at the Mayflower Hotel and throughout the country on the three national radio networks. His speech was also broadcast to some foreign countries. James A. Farley reported that the party made a profit of more than $400,000 on the Jackson Day Dinners in 1938. The Washington dinner alone yielded more than $100,000. This money was used to retire the party's $200,-000 indebtedness and to prepare the party for the Congressional battles which were to ensue.

Roosevelt's Cabinet members were scattered throughout the country giving addresses to other major Jackson Day Dinners. (This practice was continued every year after that, and is common practice today.) James Farley was in New York where he made the radio introduction of President Roosevelt to the diners at the Washington affair and to the listeners throughout the country and the world.

The *Washington Star* of January 9, 1938, described the preparations which went into the 1938 Jackson Day Dinner:

Scaling downward from the $100-per-plate banquet at the Mayflower where President Roosevelt spoke, to the more modest $25 and $50 snacks at strategic points over the country, the faithful and not so faithful came early and stayed late to eat the Democratic Party out of the red. . . .

The Democratic National Committee started sending out invitations two months ago, using a list of those who had attended similar functions last year and others who had been suggested as possessing the qualities that make for a good $100 diner-out in a worthy cause.

If no answer were received in response to the first bid, the postman rang again. If this brought no results, a third polite letter suggested that the holiday rush had been responsible for the neglect, and coupled this with a reminder that time was fleeting.

The distribution of invitations was handled efficiently and properly with deliveries being made only to the homes in view of the statute prohibiting political solicitation in federal buildings.

In one quarter it was stated that some supervisory officers were annoyed by the whole idea, and just let their staffs be guided by their conscience. Others, however, it was added, "turned on the heat."

Reports of any sort of compulsion being used to push the sale of the $100 dinner tickets were denied by Oliver A. Quayle, Jr., Acting Treasurer of the Democratic National Committee, who was in charge of the dinner arrangements.

"It is entirely a voluntary affair," he said yesterday, "giving Democrats an opportunity to contribute to the financial support of the party and to meet together with the President, such an opportunity as they have at no other time of the year."

President Roosevelt was seated at a small head table with Vice President John N. Garner; Speaker William B. Bankhead; Breckenridge Long, former Ambassador to Italy, who was Chairman; and L. W. Robert, Jr., Secretary of the Democratic National Committee, toastmaster.

Roosevelt's address at the dinner made explicit his dedication to maintain "the integrity of the morals of democracy," which he said came down to the nation as a heritage from Jefferson to Wilson. This phrase ran through Roosevelt's speech like a refrain. He used it, with variation, eight times to show that he wanted to eradicate the evils which emerge from undue concentration of economic power or from unfair business practices.

Roosevelt singled out the holding companies of public utilities as the specific "victim" against whom the people should direct their wrath, because only a few men controlled the vast utility interests of America and because they were working against the interests of the American people. This was the only specific identification provided of the so-called "minority of business." Roosevelt attacked the same generalized "selfish minority" that he had castigated on other occasions, especially in his Madison Square Garden address on October 31, 1936, during his second Presidential campaign. He mentioned then that this group had met its match during his first term and that it would meet its master during his second term. He pictured the utilities and the holding companies as a "96-inch dog being wagged by a 4-inch tail." This word picture was impressed on the minds of many of those listening to Roosevelt's speech, as was attested to by the large number of people who wrote Roosevelt about it.

Samuel I. Rosenman, one of Roosevelt's speech writers, sent the following telegram from New York to Roosevelt concerning this last quote:

> Nature abhors a vacuum and I know a few who will abhor that speech, but I love it! My dog's four-inch tail is blushing with its nation-wide publicity.

Roosevelt's remark about the 96-inch dog got the greatest applause and the greatest gales of laughter of the evening.

After President Roosevelt's speech, Speaker William Bankhead gave a brief talk. Vice President Garner was then called upon to speak, but he simply tapped President Roosevelt on the top of the head and said, "Sisters and brothers, as I say to the Senate, we dismiss you tonight until 1939 at the same hour." He sat down amid yells of applause. ★

1939

It was almost a year to the day that Franklin D. Roosevelt spoke again at the Jackson Day Dinner in 1939. Since January 8 fell on a Sunday that year, the dinner was held on Saturday, January 7, at the Mayflower Hotel. As in 1938, the only other speaker was William B. Bankhead, Speaker of the House of Representatives. There were approximately 1,200 people attending the affair, which was broadcast over the radio.

Jackson Day Dinners were held in 47 states where the diners paid up to $50 to hear Roosevelt via radio as well as other political speakers present at the dinners. The dinners in 1938 finally netted the National Committee a profit of more than $280,000. O. Max Gardner, chairman of the dinner committee and former Governor of North Carolina, aptly summarized the financial aspects of the dinner when he made the remark about James Farley's being able to sell $5 worth of groceries for $100.

Two important developments had occurred since the 1938 Jackson Day Dinner. Because some of the conservative Democrats during 1938 had combined forces with the Republicans in defeating many important New Deal measures, Roosevelt had made an unsuccessful attempt to purge the Democratic Party of Congressmen hostile to parts of the New Deal.

This coalition of anti-New Deal Democrats and Republicans in 1938 had been successful in blocking many New Deal measures. For example, the combination cut hundreds of millions of dollars from appropriation bills, defeated the bill for the Presidential reorganization of the Executive Department, refused to amend the neutrality act to give the President the right to distinguish between aggressor and nonaggressor nations in the matter of the export of war material, ignored Roosevelt's request for the establishment of six regional projects like the Tennessee Valley Authority, and favored corporations in the tax bill of 1938 which became law without Roosevelt's signature.[4]

Because of these setbacks to his program, Roosevelt intervened in the primary elections in the summer and fall of 1938 to urge the people to replace certain Democratic conservatives with liberals. Senators Tydings of Maryland, Gillette of Iowa, Smith of South Carolina, and George of Georgia were the main targets, since they were the most outspoken opponents to much of the New Deal.

The second major development was the Congressional election in the fall of 1938 when all of the Senators Roosevelt tried to purge were reelected without much trouble. In addition, the Republicans increased their representation in the House of Representatives from 89 to 170 and gained eight seats in the Senate. The recession of 1937, Roosevelt's unsuccessful attempt to "pack the Supreme Court," and his attempted purge of certain Democratic Congressmen contributed to these Republican gains.

There was special significance given to the Jackson Day speech this year because of the bitterness which evolved between the liberal New Deal and the conservative factions of the Democratic Party. Speculation arose as to whether Roosevelt would attempt to foster a friendlier atmosphere than was present when he intervened in the primary battles against candidates considered too conservative to be called Democrats. Thus, Roosevelt's chief purpose in this 1939 speech was to ask the Democrats to support the objectives of the New Deal and to request the party to restore harmony or risk defeat in the 1940 elections. He was urging a united front of Democratic liberals and independents to "continue a common, constructive service to the people of the land." Striking out at the conservative Democrats, Roosevelt suggested that they solve their differences with the liberals by debate within the party.

Roosevelt indicated in his speech that he wasn't about to give up his purge although he had been defeated in the preceding fall's elections in replacing the conservative Democrats. He said: "If there are nominal Democrats who as a matter of principle are convinced that our party should be a conservative party . . . a Democratic tweedle-dum to a Republican tweedle-dee . . . it is, on the whole, better that the issues be drawn. . . ."

One Jackson Day innovation in 1939 was an afternoon card party given by the Democratic women's organization. Mrs. Roosevelt was a guest speaker at the affair.   ★

ON Jackson Day of the following year, January 8, 1940, President Roosevelt addressed a capacity crowd of 1,500 Democrats at the Jackson Day Dinner in the Mayflower

1940

Hotel in Washington, D.C. Concerning the context of the speech, it should be pointed out that World War II had been in progress for six months. In the United States, which was supposedly neutral at this time, this was a Presidential election year. These two factors, more than any others, were the key influences on the 1940 Jackson Day affair.

Unlike the Jackson Day Dinner speech of 1939 when party disunity was paramount among the issues discussed, the speech this year did not reflect any rifts within the party. Instead, the major tone of the speech was "milk and honey, sans brickbats."[5]

Many top Democrats, as well as laymen, were speculating as to whether Roosevelt would run for an unprecedented third term. The potential candidates for the Democratic nomination for the Presidency were hoping that Roosevelt would indicate his plans for 1940 in order that they might charge ahead with their own ambitions. Although there was only one Democrat unconditionally in the Democratic Presidential race at this time, Vice President John Nance Garner, there were many others in the background ready to throw their hats into the ring as soon as Roosevelt decided not to run. Among the Democratic leaders considered by the press as possible candidates were Garner, Secretary of State Cordell Hull, Postmaster General James A. Farley, Federal Security Administrator Paul V. McNutt, and Speaker William B. Bankhead. The speech, heard nationwide on a radio hookup, was anxiously anticipated by the news media since there was general hope and belief that Roosevelt would state his political intentions. Because of this widespread speculation, the speech and the occasion drew a large attendance and listening audience.

Although the war in Europe was being fiercely waged at this time, the full effects and implications of which were not yet fully realized by Americans, Roosevelt referred only once to the foreign situation. The reasons for less emphasis on this topic were the nature of the occasion, the fact that he had spent about half his address to Congress (given a few days before the Jackson Day speech) in discussing the gravity of the European war, and the fact that isolationists and neutralists were still in control of Congress and caused Roosevelt to move slowly with his international foreign policy. Also, this was an election year, and it was natural that Roosevelt wanted to alienate as few people as possible.

A very important prelude to this speech was the unprecedented invitation to three Republican leaders in Congress to be honored guests at the Jackson Day Dinner which, from the beginning, had been attended exclusively by Democrats. Homer Cummings, former Attorney General and Chairman of the Jackson Day Committee, with the approval of President Roosevelt, sent free tickets to Republican Senate Leader Charles McNary of Oregon, Republican Assistant Leader Senator Warren Austin of Vermont, and Republican House Leader Joseph Martin of Massachusetts, who could not decide whether the offer was a joke or a trick.

Roosevelt and Cummings declared in the invitation that Roosevelt's speech would be "nonpartisan as to character." Needless to say, the Republicans were shocked and suspicious of this "political Trojan horse."

The *New York Times* noted that the invitations "provoked speculation as to whether he [Roosevelt] would devote his address to a call for national unity in solving internal and foreign problems."[6] There was also conjecture that Roosevelt's "nonpartisanship" speech would be a demonstration that he wanted to bring about nonpartisan consideration of domestic and foreign problems as he suggested previously when the neutrality bill was being considered. The Republican leaders invited to the love feast construed the invitation as a "first move by the Administration to seek non-partisan consideration of national defense appropriations."[7]

Others viewed the offer as a strategy used very adeptly by Roosevelt to put the Republican Party on the spot politically. If the Republican leaders accepted the proposition, it would appear as though they were succumbing to Roosevelt's leadership, thus enhancing his political stature. If they rejected the offer, they felt that the Republican Party would be accused of not cooperating in the face of a crisis after the Democrats had made such a gesture toward national unity.

As things turned out, the three Republican leaders declined the offer. Representative Joseph Martin's statement summed up their feelings. He said that "under the circumstances, it would be laughable for the Republicans to go to the Jackson Day Dinner, as it was arranged solely to raise funds for the Democratic campaign and was a prelude to a Democratic program for 'nonpartisanship in Congress.' "[8]

In a humorous story told by Roosevelt at the beginning of his speech, the President provided entertainment for his partisan audience by a reference to "three empty chairs" and the men who didn't want to "go to heaven" with the Democrats. Other speakers at the dinner, Homer Cummings, James Farley, and William B. Bankhead, also made humorous allusions to the action of the Republicans.

One Democratic Senator at the dinner on this Jackson Day was greeted with laughter and some good-natured boos. This was Senator Carl Hatch, who sponsored the act prohibiting political activity by state employees who are paid out of national funds. Because of the Hatch Act, solicitation of employees to attend the dinner had to be altered.

The President used the occasion to appeal to all the voters, and especially the independents, to support the New Deal program and the New Deal ticket in the fall elections. He did this in two ways—by stressing the achievements of his Administration which he suggested should be judged on the accomplishment of his major aim, and by pointing out the significance of nonpartisanship by stating that the good of the people and the country superseded any aspects of partisan politics.

Roosevelt disappointed those potential candidates who went to the dinner hoping that he would state that he was not going to run again and that he would tap one of them on the shoulder to succeed him. Instead, Roosevelt drew the image of the man the Democrats should nominate in the summer. In the light of close analysis, it could easily be seen that the Roosevelt image of the Democratic nominee emerged as a self-description.

At the dinner much fun was made of the presence of potential candidates who were eagerly awaiting Roosevelt's decision. Homer Cummings greeted the group as "Presidential possibilities and Presidential improbabilities." James A. Farley said that "fellow candidates" were so numerous that the "overflow from the head table had to be seated on the floor."

The *Washington Post's* speculation on the meaning of the speech in relation to the third term question was:

The President is getting too much enjoyment, and perhaps too much advantage out of making a mystery of his intentions but he certainly did not speak as a candidate for office. Throughout his address emphasis was laid upon disinterested public service as opposed to narrow partisan view.[9]

The *Post* had been misled as to Roosevelt's intentions because Roosevelt was seeking more of a nonpartisan appeal by his speech than the situation demanded. Roosevelt was simply laying the groundwork for his reelection to a third term.   ★

1941

IN 1941, the proposed Jackson Day Dinner in Washington, D.C., was cancelled when it was learned that Roosevelt could not attend. Roosevelt's vacation sea trip did not permit him to attend the proposed dinner.

However, on March 29, 1941, Roosevelt did give a radio address directed to the Jackson Day Dinners throughout the country. He spoke from the wardroom of the Presidential yacht *Potomac* in Port Everglades, Florida, where disturbing weather reports had driven his boat at the end of his vacation sea trip.

Although no national Jackson Day Dinner was held in Washington, D.C., that year, the speech capsule has been included in the Appendix since it was directed to the Jackson Day Dinners and since it expressed well the perspective of the times.

The year 1941 found American public opinion ambivalent toward the question of America's role in the war. Many Americans believed that if British resistance were to crumble completely and the only way to prevent total German victory was for the United States to enter the war, we should do so; at the same time, an even greater percentage was consistently opposed to immediate entry.

Actually, Great Britain's position was crucial, but the people of America were not convinced of it. Since they were not convinced, Roosevelt found himself under the continuing necessity of educating the country to the significance of a Fascist victory. At the same time, he moved steadily toward a closer identification of the United States with the Allied cause and toward the use of American power against the Nazis within the limits set by law and by public opinion.

The year 1940 started with the sending of Harry Hopkins to England while the Lend-Lease Bill was being debated in Congress. Secretaries Knox and Stimson in the Cabinet thought the United States should fight. The America First group of isolationists, like Wheeler, Nye, and Lindbergh, thought that British security was not vital to the United States. Roosevelt fought this latter group, but he had to remember that a vast majority of the people did not want the United States to enter the war.

Near the close of the year 1940, on December 29, Roosevelt gave his famous "Arsenal of Democracy" speech in which he defied the Axis and warned that there was only one decision that could be made. The United States must become the "arsenal of democracy," sending arms, munitions, and other war materials to Britain and other democratic countries which, by fighting the Fascists, were keeping them from the United States' shores. The Lend-Lease Act, authorizing the manufacture and procurement of munitions for any country whose defense the United States deemed vital to the defense of the United States, was introduced in Congress in January after Roosevelt's annual message to Congress on January 6, 1941. It became law on March 11, 1941, just 18 days before his Jackson Day Dinner speech.

In his annual message to Congress, Roosevelt based this all-out aid on the famous "Four Freedoms." He cited three "impressive expressions of the public will" as the United States' national policy:

We are committed to all-inclusive national defense; we are committed to full support of resolute peoples everywhere who are resisting aggression and are thereby keeping war from our hemisphere; and we are committed to the proposition that principles of morality and considerations for our own security would never permit us to acquiesce in a peace dictated by aggressors and sponsored by appeasers.[10]

On March 15, 1941, four days after passage of the Lend-Lease Act, Roosevelt made a worldwide broadcast in which he assured the world of aid until victory for the democracies. He stated that the decision embodied in the Lend-Lease Act ended the urging that we get along with the dictators and ended the compromise with tyranny and the forces of oppression. This announcement was made to combat totalitarian propaganda and to make clear the position of the United States against aggression.

This, then, was the general situation at the time of the 1941 Jackson Day celebration. Roosevelt's main purpose in speaking to the Jackson Day diners was to continue his appeal for a united America in the face of threatened domination by dictator nations. He discarded all political partisanship and sought the support of all citizens for the actions taken to combat the threat of the Fascists. The speech turned out to be a philosophical dissertation on the evils of totalitarian government versus the virtues of the democracy of the United States.

Of special interest in Roosevelt's Jackson Day speech in 1941 was the glowing praise Roosevelt heaped upon his Republican opponent in the 1940 Presidential race. Samuel I. Rosenman wrote:

Two weeks later, March 29, on the occasion of the Jackson Day Dinner, the President was careful to point out that the decision which the American people had made by the passage of the Lend-Lease Bill was not a partisan decision. He paid particular tribute to his old opponent, Wendell Willkie, who had helped secure the passage of the bill and who, he stated, "in word and in action is showing what patriotic Americans mean by rising above partisanship and rallying to the common cause. . . ."

He never forgot the help that Willkie gave in getting lend-lease adopted by the Congress.[11]   ★

BECAUSE of the bombing of Pearl Harbor on December 7, 1941, just a month prior to the usual date for the Jackson Day Dinners, the Democratic National Committee postponed the celebration until February 23, 1942. The dinner, held in the Mayflower Hotel, was called a Washington Day Dinner for the purpose of giving the affair a patriotic and nonpartisan appearance.

1942

Franklin D. Roosevelt did not attend the dinner, but he did give a nationwide and worldwide address on the evening of February 23. Arrangements were made to pipe Roosevelt's radio address to the 60 Democratic dinners held throughout the country. Edward J. Flynn, Chairman of the Democratic National Committee, stated that Roosevelt's speech would be nonpolitical and that there was no connection between his speaking and the holding of the banquets. However, some newsmen and Republicans thought the two affairs were more than just coincidental. For example, David Lawrence wrote:

> The President, moreover, had plenty of other nights available in which to deliver his fireside chat, and even after his attention was called publicly to the fact that political dinners of his own party were being held throughout the country "coincidental" with his fireside chat, no move was made to meet public criticism.[12]

At any rate, a $600,000 debt resulting from the Presidential election of 1940 had to be paid, and the most successful means of getting the money was through these $100-a-plate dinners. Although Roosevelt did not attend, Mrs. Eleanor Roosevelt, Secretary of State Cordell Hull, Vice President Henry A. Wallace, Speaker Sam Rayburn, and Sergeant Alvin York, hero of World War I, spoke at the Washington dinner. Roosevelt's speech, beamed into the banquet hall, would have to be labeled the major address of the evening although it was not connected *prima facie* with the diners at these banquets.

The 4,156-word address, delivered on the occasion of the 210th anniversary of George Washington's birth, was

the President's third major broadcast since Pearl Harbor. The first speech was on December 9, two days after Pearl Harbor, and the second was on the 7th of January, 1942, when he delivered the State of the Union Address.

Just prior to this Washington Day celebration, Japan had jumped from one great victory to another in the Pacific until she had expanded almost all the way to Australia. Singapore had fallen. A Japanese torpedo plane had sunk the *Prince of Wales,* one of Britain's strongest and most modern battleships. The American heroes on Bataan Peninsula were doomed. The German army in North Africa had rumbled rapidly along the roads leading to the East. German U-boats had taken their toll of American tankers. Japanese and German propaganda, praising their own victories, had pronounced the weakness and inevitable defeat of the "soft" Americans.

Because of these events, Roosevelt decided that a fireside chat should be made to allay defeatist thoughts during this time of America's blackest hour. Rumors had exaggerated the losses of the United States Navy at Pearl Harbor. Japanese and German propaganda had to be answered.

When Roosevelt first talked to his speech writers about giving the speech on this occasion, he said:

> I'm going to ask the American people to take out their maps. I'm going to speak about strange places that many of them never heard of—places that are now the battleground for civilization. I'm going to ask the newspapers to print maps of the whole world. I want to explain to the people something about geography—what our problem is—what the overall strategy of this war has to be. I want to tell it to them in simple terms of A B C so that they will understand what is going on and how each battle fits into the picture. I want to explain the war in laymen's language; if they understand the problem and what we are driving at, I am sure that they can take any kind of bad news right on the chin.[13]

Newspapers did print the world maps which people could use in following Roosevelt's speech. This proved to be a very effective device of identification and interest in what President Roosevelt was going to say. It also insured the President of a large audience.

The spirit and morale of the American people was at its lowest ebb during these first few months after Pearl Harbor. Japan and Germany were at their peak in military strength and conquest. The oceans which had protected America throughout its entire history no longer seemed sufficient. Invincible America had lost many planes, ships, and men in the unsuccessful battles of the war. The shadow of doubt and gloom had descended. This was the situation in which Roosevelt made his Washington Day address on February 23, 1942—the occasion which was a substitute for the regular Jackson Day affair.

The President had several purposes which he sought to accomplish when speaking on that occasion. First, he wanted to explain the Allied global strategy of the war, what the United States was doing to carry out war plans, and what the war situation was at the time of the speech. Second, he wanted to give the people as much factual information about the war plans as he could without jeopardizing the Allied cause. Third, he wanted to explain to the people why the outlook for the United States was dismal at this time and why and how the ultimate victory would go to the Allies. In other words, he tried to keep the nation unified by reassuring the people the United States would win the "inevitable triumph."

Roosevelt drew parallels between the vicissitudes of George Washington's army during the Revolutionary War and those of the United States in the first few months of World War II. He did this to suggest to the people that they associate themselves with the courage of the great leaders of America who had faced recurring defeats in their eras.

An effort was made by the Japanese to steal the headlines from Roosevelt's address by dispatching a Japanese submarine to a point off the coast of Goleta, California, for the purpose of shelling the West Coast of the United States. Exactly at the time of Roosevelt's speech, twenty-five badly aimed shells from the submarine were fired at an oil field. No real damage was done, however. By carrying out this feat, the Japanese hoped to take away the credibility of anything Roosevelt might say. This was the first attack on continental United States soil in World War II.

But the Japanese attempt at grabbing the headlines was very feeble compared to the wide coverage of and reaction to President Roosevelt's speech. He spoke over all the domestic radio networks and throughout the world in rebroadcasts in almost twenty foreign languages.

The national party officials predicted that the local dinners held concurrently with the national Washington Day Dinner would completely erase the $600,000 debt left from the 1940 Presidential campaign. From all reports, this goal was attained. ★

WITH World War II still being waged throughout the world in 1943, the Jackson Day celebrations took on a pattern similar to the 1942 affair. At the request of Frank Walker, Democratic National Committee Chairman, President Roosevelt spoke by radio from the White House to Democrats at thirty fund-raising dinners held throughout the country. This was the 211th anniversary of George Washington's birth, February 22, 1943, on which the celebrations were held. During these war years the Democratic National Committee Dinners were held on Washington's birthday instead of Jackson Day, in keeping with the nonpartisan policies of the President.

1943

Speakers at the Washington dinner in the Mayflower Hotel were Vice President Henry Wallace, Speaker Sam Rayburn, Democratic National Committee Chairman Frank Walker, and Major General Alexander Vandegrift, the leader of American forces on Guadalcanal. This array of speakers was used to attract the Democrats to the $100-a-plate dinner in the absence of President Roosevelt. World War II was at its turning point at this time with the Allied forces in the South Pacific halting the Japanese advance and even starting an offensive. In Europe the Russians had staved off the German blitzkriegs. In retrospect, World War II was at its midpoint, for the big Axis victories became fewer and fewer while the Allies started their major offensive campaign. Because of the successes of the Allies in stopping the Axis, many people started saying that victory was just around the corner. On the opposite side, as described by Roosevelt, were the cynics and skeptics who sneered at the "determination to attain freedom from want and freedom from fear."

In general, however, the morale of the people had improved greatly since the nadir of public sentiment at the time of the 1942 Washington Day address. Allied successes in North Africa heightened confidence in the American people. In his State of the Union message on January 7,

1943, Roosevelt said that "the period of our defensive attrition in the Pacific is drawing to a close. Now our aim is to force the Japanese to fight. Last year, we stopped them. This year, we intend to advance."

Roosevelt had just returned from the Casablanca conference where the issues of unconditional surrender of the enemy and punishment of the Axis leaders, not the people, were agreed upon. All in all, the situation at this 1943 Washington Day or Jackson Day celebration could be called "the turning of the tide."

President Roosevelt gave the shortest of all the Jackson Day speeches in modern times at this 1943 affair. He tried to convince the American people that they should continue to work hard and sacrifice since "we still face reverses and misfortunes." Such continuous action was advocated by comparing the deeds and hardships of Washington's times, as he had done in the 1942 address, with those actions and tribulations of World War II.

Demonstrating that Americans do have faith, and reinforcing the beliefs of Americans, Roosevelt read the Ten Beatitudes for the stated purpose of giving "heart and comfort to all men and women everywhere who fight for freedom." This was an appeal by Roosevelt for Americans to follow the "guiding light" provided by the truths in the Beatitudes in order that the United States could fulfill its "hopes for victory, for freedom, and for peace."

More than a thousand people attended the $100-a-plate dinner in Washington, D.C., at the Mayflower Hotel and ate the rationed menu which left out sugar, coffee, and butter. ★

1944 PRESIDENT Franklin D. Roosevelt, who could not attend the Jackson Day Dinner on January 22, 1944, and could not make a speech because of pressing world affairs, requested Speaker Sam Rayburn to address the diners. For the first time since these $100-a-plate dinners started in 1936, someone besides Roosevelt would be the main speaker. On the program with Rayburn were Vice President Henry Wallace and Mrs. Charles W. Tillett, who gave very short speeches.

The approaching Presidential election in the fall precipitated most of the discussion on this Jackson Day occasion. With the war still going full force, it was evident that the Democratic Party and its leaders did not want to "change horses in the middle of the stream"; Roosevelt was viewed as the only possible nominee for the Democrats.[1]

However, a "battle royal" was taking shape over the Vice Presidential nomination. Opposition to Roosevelt's 1940 eleventh-hour choice of a running mate, Henry A. Wallace, was obvious, particularly among Southerners and Middle Westerners. The Democratic House of Representatives members were booming Speaker Sam Rayburn for the second spot, and there was also talk of Senator Harry S. Truman of Missouri and Senator Scott Lucas of Illinois for the role. Because of Roosevelt's giving the nod to Rayburn for the top speaking assignment at this important party occasion, the city of Washington buzzed with the rumor of the possibility that Rayburn might be the Vice Presidential candidate.[15]

The situation was made even more exciting by the addition of a five-minute speech by Wallace to the rostrum schedule. Rumor had it that there would be a speaking contest between Rayburn and Wallace, but this never materialized.

In addition to the speculation about the running mate of Roosevelt, and there was practically no doubt that Roosevelt would run again, the background of the speech and the occasion indicated that the war was running in favor of the Allies. The tenor of thought at this time was that the war would be over before too long. Thus, many thoughts of the people were turned to the reconversion of life after the war. What would happen to all the war industries? Would there be jobs for everyone? What would happen to the many fighting men who would return? How could they be employed and cared for? These were questions which people were thinking or asking at this time.

Rayburn's immediate aims in his speech were: first, to kick off the Presidential campaign by stating what type of candidate the Democratic Party would not nominate, by reviewing the accomplishments of the Democratic Party, and by predicting what the Democratic Party would do after the war was won; and second, to seek unity on the home front.

Rayburn reflected the ideas of his time when he suggested the following courses of action: first, the party and the people should support nobody of "any smaller caliber" than Roosevelt (which was really saying that everyone should back Roosevelt for a fourth term); second, the Democratic Party should not forget servicemen and their families, subject postwar jobs to "boom and slump economy," upset free enterprise in its broadest meaning of "equal opportunity," or turn back to "the sorry mirage of isolationism"; third, the Democratic Party should not "palm off an imitation liberal" (this seemed to be an attack on the leading Republican, Wendell Willkie); fourth, the Democratic Party should keep the factories running to provide jobs for the people, keep the economy healthy, help the farmers, find the way to internal and external security, and give the armed forces the right to vote.

Postmaster General Walker, the retiring Chairman of the National Committee, presided at the dinner and introduced Vice President Wallace and Mrs. Tillett, the Assistant Chairman. Later in the evening, the outgoing National Committee Chairman presented Robert E. Hannegan, the new National Committee Chairman, to the 1,200 Democrats who flocked to the Mayflower Hotel for the fund-raising affair. ★

1945 On April 13, 1945, 350 Jefferson Day Dinners were scheduled throughout the United States with the total contribution to go into the Congressional campaign of 1946.[16] Roosevelt, not planning to attend the Washington dinner because of his schedule, was to deliver a 30-minute radio address to all of the dinners, as had been his custom throughout World War II with the exception of 1944. These dinners were "conceived as the demonstration 'stock-taking' preparatory to strengthening the Roosevelt Administration and the Democratic Party on all fronts to win the war and the peace and then embark on the President's program of providing millions of jobs for all of us, including the servicemen and women returning from all corners of the world."[17]

On April 12, 1945, the day before the Jefferson Day Dinners, President Franklin D. Roosevelt died suddenly. His speech was typed in final form for the next day, but it remained undelivered.

Other speakers at the proposed 1945 dinner in Washington included Governor Ellis Arnall of Georgia, Governor Maurice J. Tobin of Massachusetts, Fannie Hurst, and Milton Berle.

The Democratic National Committee set a goal of $1,500,000 to be raised at these Jefferson Day celebrations throughout the country. Two important departures from practices of traditional Jackson Day affairs were planned for this 1945 Jefferson Day Dinner. Normally, the funds gathered at these dinners were simply added to the general fund of the National Committee, but in 1945, plans were to earmark every dollar of the contributions coming in from the Jefferson Day Dinners for just one purpose—the Congressional campaign of 1946. The second departure from custom resulted from an Office of Defense Transportation ruling that after February 1, purely local meetings of more than 50 persons using only city or suburban transit facilities in the case of rural communities were not required to file application for a special permit. Robert Hannegan, the National Committee Chairman, explained to national and state party officers that the states should abandon the customary state dinners and have a number of local or city dinners within each state. He suggested this as an illustration of the cooperation of the Democratic Party with the Administration in restricting unnecessary travel.

But because of President Roosevelt's death, all the dinners were cancelled.

The Jackson Day celebrations during Roosevelt's regime represented a reprise or resurrection of annually honoring Andrew Jackson and Thomas Jefferson. Using the occasion for the major fund-raising affair of the party, for presenting the party's policies and principles to the workers and to the people of the country, and for rededicating all Democrats to the party's principles remained the constants in the annual party ritual. ★

Chapter 14

TESTIMONIALS IN TRUMAN'S TIME

THE $100-a-plate dinners held usually on Jackson Day or Jefferson Day had become a firm tradition in the Democratic Party by 1946. Within ten years, the Democratic Party had built the $100-a-plate affairs into a million-dollar operation. President Harry S. Truman became the focal point of the Jefferson-Jackson Day celebrations during the period of 1946 through 1952.

SPEAKING before the Democratic faithful and to a radio audience from the Mayflower Hotel in Washington, D.C., on March 23, 1946, President Harry S. Truman gave his first truly partisan speech as President. At President Truman's suggestion, the menu for this Jackson Day Dinner was planned on a 700-calorie basis. This was one-half of the daily allotment for people in the food-shortage areas of Europe. The menu card at the 1946 Jackson Day Dinner contained this description of the dinner:

1946

> Tonight, you are being served a simple dinner. There are not many trimmings. In fact, you are being limited to 700 calories, and those are provided in foods which are not needed for shipment elsewhere in this hungering world. You will notice that grains, red meats, fats, and oils have been eliminated.
>
> Tonight, in Europe, millions of families are sitting down to a meal that corresponds, in calorie value, with the one that will be served to you. Their dinners probably will not be as well cooked. They will not have as many items on the menu. But the amount of nourishment will be about the same.
>
> This is not an apology. We of the Democratic Party are proud of the simplicity of our Jackson Day Dinner in this year of 1946. We feel—and we are sure you share the feeling with us—that this voluntary limitation of our menu is characteristically American and characteristically Democratic.

About twelve Southern Congressmen refused to attend the Jackson Day Dinner because Secretary of Commerce Henry A. Wallace was listed as a speaker. Just a few days before the dinner, Wallace made the statement that those

Democrats in Congress who bolt the leadership on major issues should be expelled from the party. He was referring mainly to the conservative Southern Democrats who had frequently joined the Republicans in opposing Administration measures.[1]

Prior to this dinner, Congress had passed only one of a score of Truman's major measures—a watered-down version of the unemployment bill. President Truman realized that his measures had to be passed by the Democratic-controlled Congress if the Democratic Party was to keep that majority after the coming elections in the fall.

On January 3, 1946, Truman "went to the country" with an unprecedented speech asking the American people to use their influence on Congress to get them to enact the measures he thought the people needed. This device was a favorite one which Truman used many times thereafter.

World War II had been won by the Allies, and now there were the many problems of transition, reconstruction, and rehabilitation. The United Nations organization had been established almost a year, and it presented many issues for the United States government to decide. Millions of returning American servicemen and thousands of displaced persons had to be properly settled and employed. All of these problems were presented to Truman and the United States government for solution. The Truman program was being blocked by a coalition of Democratic conservatives and the Republicans in Congress.

What was President Truman to do in order to get his program moving? He used the Jackson Day Dinner speech as an agent for appealing to the Democratic Party and to the American people for support. His main purposes were to seek party unity and responsibility in support of price control and the Administration's housing bill to prevent inflation and distress, for world peace through the United Nations, and for industrial productivity. Above all, he sought support from Congress for his measures. Not only were the measures necessary, in his estimation, but failure

President Harry S. Truman used the fund-raising dinners to help bolster party solidarity and morale in the 1950's. (Courtesy of Devlin O'Neil)

to pass them could cost the Democrats the Congressional elections in the fall.

Specifically, Truman sought support for policies dealing with: first, establishing higher standards of living; second, checking inflation and getting production going; third, making wages and prices more compatible; fourth, building more homes while keeping prices from "skyrocketing"; fifth, providing for veterans' housing; sixth, balancing the budget and reducing the debt; seventh, returning trade to private enterprise; eighth, strengthening the foundations of the United Nations. Above all, he was asking for party unity to carry out these things.

During Truman's time and thereafter, the date for the $100-a-plate dinners became more flexible. Generally, the time of the dinners has been in the vicinity of January 8, the anniversary of the Battle of New Orleans, or April 13, Jefferson's birthday.   ★

1947   ON April 5, 1947, in the Mayflower Hotel in Washington, D.C., before an audience of 2,000, President Truman suggested in his Jefferson Day speech that the United States "take a positive stand" against all types of aggression and "act ahead of time" to prevent another World War.

On March 12, 1947, approximately a month before his Jefferson Day speech, Truman laid before Congress his now-famous Truman Doctrine. He asked for $400 million for military and economic aid to Greece and Turkey. Prompted by the removal of British forces from Greece and the fear of the spread of Communism to these areas, Truman declared that it was in the interest of the United States to provide moral and financial assistance to countries whose political integrity was threatened by Communism or totalitarian ideology. Russia was infiltrating and setting up her satellites in Eastern Europe at this time, and Truman wanted to contain Communism by helping the European countries retain their freedom.

A second major influence on his speech at the Jefferson Day Dinner was the slow movement through Congress of his legislative program, including fiscal stabilization, better housing, increased public health care, and improved labor relations structures.

In the fall elections of 1946, the Republicans had gained control of Congress. If Truman was to get his program through Congress, he had to deal with the Republicans, and he chose to seek cooperation with them rather than to criticize them harshly.

Not as kind to the Democrats, however, the Republicans were rapping very hard at this particular time; the "tax and spend" label was being applied to the Democratic Party. Truman had placed his budget before a Republican Congress which was threatening to cut it and the taxes at the same time.

Truman sought support for his legislative program, asked for popular and Congressional approval of his financial policies, and requested support for the Truman Doctrine and the United Nations.

Speaking to the $200,000 crowd in Washington and to scores of similar gatherings throughout the nation, he delivered his 20-minute speech over a nationwide radio hookup. His speech was taken by Republicans and Democrats alike as an indication that he would be available as the Democratic nominee for President in 1948.

The *Washington Star* described Truman's nonpartisan speech with these words:

> It was a message which carried an impression of maturity and earnestness—an expression from a man who spoke, not as the leader of a political party, but as the President of a great people who are reluctantly beginning to realize that they have been pushed to center of the world stage at a decisive moment in history.
> One might say . . . without any intent to give offense . . . that here is a man who has found himself.[2]

Henry Wallace, the former Secretary of Commerce who was ousted by President Truman in 1946 over a foreign policy controversy, did not appear at the dinner. He stated that he was sailing for Europe and that he had to get back to New York immediately. Just the same, participants at the dinner were craning their necks to see if he were in attendance. ★

1948 ON February 19, 1948, the Jefferson-Jackson Day Dinner was held in commemoration of the 100th anniversary of the Democratic National Committee. Because of the record number of people (2,900) who wanted to attend the dinner, it had to be held at two hotels, the Mayflower and the Statler. The only time prior to this that a celebration was held in two hotels was in 1920.

President Harry Truman appeared at both hotels with his wife and daughter. They dined at the Statler Hotel where he gave a two-minute impromptu talk; later, he gave his main oratorical effort at the Mayflower Hotel.

The Truman-Wallace split in 1946 precipitated a direct confrontation in 1948 when Wallace put his third party in motion. Wallace's candidate in the 24th Congressional district in New York City had won an upset victory over the regular Democratic candidate just a few days prior to this celebration. There was no mention made of the event or of Wallace in President Truman's speech.

Also Truman did not mention directly his ten-point civil liberties program, which resulted in a threatened bolt of Southern Democrats. Actually, this bolt became a reality a few months after this speech by the formation of the Dixiecrats. Probably Truman avoided the topic in deference to party harmony. A considerable number of Southern Congressmen were conspicuous by their absence from the dinner. A table in the center of the banquet hall at the Mayflower Hotel was kept vacant as a reminder of Southern objection to Truman's civil rights program. Senator Olin Johnston of South Carolina and his party paid for their seats in order to keep the table vacant as a visible reminder.[3]

When President Truman later was asked if the Southern walk-out of the 1948 Jefferson-Jackson Day Dinner affected him in any way, he retorted, "Not the slightest, I went ahead and beat them anyway."[4]

These two developments are significant in the context within which the speech was given, even though no mention was made of either event. What Truman did not say at the dinner was almost as important as what he did say.

As was very often the situation, this Jefferson-Jackson Day Dinner was the springboard for the coming campaign. The Republicans had become the majority party in Congress as a result of the 1946 Congressional elections. President Truman, if he decided to run, faced tremendous odds in view of the Republican gains, the failure of much of his program to squeeze through the Congress, the splinter of a Wallace third party, and the threatened bolt of some Southern Democrats. One of Truman's main tasks in the speech was to put some fire under the party workers and give them the feeling that he was going to win the election.

This 1948 dinner was the first official recognition of these celebrations as the "Jefferson-Jackson Day Dinners." The Senate Minority Leader, Alben Barkley, presided at the Mayflower dinner, and House Minority Leader Sam Rayburn was host at the Statler Hotel. Wilson W. Wyatt, the dinner chairman, presented President Truman to the diners at the Mayflower Hotel, where the President broadcast his speech over radio and television—probably the first time that a Jefferson-Jackson Day affair was seen on television. Part of the success of this dinner was attributable to Mrs. Perle Mesta, who acted as cochairman for the double-header dinner.

A touch of humor was injected inadvertently into the delivery of Truman's speech when he concluded:

The ten-year program that I have outlined for American prosperity is founded on our faith in the ability of the American people to plan their future boldly and to move steadfastly toward their goal.

If anyone chooses to call this politics, then it is the politics of Jefferson and Jackson, Wilson and Theodore Roosevelt—and it is good enough for me.[5]

It was this final "Theodore" before "Roosevelt" that made the audience laugh. President Truman, not realizing what he had said to make them laugh, asked several people near him as he sat down. They told him of his use of "Theodore Roosevelt" instead of "Franklin D. Roosevelt," and he also laughed. ★

1949

THE 1949 Jefferson-Jackson Day Victory Dinner was almost an identical repeat of the 1948 affair. Mrs. Perle Mesta and Wilson Wyatt again served as cochairmen, and the record-breaking 3,500 people at the affair had to be fed at two hotels again, the Mayflower and the Statler. The dinner, held on February 24, after President Truman's "surprising" defeat of Thomas E. Dewey, attracted both the believers and the nonbelievers in "Truman the Vote-getter." This year, Truman gave his off-the-cuff speech at the Mayflower Hotel and his principal address at the Statler, where it was broadcast and televised.

The atmosphere at this dinner was very different from the one held the previous year when the Southerners were conspicuously absent because of the civil rights issue and when Henry Wallace attempted to create a left-wing third party. The audience was composed of practically the same people, but this dinner, with most of the Southerners back in the fold, was marked by happiness, assurance, and cordiality.

The historic upset victory of President Truman over Thomas Dewey and the return of Congress to Democratic control gave the Democrats faith in a leader who many people thought could not win.

With such a great victory under his belt, Truman believed that the people had given approval of his program which he was determined to put through Congress despite his foes. He threatened early in his speech to take his case to the people again if the Democratic-controlled 81st Congress failed to put his program into effect. He said, "If I get on that train again, I'm going to tell the people how their government is getting along—and I know how to tell them."

Truman wanted to repeal the Taft-Hartley Act which was passed by the Republican-controlled Congress on June 23, 1947. This law amended the National Labor Relations Act, outlawed the closed shop, provided for a cooling-off period of 60 days before resorting to strike and lockout, required labor unions to file copies of their constitutions, and forbade unions or employers to make direct or indirect contributions to party campaign funds. The repeal of this act was one of the principal planks of the Democratic platform. Truman's program also included "measures for the welfare of the people" such as the expansion of social security, housing, increase of statutory minimum wages, and waterways development. His main object on this occasion was to use his speech as a vise to squeeze the legislators between the public and his program.

The confident and triumphant Truman, after his exhaustive campaign tour and victory of the previous fall, started his speech by saying: "I am happy to be up here talking to you once more from the same old stand. Incidentally, this is right where I expected to be."

Senator J. Howard McGrath of Rhode Island, the Democratic National Committee Chairman, introduced President Truman at the dinner. The *Washington Post* made this comparison between the 1948 and 1949 dinners:

Then [1948] President Truman was a man on the defensive, undismayed and defiant, it was true, but almost alone in his cocky assurance of victory. He was far from alone last night; every Democrat who could pack into either hotel was there to be seen, to shout himself hoarse and to congratulate himself on the leader for whom a year ago many had only gloomy pessimism.

The man who stood up in the two crowded banquet halls last night was exactly the same man who had stood there a year ago to promise victory to a lot of people who didn't believe him. It was the crowd itself last night that was different; it was made up of the same men and women, but victory had been thrust upon it by the unpretentious man they had discounted a year before.[6]   ★

1950

PRESIDENT TRUMAN opened the 1950 Congressional campaign at the Jefferson-Jackson Day celebration where the largest audience ever to eat under one roof in Washington, D.C., assembled. More than 5,300 Democrats paid $100 apiece to attend this dinner held on February 16, 1950, in the four-acre National Guard Armory. With more and more people attending these affairs, the Jefferson-Jackson Day celebration had to move from one hotel into two hotels, and now it was to be held in the huge National Guard Armory. The hot meal, kept warm by charcoal ovens, was trucked four miles from the Mayflower and Statler Hotels which hired 550 waiters and 75 captains to see that service was efficient.[7]

This prodigious banquet prompted Truman to ad lib at the beginning of his speech: "This is the most remarkable dinner I have ever seen. And during my 30 years in politics, I have seen many a dinner. I have attended many Democratic meetings such as this and I think this has been the grandest of all." There is no doubt that this dinner broke all records up to that time as far as numbers are concerned. Never had so many assembled for a dinner in the whole history of such affairs.

In addition to the large immediate audience, Truman's speech was once again broadcast by all the major networks on radio and television. Truman had laid plans to stump and campaign for the Democratic candidates up for election in this Congressional year of 1950.

The Republicans, seeking to regain control of Congress after losing it in the 1948 election, had already stated that the major issue in the campaign was going to be "liberty versus socialism." The Republicans had been trying to pin the label of "socialism" on the Truman programs.

President Truman, in a highly partisan speech, took the offensive in advocating that the Republican "rascals" not be allowed to gain control of Congress because of their proven inability to provide the leadership necessary to promote the programs beneficial to all the people. Truman's main aim was to contrast the two major parties by looking at their records over the years, a common theme at these Jefferson-Jackson Day Dinners. He also sought to soften the effect of the many Republican slogans which were being used to get votes in the fall.

William Boyle and Charles Luckman, cochairmen of the Jefferson-Jackson Day Dinner in 1950, planned the fund raiser where the diners were assembled at tables placed in the form of a gigantic fan on the Armory's drill floor.

During the early years of these $100-a-plate dinners, the Republicans ridiculed the Democrats for claiming to be the party of the common man while charging the diners $100 a plate. In the years of the 1930's and 40's, the Republicans held $1 box-lunch affairs on Lincoln Day as a contrast to the $100-a-plate dinners. But when they realized the great amounts of money that could be raised by the $100-a-plate dinners, the Republican scorn and ridicule turned to envy and desire to hold similar affairs for their own party, and they joined the bandwagon by setting up their own $100-a-plate dinners throughout the country. Today, both Republican and Democratic Parties hold such dinners as their major fund-raising devices.   ★

THE 1951 Jefferson-Jackson Day Dinner, held on April 14, was very much a repeat of the 1950 dinner. Again, 5,300 of the Democratic Party faithful attended the affair held at the National Guard Armory. Several important events occurred in the intervening months between the Jefferson-Jackson Day Dinner of 1950 and this one in 1951. The most important was the outbreak of war in Korea on June

1951

25, 1950, ultimately between the Communist Chinese and the North Koreans on the one side and the South Koreans and the United Nations, mainly composed of United States troops, on the other side. With the sudden attack on South Korea, President Truman made his most crucial decision to resist the attack. In his Jefferson-Jackson Day speech, Truman said that this action was heralded at the time as brave, courageous, and proper procedure in light of the alternatives. However, as the Korean War, sometimes referred to as the United Nations police action in Korea, seesawed back and forth, with no apparent end in sight because of the vast numbers of Communist Chinese and the United States policy of not invading Communist China for fear of touching off a third World War, many began to criticize Truman's initial action of sending troops into Korea and his policy of noninvasion of Communist China from whence came Communist supplies. To many it appeared that the war was very distant, useless, and wasteful of American men and materiel. Many of the Republican leaders were especially critical.

To add fuel to the flames of emotional feeling and of criticism concerning Truman's conduct of the Korean War, he fired General Douglas MacArthur, dramatic hero of World War II, from his post as Far East Commander, just a week before the dinner. In an address to the nation a few days before this Jefferson-Jackson Day affair, Truman gave his reasons for the MacArthur dismissal. Republican critics of Truman's foreign policy included Senator Robert A. Taft of Ohio, Senator Kenneth S. Wherry of Nebraska, and Representative Joseph Martin of Massachusetts. These and many others were attacking Truman for his refusal to permit General MacArthur to bomb Chinese Communist installations in Manchuria and for his refusal to use Chiang Kai-shek's Formosan troops to invade the Chinese mainland. For these refusals, he was charged with appeasement and with producing "another Munich" in Asia.

At the Jefferson-Jackson Day Dinner, Truman sought

mainly to gain the people's confidence in his foreign policy by answering criticism of it and by charting courses which America should follow. He charged that his critics were seeking to spread confusion for political gain and that they were playing politics at the expense of his efforts to prevent a third World War.

President Truman ridiculed his opposition because of the contradictory nature of their assertions; for example, he pointed out that "they want us to get out of Korea—but they urge us to wage an aggressive war against China." It was at this point that he ad libbed his only direct reference to the MacArthur case. He said: "It has been categorically said that Russia will not come in if we bomb Manchuria. The statement was made to me about the Chinese not coming into Korea, and it was made on good authority, too, and I believed it." This was a reference to the President's conference with General MacArthur on Wake Island in October of 1950 before the Yalu River offensive.

Ironically, President Truman ignored the displaced MacArthur but went out of his way to praise General Dwight D. Eisenhower, Commander of the North Atlantic Treaty Organization forces in Europe, as a "great American." At this point in history, General Eisenhower was not in consideration as running for President on either the Democratic or Republican ticket. He had been mentioned obliquely during the years after World War II as a candidate for the Democrats *and* for the Republicans, but nothing was definite at the time President Truman made this speech. But before a year had passed, General Eisenhower was in the thick of the running as the Presidential nominee on the Republican ticket. ★

AT THE 1952 Jefferson-Jackson Day Dinner in Washington, D.C., President Harry S. Truman sat at two head tables during the evening and talked to another record-breaking

1952

crowd. While he ate his dinner, he sat at one end of the large National Guard Armory. When he had finished, he traveled across the room to the other end of the Armory where he delivered his address over radio and television. A crowd in excess of 5,300 swarmed into the building until the fire marshals became so concerned that they prevented others from entering.

An illustration of the immense size of the gathering can be seen in the amounts of food consumed at the dinner—3,100 pounds of meat, 3,466 pink grapefruit, 1,800 bunches of celery, 2,640 heads of lettuce, 40 gallons of olives, 3,000 pounds of string beans, 7,500 pounds of potatoes, 15,000 rolls, 200 pounds of butter, 300 gallons of coffee, 5,200 ice cream rolls, and 4 tons of ice. It was estimated that each dinner cost $7.50 and that the promotion cost $2.50 apiece, which would leave $90 of each contribution for the Democratic National Committee treasury.[8]

In addition to the size of the dinner, given on March 29, 1952, the Jefferson-Jackson Day speech was one of the landmarks in the history of such speeches because Truman ad libbed an announcement at the end of his speech that he would not be a candidate for President in this Presidential election year and that he would not accept a renomination. This statement completely surprised the audience, who had been speculating for months about Truman's plans but had not been expecting him to make the statement at the dinner. Even the Presidential aides did not know that he was going to make the announcement.

In a personal interview with President Truman, he said: "I had made up my mind long before the dinner that I would not run again for the Presidency. . . . I didn't tell anyone I was going to make the announcement because I wanted to make the announcement myself. . . . I didn't let the press know because you can't trust those fellows."[9]

According to Truman, then, he had made up his mind not to run again even before his defeat at the hands of Senator Estes Kefauver in the New Hampshire primary.

Yells of "No! No!" came from the audience after he completed his statement; but with Truman's position made clear, the big scramble for the nomination began. The Twenty-second Amendment to the Constitution limiting the President to two terms had been ratified at this time although the amendment exempted President Truman from such a limitation.

Another factor giving perspective to the situation was the Republican charge that the Democratic Administration was flooded with corruption and Communism. Some of Truman's appointees had been charged with using their official positions for obtaining undue private gains. Also, his critics had been suggesting that the Democratic Administration had allowed Communists to infiltrate high positions of the government. These accusations were preliminary probes into public feeling in order to find good campaign issues.

Added to these two issues of corruption and Communism was the third issue of the Korean War. The Republican critics harassed Truman about his policies concerning Korea. It was not long before "Communism, corruption, and Korea" became the slogan of the anti-Democratic, anti-Truman forces.

In view of these charges, President Truman sought in his speech to defend his record and to attack the Republicans. His object was simply to negate the charges which "Republican propagandists" were spreading. He appealed to the voters to accept his version of his Administration's achievements and to ignore the talk of Communism, corruption, and Korea sponsored by Republican "fakers" and "phony propagandists."

With Frank E. McKinney, Chairman of the Democratic National Committee, Wash B. Williams, a Washington, D.C., businessman and civic leader, served as chairman of the 1952 Jefferson-Jackson Day Dinner committee. The National Committee, being very careful not to violate the Hatch Act, printed in red ink at the bottom of the campaign fund pledge cards for this year a statement warning solicitors not to seek contributions from people on federal relief, working on federal projects, or those holding federal contracts with the government. It did state, however, that employees of firms holding government contracts could be approached. The printing of this warning on the pledge cards had been customary for several years.

The testimonial dinners in Truman's time, from 1946 through 1952, assiduously followed the celebrations begun during Roosevelt's era. During this time, the dinners became known officially as a combination Jefferson-Jackson Day affair. Prior to this, the dinners had many names, but mostly either Jackson Day Dinners or Jefferson Day Dinners. The popularity of these affairs during Truman's time surged to an all-time high.

By President Truman's time, the Jefferson-Jackson Day fund-raising device was a tried, tested, and accepted means of raising annually the greatest single sum of money for past and present campaigns. ★

Chapter 15

FUND RAISING
IN THE FIFTIES

WITH THE ELECTION of Dwight D. Eisenhower, a Republican, in the Presidential election of 1952, the perquisites and privileges of the party in power shifted to the Republican Party after 20 years of Democratic control. Unaccustomed to the role of the "outs," the Democratic Party found fund raising somewhat more difficult in their new position.

No longer did the Democratic Party have the President of the United States as a drawing card for their huge fundraising dinners. No longer did they have control of the many financial ramifications accompanying control of the government. The sunshine Democrats suddenly switched to supporting Republicans—at least, those interested in government and the United States purely for financial gain. No longer did the Democrats have the financial backing of this group of people. The fair-weather financial fat-cats suddenly found the Republican Party the most remunerative return on their investments.

1953

INDICATIVE of this reversal of situations is the absence of a Jefferson-Jackson Day Dinner in Washington, D.C., in 1953. Without a Democratic President and without patronage workers in the city for the first time since the fundraising dinners started in 1936, the Democratic Party resorted to a series of regional Jefferson-Jackson Day Dinners. The shock of the Democratic loss in the 1952 election was felt very deeply, and the absence of the traditional drives reflected this feeling. ★

1954

BUT the Democrats quickly regained their confidence in 1954 and held a national Jefferson-Jackson Day Dinner on May 6. The Republican Administration was beset with the McCarthy Communist purge in America. Not one of the Democratic measures labeled as socialistic in the 1952 campaign had been repealed.

*Speaker Sam Rayburn
was most frequently in the
spotlight at the Jefferson-
Jackson Day Dinners
when the Democratic
Party was out of power.
(Courtesy of Devlin O'Neil)*

President Eisenhower, though still riding the crest of
the wave of his popularity, could not get his program
through the Republican-controlled Congress. According
to Sam Rayburn's speech this year, only two positive pieces
of legislation were passed during the First Session of the
83rd Congress, and only one major bill, the Excise Tax Bill,
had been enacted by the date of the dinner.

Rayburn charged that Republican promises during the
campaign of 1952 had, for the most part, not been kept.
Prices and unemployment had risen. All of this background
indicated that the Republican-controlled Congress was ripe
for change, at least so the Democratic Party members
thought.

Former President Harry S. Truman attended the dinner and spoke extemporaneously for a few minutes but gave
no formal address. Adlai Stevenson, who had been defeated
in the Presidential election of 1952, was in the hospital and
could not attend the dinner. This meant that the third top-
ranking Democrat in the party, Sam Rayburn, former
Speaker of the House of Representatives, was the major
speaker of the day. The House Minority Leader had been
present and had spoken at almost every dinner in Washing-

ton from 1942 to this time, but he had been the principal speaker only once before, in 1944.

Rayburn sought to arouse the party faithful in preparation for the coming Congressional elections. He attacked the Republicans for not living up to their 1952 campaign promises and for their poor leadership in the government.

Approximately 1,500 people meandered into the Mayflower Hotel for the dinner. Compared to the 5,300-plus attendance at the 1952 celebration, this affair appeared very anemic. However, the $150,000 raised at the dinner was very welcome to Stephen Mitchell, the Democratic National Committee Chairman, who was still paying off the 1952 campaign debt.   ★

1955

GRADUALLY, the Democratic Party regained its attractiveness, and the attendance at the dinners began to rise. On April 16, 1955, at the National Guard Armory, over 3,300 people attended the Jefferson-Jackson Day banquet. The increased attendance was aided and abetted by the victory of the Democrats in the Congressional elections of the preceding November.

Between the 1954 and 1955 dinners, the Democrats had won control of both houses of Congress, and the United States had signed a mutual defense pact with the Chinese Nationalists. Senator Joseph McCarthy of Wisconsin was up for censure by the United States Senate because of alleged misconduct in the Army-McCarthy hearings. On March 1, 1954, the first hydrogen bomb was set off at Bikini Island in the Pacific. On January 28, 1955, President Eisenhower ordered United States Armed Forces into action to protect Formosa and the Pescadores Islands against attack. The United States Senate approved the Southeast Asia Treaty Organization.

Ignoring almost all of these events, Sam Rayburn turned his attention to the accomplishments and activities of the Democratic Party. He sought to rededicate the party to the principles which it had always held and to praise the men who formulated these principles.

Rather than attack the Republicans this year, Rayburn tried to portray positively the Democratic Party and its leaders. After all, the Democrats were now in control of Congress again, attacks on President Eisenhower had proven ineffective because of his immense popularity, and the recounting of the achievements of the great Democrats of the past and the rededicating of the party to its principles were designed to rebuild the party.

Rayburn asked for nonpartisan support "in all things that pertain to war and peace, since they pertain also to the life and death of all men." Trying to get people to huddle together in this time of crisis regardless of their political leanings was a nonpartisan means of gaining identification. Self-preservation, one of the strongest motives for unifying people behind a given cause against a common enemy, was Rayburn's purpose. He appealed to the people to follow in the footsteps of the founders of the Republic in this time of crisis and to fight the evil which "stalks the hills." ★

1956

THE $100-a-plate Democratic National Committee Dinner in 1956, called the Woodrow Wilson Centennial Dinner, was given April 21 in the National Guard Armory with 2,500 people attending. Speaker Sam Rayburn, the principal speaker, was accompanied at the rostrum by other speakers—Senator Alben Barkley at Kentucky, Governor Robert Meyner of New Jersey, Governor John Battle of Virginia, and Representative Edna Kelly of New York.

In this Presidential and Congressional election year, the front runners for the Democratic Presidential nomination, Adlai Stevenson, Estes Kefauver, and Governor Averell Harriman, were not included as speakers in order that no charge of favoritism could be affixed to the Democratic National Committee.

Adlai Stevenson, a major speaker at the fund-raising dinners in the 1950's, discusses some of the party's problems with Paul Butler, Chairman of the Democratic National Committee at that time, and Mrs. Butler. (Courtesy of City News Bureau of Washington, D.C.)

Stevenson and Harriman did attend the dinner, however, and received great applause, with the greater applause going to Stevenson. (For several years, an applause meter has been applied to those speaking and attending these affairs to measure the party response to potential Presidential candidates. The reliability of this measuring device for gauging potential candidates has been fairly high.) Estes Kefauver did not attend the dinner because he was actively campaigning in the state of Oregon.

The major theme of the dinner speeches was the life and achievements of Woodrow Wilson as Governor, President, and the leader who tried to establish world peace and social betterment. However, the main speaker, Sam Rayburn, talked of the current situation in terms of the accomplishments of the Wilson Administration.

Just a few days before this dinner, President Eisenhower vetoed the controversial farm bill which included the soil bank plan and which would have restored rigid 90 per cent parity price supports. Rayburn, seeking to make political capital out of this in the campaign, brought it up in his speech. He tried to convince the people that the Democratic Party was more capable of running the country than the Republicans, to create enthusiasm in the Democratic ranks, and to promote unity within the party—aims usually sought at these occasions. This dinner lifted the lid off the Presidential campaign.

The dinner came as a climax to a two-day gathering of the Democratic National Committee, state chairmen, and other party officials. Paul M. Butler, the new Democratic National Committee Chairman, designed the dinner to raise funds for the 1956 political campaign, at a time when Democratic funds were extremely low. Former President Truman could not attend the dinner because of the wedding of his daughter, Margaret, in Independence, Missouri.

The now-familiar prestige clubs for $1,000 contributors were conceived by Paul Butler in 1956 when he started the "750 Club." It was six years later that the Kennedy clan carried on this idea with more finesse in the form of the "President's Club." In 1960, the "750 Club" members received preferential treatment at the convention and at the inaugural parade and ball in 1961.

In addition to the "750 Club" idea, Butler initiated the $10 sustaining fund party membership in 1957. This important but less showy idea helps the National Committee with its operating expenses.

Former Secretary of State Dean Acheson, a speaker at the 1957 dinner, talks with Mrs. Estes Kefauver prior to the dinner. (Courtesy of City News Bureau of Washington, D.C.)

But disaster hit the Democrats again in 1956 in the form of the second Eisenhower landslide. ★

AFTER this Presidential defeat, the Democratic Party's $100-a-plate dinner in 1957 was attended by only 1,600. The dinner, held on May 4, was given in the huge National Guard Armory. Formerly, more than 5,000 people had attended these affairs in the Armory, and the 1,600 this year looked very small in comparison.

1957

However, the Democrats made up for the small numbers by the roster of enthusiastic speakers, in addition to former President Harry S. Truman, who delivered the major address. Other speakers included Adlai Stevenson, Dean Acheson, John W. McCormack, G. Mennen Williams, Russell B. Long, and Edith Green. This long line of Democrats severely attacked President Eisenhower who, until the campaign of 1956, was almost immune from attack. In fact, the party "turned into a sort of 'swat' Eisenhower night."[1] Now that the Presidential election was over, the Democrats, who had been treading lightly upon Eisenhower because of his popularity, felt that no harm could come from attacking him. The Democratic guns were pointed at the 1958 Congressional elections and the 1960 Presidential election, although both were relatively far into the future.

Former President Truman's speech was unique since it dealt entirely with only one specific topic—the budget. Truman used his speech to attack Eisenhower, his Cabinet, and big business for the $71.8 billion budget Eisenhower sent to Congress. The two main courses of action proposed by Truman were: first, the United States must spend what is necessary for the welfare and the safety of the people; and, second, the Democrats and the people must fight special interests which are attempting to take over the economic control of the country.

He sought to alert the people to the Presidential tactics concerning the budget and to soften the attacks on the Democratic Congress which might result from Republican maneuvers. He showed that Eisenhower was shifting the blame for the size of the budget to Congress so he could "remain above the battle" and still be popular with the people.

On the day that President Eisenhower sent his record-breaking budget to Congress, January 16, 1957, Secretary of the Treasury George Humphrey said that Congress ought to cut it. A little later, President Eisenhower said that "if Congress made any big cuts it would seriously impair great programs for the safety and welfare of the people."[2] Finally, President Eisenhower sent a letter to Congress on April 18, in which he proposed cuts in the budget. All of this activity "confused" Truman and provided him with his one-point speech. Truman said he had changed glasses and read several newspapers, but still he saw the same confusing statements. This humorous bit of exposition, designed to set the people against the Republicans, was aimed at labeling Eisenhower and the Republicans as confused and deceptive.

Truman charged that the budget cuts suggested by the Republicans were nothing "but robbing Peter to pay Paul." He called such Republican actions "political bunk," "evasion," and "buck-passing."

In this post-Presidential election year, the Democratic Party had a $660,000 party deficit. The dinner provided only one-fourth of the amount necessary to retire the debt. ★

1958 THE 1958 Jefferson-Jackson Day Dinner, held at the Sheraton Park Hotel on February 22, attracted 3,000 diners who ate in two different dining rooms of the hotel. In his traditional "give-'em-hell" style, former President Harry S. Truman blasted the Eisenhower Administration and the Republicans in the manner which made President Truman famous in 1948. Sensing a possible Democratic victory in this Congressional election year, which eventually turned out extremely successfully for the Democrats, a greater number of Democrats appeared at this $100-a-plate dinner than at any dinner in Washington since 1952. It was the largest crowd ever to dine under one *hotel* roof in the history of Washington; larger crowds at these dinners have been in attendance, but these were held in the National Guard Armory and not in a hotel. The dinner was given in honor of former President Truman to kick off the approaching Congressional campaign, and party leaders from all over the nation attended.

Other speakers at this dinner included Adlai Stevenson, Sam Rayburn, Lyndon Johnson, and Paul Butler. Since the audience was split into two sections, the speakers addressed both groups in a rotating fashion. Truman ate in the downstairs banquet hall and then appeared before the audience in the main ballroom to give his radio and television address. Because of the political nature of his speech, Republicans were offered equal time. Also, because of his ad libbing at the beginning of his speech, Truman ran over the allotted 30 minutes and was cut off the air.

The tone of his speech was suggested the day before he spoke. At an Electrical Consumers Committee breakfast meeting, Truman said, "I understand they are going to

Three powerful Democratic leaders in an informal moment during the 1958 $100-a-plate dinner at the Sheraton Park Hotel— former President Harry S. Truman, former Governor of North Carolina Luther Hodges, and Lyndon B. Johnson. (Courtesy of City News Bureau of Washington, D.C.)

broadcast this spasm of mine Saturday night. . . . Tune in and hear the facts of life from an old retired farmer."[3] He hinted that the speech would be a "scorcher." Sam Rayburn chimed in that Truman would make the Republicans "squeal like stuck pigs."

Since the 1957 dinner, several significant events had occurred which gave Truman the necessary ammunition for his onslaught. Russia, displaying its great strength and progress, had launched the first man-made earth satellite and followed it with other spectacular achievements, while the United States' efforts fizzled on the launching pad. The psychological impact of these achievements probably took its toll in the battle for uncommitted nations in the cold war. At any rate, the United States' superiority as the Number One power began to be questioned.

The United States had slipped into a "Republican recession" which brought about large unemployment and other economic difficulties. Despite the recession, price inflation was on the increase.

There were integration troubles in schools throughout the South. On September 24, 1957, President Eisenhower ordered United States troops to enforce the Supreme Court racial integration order at Little Rock, Arkansas. There was much publicity and concern over this matter, not only because of the domestic troubles but also because of the effect this would have on the United States' prestige abroad.

In direct contrast to the 1957 speech, Truman's address this year covered many topics and contained a more positive and constructive outline of policies which the Democrats should follow. With the 1958 Congressional elections approaching, Truman set the example for the campaign. He had several purposes in mind: first, to seek support for the Democrats in the November election; second, to elucidate the weaknesses and failures of the Republicans; third, to give the Democratic Party arguments and a program to offer in the coming campaign.

The five specific courses of action which Truman

recommended for the Democrats to follow during and after the campaign were:

1. The Democratic Party must remain the Party of the People—"Our primary concern is with the little fellow . . . the working men and women, farmers, people on salaries, and people of moderate incomes."
2. The Democratic Party must stand for full employment and protection of civil rights and liberties of every citizen regardless of race, creed, or nationality.
3. The Democratic Party must develop plans and programs for creating conditions in which steady economic growth will take place.
4. The Democratic Party must support an adequate national defense, whatever the cost.
5. In foreign policy, the Democratic Party must stand firmly for cooperative and concerted action with other free nations.[4]

In addition to attacking the Republicans for their shortcomings, as was the *modus operandi* during the years since he left office, Truman proposed a positive program for Democrats to pursue during the campaign. The "out party's" natural means of replacing the "in party" is gen-

Former Governor of Michigan G. Mennen Williams was a speaker at the 1957 and 1960 dinners. Here his dinner partner is Mrs. Katie Loucheim, former director of women's activities of the Democratic National Committee. (Courtesy of City News Bureau of Washington, D.C.)

erally by attacking the efforts of the "in party" by implying that the "out party" can do a better job. Sometimes the "out party" will present its own programs or plans, much as Truman did in this speech.

Former President Truman gave his version of what he considered to be the "Republican program":

In regard to overcrowded schools and underpaid teachers: nothing.

Aid to hospitals: cut it back or out.

Slum clearance: abandon it.

Public assistance: turn it back to the states or repeal it.

Stop stream pollution: don't do it.

REA co-ops: turn them over to private power companies and strangle them.

GI loans: jack up the interest rates.

The aged: do nothing.

The unemployed: they have the "right to suffer"—so a Republican spokesman said. Republicans haven't overlooked anybody in dishing out punishment. In fact, if you are not on this list in any other way, you haven't been forgotten . . . you'll get a five-cent stamp.[5]

At this 1958 dinner the Democratic crowd was larger and more enthusiastic than at any time during the prior eight lean years. After the 1958 dinner, the Democrats were on the move again toward extending their control in Congress and gaining the Presidency in 1960. The real buildup for the Presidential campaign which elected John F. Kennedy was actively started at this dinner. The party workers began to feel the public's desire for change, and they were willing and able to assist in bringing about this change. ★

1959 THE 1959 Democratic National Committee Dinner was held on February 28 at the Sheraton Park Hotel. The dinner was called the National Victory Dinner, held in honor of the newly elected Democratic Senators, governors, and Congressmen who helped win one of the greatest Demo-

cratic victories of all time in the preceding fall election.
The victories in the fall of 1958 provided the Democrats
with more governorships than they had had at any time
since 1938 (35), more United States Senate seats than at
any time since 1940 (64), and more seats in the House of
Representatives than at any time since 1936 (283).

House Speaker Sam Rayburn was the major speaker,

*Jefferson-Jackson Day Dinners have tradi-
tionally been a rallying point for the
party faithful. Senators Kennedy
and Johnson, born and bred in the 20th
century, join hands with elder statesman
Speaker Rayburn.*

accompanied by other speakers: Representative David King of Utah; Ella Grasso, Secretary of State in Connecticut; Senator Philip Hart of Michigan; Senate Majority Leader Lyndon B. Johnson; Governor J. Millard Tawes of Maryland; Governor Stephen McNichols of Colorado; Senator J. William Fulbright of Arkansas; Representative Samuel Stratton of New York; Genevieve Blatt, Secretary for Internal Affairs of Pennsylvania; Senator Harrison A. Williams, Jr., of New Jersey; Senator Mike Mansfield, Majority Whip; Governor J. Howard Edmondson of Oklahoma; Governor LeRoy Collins of Florida. Half of these additional speakers appeared in the banquet hall and the other half appeared in another room called the Sheraton Hall. Speaker Rayburn, who appeared in both halls, described the Democratic Party as embracing people of every type of economic and political interest. He suggested that all shades of opinion and belief are represented in the Democratic Party.

As has been the custom in the twentieth century, the Democratic National Committee tried to avoid showing any favoritism toward any Presidential hopeful. Lyndon B. Johnson was the only Presidential aspirant who was allowed to talk at the dinner. Other Democrats desiring a crack at the Presidency and present at the dinner were: Senator John F. Kennedy of Massachusetts, Senator Hubert H. Humphrey of Minnesota, Senator Stuart Symington of Missouri, Governor G. Mennen Williams of Michigan, and Governor Robert Meyner of New Jersey.

The first two years in the fifties produced the largest Jefferson-Jackson Day Dinners ever held, with more than 5,300 people attending each dinner. Then, after they lost the Presidency in 1952 and became the "out party," the Democrats had a more difficult time raising funds. The failing fifties found the Democratic Party wanting, both politically and economically. However, determined efforts by Democratic National Committee leaders Stephen Mitchell and Paul Butler succeeded in raising the party from its financial depths to a party equipped—both in candidates and in finances—for the 1960 Presidential battle. The Jefferson-Jackson Day fund raisers formed the firm foundation of the Democratic Party's finances in the fifties. ★

Chapter 16

JEFFERSON, JACKSON, JFK, AND JOHNSON

CHARISMATIC John F. Kennedy became the nucleus of attraction for rallying the people around himself and the Democratic Party in the early 1960's. He charmed the public with an electricity found in few men since Franklin D. Roosevelt.

Added to the many fine qualities brought to the Democratic Party and to the Presidency by John F. Kennedy was his magical ability to raise funds for his campaign and for the party.

AT THE 1960 $100-a-plate dinner in Washington, all the Presidential hopefuls spoke to 2,500 diners gathered in the two huge dining rooms of the Sheraton Park Hotel. The dinner, held on January 23, served as the official kickoff of the Presidential campaign. Speaking at the affair, in addition to former President Harry S. Truman, were such Presidential prospects as Senator John F. Kennedy of Massachusetts, Senator Hubert H. Humphrey of Minnesota, Senator Stuart Symington of Missouri, Senator Lyndon B. Johnson of Texas, Governor Robert B. Meyner of New Jersey, Governor Edmund G. Brown of California, and Governor G. Mennen Williams of Michigan. The only potential candidate who didn't attend the dinner and speak was the two-time Presidential aspirant Adlai Stevenson. However, a telegram from Stevenson was read at the gathering.

1960

Since most of the Presidential hopefuls were seeking delegate support, they centered their attack upon Richard Nixon, the only Republican in sight for his party's nomination. Governor Nelson Rockefeller of New York had withdrawn his attempt to gain the Republican nomination.

In most of the previous Presidential election years, the Democratic National Committee had tried to keep any potential Presidential candidates from gaining unfair advantage by speaking at the dinners. But in 1960 there was a direct attempt to see that anyone interested in the Presidency had a chance to speak to the party faithful and to round up as much support as each man could. There was intense political maneuvering before, during, and after the dinner by the Presidential candidates. Hotel suites, lobbies, and luncheons became important meeting places for these aspirants. The governors and Senators of big electoral-vote states were being wooed throughout the dinner without abatement.

John F. Kennedy, Senator from Massachusetts at this time, attacked the Republican slogan of "peace and prosperity." Senator Kennedy said:

We are not enjoying a period of peace—only a period of stagnation and retreat, while America becomes second in missiles, second in space, second in education, and, if we don't act fast and effectively, second in production and industrial might.

Senator Hubert H. Humphrey of Minnesota accused the Republicans of running a "payola government." He characterized the Republican record as the final triumph of the "payola age." Senator Humphrey continued:

He [Nixon] cannot avoid responsibility for the erosion of our national power and prestige which has taken place in the last seven years. He cannot dodge or duck responsibility for the slowdown in our national growth which has taken place in the last seven years. He cannot beg out of the stagnation in our national morality and character which has taken place in the last seven years.

Senator Stuart Symington of Missouri nicknamed Vice President Richard Nixon as "Sir Richard the Nimble" and ripped into Nixon's voting record in the House and the Senate. He said that Nixon opposed the expansion of Social Security, extension of minimum wage coverage, and slum clearance; voted to cut Rural Electrification Administration funds; voted against "fair prices" for farmers; and voted to

President John F. Kennedy in one of his winsome moments in a 1963 news conference. (Courtesy of the White House, Abbie Rowe)

slash funds for flood control and reclamation.

Senator Lyndon B. Johnson ridiculed Rockefeller's withdrawal from the Republican Presidential race, and labeled it "political birth control." He said that it was Democratic "responsibility" which had assured the party victories in the past and that it would be "responsibility" which would assure widespread victories in 1960. Continuing with the "responsibility" theme, Senator Johnson stated:

> Responsibility doesn't have a veto for a heart. Responsibility doesn't wait eight months to settle the steel strike or eighty months to start balancing budgets, or eighty years to pass a civil rights bill. Responsibility keeps its heart without losing its head.

Assessing the effect of the Presidential prospects at the dinner, James Reston of the *New York Times* indicated that Senators Kennedy and Humphrey showed the greatest gains in influence. He predicted that the young Democrats — "particularly Senators John F. Kennedy and Hubert H. Humphrey"— were "coming up fast" and that the older Democrats, such as former President Truman, were gradually losing some of their power and authority.

The $100-a-plate dinner had become so successful in these prosperous times that many cities outside Washington were holding $100-a-plate dinners. When the dinners first began in 1936, the only $100-a-plate dinner was held in Washington, D.C. In 1960, the city of Boston held a $100-a-plate dinner where Senator Kennedy spoke just one day after the national dinner. That dinner cleared $175,000 for the use of the state party, and it gave Senator Kennedy $50,000 for his campaign. The cities of New York and Philadelphia were probably the first cities outside Washington to hold $100-a-plate dinners shortly after their initiation on the national level in 1936.

The Democratic Party had emerged with a deficit of more than $800,000 after the unsuccessful 1956 Presidential campaign. The party was still $250,000 in debt when the

1960 Jefferson-Jackson Day Dinner was held. Most of the money raised at this affair went toward that deficit. The Democrats tried a house-to-house canvass in what they called a "Dollars for Democrats" drive but were very unsuccessful, raising only $62,000 by this device. This points up once again the great success and need of the Jefferson-Jackson Day $100-a-plate dinners.

The Republicans, realizing the great potentialities of the $100-a-plate dinner, fattened their treasury by almost $3 million at their "Dinner with Ike," held just four days after the Democratic Jefferson-Jackson Day Dinner. This was the total amount the Republicans raised from about 80 dinners throughout the country. During Eisenhower's Administration, the Republican Party broadened the base for the $100-a-plate dinners by holding a coast-to-coast closed-circuit television program with President Eisenhower performing the major speaking chores.

Another $100-a-plate dinner was held in Washington, D.C., in 1960 for the purpose of raising funds for the campaigns of members of the House of Representatives and the Senate. Former President Harry S. Truman was the major speaker at the affair which attracted 5,200 people in the National Guard Armory. This was the largest group to attend such an affair since the early 1950's.

Making contacts for people to attend these $100-a-plate affairs has always been a touchy and most difficult task. Throughout the history of these celebrations, the Republicans have charged the Democrats with soliciting federal employees and with using undue pressure on them.

The case was no different in 1961 when Secretary of the Interior Stewart L. Udall was caught in the middle of Republican barrages from many barrels. A letter sent by J. K. Evans, an oil executive in Washington, D.C., to 56 of his friends stated that Secretary Udall "has asked me . . . to solicit the oil and gas industries" to buy $100 tickets to the Jefferson-Jackson Day Dinner on May 27 in celebration of President John F. Kennedy's birthday.

Secretary Udall quickly called a news conference and denied categorically that he had asked Evans to "solicit the industry." He indicated that he simply suggested that Evans bring a few of his friends. The Secretary asked Evans to withdraw the letter, but this was not forthcoming.

Republicans in and out of Congress charged Secretary Udall with unduly using his influence to obtain political contributions. Several demands were made that President Kennedy ask him to resign. President Kennedy, although upset by the letter, told his news conference that Secretary Udall was "embarrassed" and, to prevent such incidents, he suggested that there be "some other way" to raise party funds. He even suggested that the federal government bear the "major burdens of Presidential campaigns."

Secretary of Agriculture Orville L. Freeman stated at his news conference that he sold tickets to the Democratic Party fund-raising dinner. He said proudly that he had been in the habit of selling tickets to Democratic affairs for 20 years and that he expected to continue to do so. He said that this method of raising money had been used for a long time by both major parties. Secretary Freeman continued:

> I personally have bought a ticket to the dinner, and I expect to attend. I would hope that many good Democrats and some Republicans who believe in the two-party system will want to buy them. If they do, I would be glad to accommodate them. ★

1961 THE PURPOSE of the 1961 "Birthday Dinner" on May 27 was to help wipe out the party's 1960 campaign deficit which had been reduced to $2,500,000. In his first "political" appearance since inauguration on January 20, 1961, President John F. Kennedy addressed the 6,000 Democrats who gathered at the National Guard Armory to celebrate his birthday at a price of $100-a-plate. The party faithful also met to wish him bon voyage on his European trip which was to begin the following Tuesday. The trip included visits to France's President de Gaulle, Great Britain's Prime Minister Macmillan, and Premier Khrushchev in Vienna.

Speaking before the largest gathering of $100-a-plate diners in the national capital's history, President Kennedy described his anticipated meeting with Khrushchev as "seeking not solutions to all our problems" but "insight" into East-West problems.

His speech was designed to prepare the American people for the proposed talks, warning them that no quick, simple solutions would be readily found. He praised former President Harry S. Truman for making Europe strong.

For one of the very few times since the beginning of these $100-a-plate dinners, no arrangements were made for radio coverage. Other major speakers at the dinner were former President Harry S. Truman, Vice President Lyndon Johnson, and Speaker Sam Rayburn.

Former President Truman, who had opposed President Kennedy's nomination, gave him ringing tribute on this occasion:

> The new President has his work cut out for him. But I have every confidence in his capacity, his ability, and his judgment to deal with the unsolved problems of the previous Administration and the new problems as they develop.

Matthew H. McCloskey, the Democratic National Committee treasurer, reported that $5,280,000 had to be raised in 1961 to pay off their debts and to meet the operating costs of the National Committee and the Congressional Campaign Committees.

The Democratic deficit after this dinner was reduced to $1,926,785. About $400,000 or more was expected from a second Kennedy Birthday Dinner held at Boston on Monday, May 29, the real birthday of President Kennedy.

John M. Bailey of Connecticut, the new Democratic National Committee Chairman, told the diners that only once in the last half-century had the party in control of the

White House gained Congressional seats in the midterm elections. He made it the goal of the party to break the off-Presidential-election-year jinx.

President Kennedy thanked Chairman John Bailey and the other Democrats for his birthday party and stated that he also wanted to thank his Secretary of Interior, Stewart Udall, who, he said smilingly, had "handled all the publicity."

The Democratic Senatorial and Congressional Campaign Committees joined forces this year with the Democratic National Committee to organize and promote the fund-raising event. A Hartford, Connecticut, baker whipped up a 4,400-pound birthday cake, topped by a 4-foot-long hard sugar White House. The cake was brought to Washington in two sections in armored cars.   ★

1962

THE OCCASION for the 1962 $100-a-plate dinner was the celebration of the first completed year of the Kennedy Administration. President Kennedy, speaking to the more than 5,000 delirious Democrats in the National Guard Armory on January 20, kicked off the Congressional campaign by predicting that the Democratic Party could hold its own in the forthcoming elections if it continued acting as "a party of progress." The funds raised at this dinner were earmarked for assistance to the Democratic House and Senate candidates who would be running in the fall elections.

President Kennedy reviewed the record to show that the party in power is supposed to lose seats in Congress during off-year elections. However, he said:

> We believe the Democratic Party at home and abroad is best fitted to lead this country, and therefore we start tonight.

Kennedy, always quick with a quip, provided the humor of the evening when he paraphrased his own inaugural address. He said:

Our deficit [the party campaign deficit] will not be paid off in the next hundred days, nor will it be paid off in the first one thousand days, nor in the life of this Administration, nor, perhaps, even in our lifetime on this planet, but let us begin—remembering that generosity is not a sign of weakness and that Ambassadors are always subject to Senate confirmation, for if the Democratic Party cannot be helped by the many who are poor, it cannot be saved by the few who are rich. So let us begin.

In his brief speech, the President also paid high tribute to Vice President Johnson when he said that "we have worked together better than any President and Vice President in history, at least since Franklin Roosevelt and Harry S. Truman."

Mrs. Jacqueline Kennedy attended the dinner with her husband and sat at a head table on the south side of the Armory between Mr. Truman and Attorney General Robert F. Kennedy. As had become the custom at these massive dinners held in the Armory, the First Lady later moved to the north side of the Armory with the President, where they exchanged places with Vice President and Mrs. Lyndon B. Johnson. Because the Armory was so large and so many people attended the dinner, two head tables were set up, one at each end of the Armory, to give people in all parts of the building a chance to see and hear the President.

Former President Harry S. Truman enthusiastically endorsed Kennedy's new trade program and compared it to the Marshall Plan of his own Administration. He suggested that Kennedy be given increased power to negotiate trade agreements with the Common Market "to strike the great bargain which will redouble the economic power of the free world."

Vice President Lyndon Johnson spoke mainly in tribute to the late Speaker Sam Rayburn who had died the previous November. Johnson called Rayburn the personification of the Democratic Party. He eulogized him as being "as old as Thomas Jefferson and as young as John F. Kennedy."

Matthew McCloskey, the retiring Democratic treasurer, reported that the Democratic National Committee had raised more money than ever before in the history of the country in a nonelection year—over $4 million! Despite such far-reaching fund raising, the party still needed to raise about the same amount in 1962 to pay off its remaining debt of approximately $1 million and to meet the expenses of the 1962 Congressional campaign.

Former President Harry S. Truman, though he had opposed the nomination of President Kennedy, pictured him as "wise, brilliant, and vigorous." He continued: "I am proud of his record, I am proud of what he has done as President, and I am confident of the even greater achievements that lie in store for him in the years ahead.

Carroll Rosenbloom, the chairman of the dinner, planned the program of entertainment following the dinner and before the formal speeches.

Earlier in the day of the dinner, Democratic National Committee Chairman John Bailey and House Speaker John W. McCormack visualized the 1962 Congressional campaign as a contest between the Republicans of the right and the Democrats of the people. Chairman Bailey said:

> The American people have not gone right with the Republicans; the American people have gone forward with the Democrats. . . . Republicans say there is a tremendous upsurge of right-wing conservatism sweeping the country. I won't believe it until I see the Republicans match this crowd in size, in enthusiasm, and in party loyalty. They can't do it.

In this same year of 1962, on Saturday, June 9, a $250-a-plate dinner was given in honor of Matthew McCloskey, the retired Democratic National Committee Treasurer, who had accepted an appointment as Ambassador to Ireland. It is ironical that the Democratic National Committee should honor this Irish millionaire with a $250-a-plate dinner instead of a $100-a-plate dinner since he has often been credited with initiating the first $100-a-plate dinner on a local level in 1935 in Pennsylvania.

Whether the $100-a-plate dinners originated with Matthew McCloskey or W. Forbes Morgan or James Farley, they all deserve major credit for making the fund-raising idea successful. James Farley and W. Forbes Morgan tied in the $100-a-plate idea with the Jefferson and Jackson Day celebrations on the national level. Matthew McCloskey started the $100-a-plate dinners on the local scene in 1935 when he presented the idea to David Lawrence, the Pennsylvania Democratic State Chairman at that time, for a dinner which was held in Philadelphia.

John Bailey presented Matthew McCloskey with a lifetime card which would admit him to any Democratic fund-raising dinner—provided he paid the price. But the $250-a-plate dinner for Matthew McCloskey was merely a prelude and portent of things to come at the 1963 celebration. ★

THE PRICE of political dinners skyrocketed into space on January 18, 1963, when a $1,000-a-plate dinner was held in the banquet room of the International Inn in Washington, D.C. More than 700 guests in formal attire satisfied their appetites on the main course of filet of sole, since the dinner was held on Friday. There was some reluctance and anxiety over the plans and success of the $1,000-a-plate dinner, but this anxiety was soon relieved when it became apparent that more than 700 people were willing to pay such a price to have dinner with the President of the United States. The chairman of the dinner was Bedford S. Wynne, an attorney and co-owner of the Dallas Cowboys football team. The dinner was followed by a $100-a-seat gala held in the National Guard Armory.

For the first time since 1952, the Democratic Party was solvent. The party, long ridden by debt, raised almost $1 million at the $1,000-a-plate dinner and at the foodless gala attended by 4,000 to 5,000 people. The funds from these events erased the $800,000 Democratic deficit and provided a surplus for the 1964 Presidential election.

The diners attending the $1,000-a-plate dinner auto-

1963

matically became members of the President's Club. Un-
doubtedly the President's Club fund-raising device will become an adjunct to the traditional Jefferson-Jackson Day
Dinners or the $100-a-plate or even $100-no-plate celebrations.

President John F. Kennedy gave a very brief talk at the
National Guard Armory after the entertainers had performed. The witty and winsome President brought loud
laughter to the huge audience when he remarked that
Matthew McCloskey originated the $100-a-plate dinner in
the 1930's: "We have revolutionized that by removing the
dinner, but we are hanging on to the $100. The day will
come when we will let you go."

President Kennedy was referring of course to the dinners which were served as at least some recompense for the
$100 contribution. Now those attending the gala did not
get a dinner. Instead they were entertained by some of the
top performers in the nation. Only those who had joined
the President's Club and had paid $1,000 received a dinner
in 1963.

Still in a party mood, President Kennedy joked about
the complaints of pressure being applied to get people to
attend the $100 gala:

> Actually, I have been asked by Mr. Wynne, the chairman of
> the Inaugural Salute Celebration, to announce the man who sold
> the most tickets tonight.
> It is Mr. Jerry Kluttz of the *Washington Post*. Actually, I was
> invited to a cocktail party by Mr. Kenny O'Donnell and that is the
> way I happened to get my ticket.

The President was referring to several stories which
Washington Post reporter Jerry Kluttz had written describing the complaints from federal workers that pressure had
been put on them to buy $100 tickets to the gala. It was re-
called that members of Congress had even talked about an
investigation. Throughout the many years that these fund-
raising dinners have been held, there has always been a

plethora of complaints and implications of investigations concerning the soliciting of funds for the dinner. However, this is as far as the complaints have gone.

President Kennedy concluded his talk by saying:

A party is of no use unless it fulfills some national purpose. I said the other day, in the State of the Union message, that we were not on the top of the hill but on the side of the hill. I don't think in this Administration or in our generation or time will this country be at the top of the hill. But someday it will be, and I hope when it is, they will think we have done our part.

International talent as well as domestic talent provided the entertainment for the gala: Yves Montand, Shirley Bassey, Antonio and his Flamenco Ballet Espagnol, and Joan Sutherland. The United States performers were Master of Ceremonies Gene Kelly, George Burns and Carol Channing, Kirk Douglas, Carol Burnett assisted by Dick Altman, Diahann Carroll, and Peter Matz, conducting. The finale was the New York City Ballet's Balanchine Inspiration from John Philip Sousa's "The Stars and Stripes Forever."

Producer and composer Richard Adler produced the gala for President Kennedy's second inaugural anniversary. A stage was located at the south wall of the National Guard Armory where a high platform was built. An orchestra pit with 50 musicians, directed by Hal Hastings, was directly in front of the stage.

The ultimate in fund-raising affairs was achieved at this 1963 combination $1,000 dinner and $100 gala. It can be assumed that such a combination affair will continue in the future. Whether it will replace the old-fashioned $100-a-plate Jefferson-Jackson Day Dinner remains to be seen. From a financial viewpoint, there is little doubt that an affair as successful as this one will not be forgotten. Much of the credit for the raising of such huge sums, however, belongs to the late President John F. Kennedy. His dynamic personality and the devotion of his many ardent supporters who were willing to sacrifice large amounts of money to see him continue in office account for the success of the fund raisers. As in so many other areas, President Kennedy had the magical affinity for attracting the American people, rich and poor, toward the goal of promoting democracy.

Dorothy McCardle, in the January 19, 1963, edition of the *Washington Post,* gave a comprehensive and detailed description of the $1,000-a-plate dinner and the role of President Kennedy at the affair. In addition to discussing the intimate conversations of those gathered at the dinner, Dorothy McCardle indirectly presented humanistic insight into the personalities of President Kennedy and Vice President Johnson.

President Kennedy went table-hopping last night to greet personally each of the 700 men and women whose dinner tickets at International Inn had cost $1,000 per plate.

The young President astonished many an old-timer in his party by his uncanny memory for facts and faces. He turned their salute to him on the second anniversary of his inauguration into a salute to their industry in tackling such a gigantic fund-raising campaign.

The private, high-priced dinner, which wouldn't have cost a cent above $10 per person on any other occasion, was attended by Democratic governors, Senators, Congressmen, party officials and their glamorously attired wives from every state in the Union. It was the preamble to the $100-per-seat gala entertainment at the D.C. National Guard Armory later in the evening.

Because it was Friday, the party faithful were served a meatless menu built around a main course of filet of sole. Beginning with the avocado filled with seafood, it progressed through green turtle soup with cheese sticks to the fish, served with broiled tomato and French peas. Salad was hearts of palm on Boston lettuce and dessert was flag-topped Cherry Blossom International.

President and Mrs. Kennedy, together with Vice President and Mrs. Johnson, were the last to leave the dinner for the Armory. That was because they had not dined while the others ate, but spent their time socializing and hand-shaking.

At 8:30 P.M., when everyone else was taking to limousines or to buses to head for the Armory, President and Mrs. Kennedy and Vice President and Mrs. Johnson sat down together in an adjoining small dining room for the same menu.

Then at 9 P.M., the President and First Lady headed for the White House limousine. Mrs. Kennedy's gown, with its white satin skirt and crimson beaded top, was keyed to the red, white and blue table decorations of the evening's affair.

After the big show at the Armory, President and Mrs. Kennedy put in an appearance, shortly after midnight, at The Elms, home of Vice President and Mrs. Johnson, where the Johnsons were giving a late supper for the performers who starred at the Gala.

With the Kennedys was First Lady Jacqueline Kennedy's sister, Princess Radziwill.

President Kennedy stayed more than an hour and met all the performers, chatting with them, just as he had done with many attending the $1,000-a-plate dinner earlier in the evening.

The Vice President and Mrs. Johnson had pulled one of the neatest bits of timing earlier when they both arrived at the hotel, by separate cars, exactly on the dot of 6:45 P.M. As the Vice President climbed out of his car, his wife, wearing a handsome golden satin gown, walked from her car.

"Howdy, Lyndon," said Lady Bird Johnson to her husband. "How's that for connecting!"

She had come from home, and he from his office on Capitol Hill.

At 7:15, President and Mrs. Kennedy arrived and walked into the dining room as everyone rose and applauded.

President and Mrs. Kennedy were escorted to table number 25 in the center of the room. They greeted the others at the table who were the Vice President and Mrs. Johnson, the Chairman of the Democratic National Committee and Mrs. John Bailey, Special Assistant to the President and Mrs. Lawrence F. O'Brien, and the Chairman of the Inaugural Anniversary Committee and Mrs. Bedford Wynne of Texas.

Then the President and Vice President had a quick conference and both rose. The Vice President began table-hopping to the left of the huge room. The President went to the right straight to table 26, where he shook hands with one of the most surprised couples of the evening, Mr. and Mrs. Angus Wynne, parents of the Anniversary Chairman. They were astonished that the President headed straight for them and recognized them so warmly.

"I want to thank you for the wonderful job your son has done," said President Kennedy. "I deeply appreciate it."

President Kennedy chatted with Assistant Secretary of Commerce Hickman Price, who is leaving government to go into business. The President wanted details of Price's new post and got a pledge for future support, too.

"I hope to come to Washington during your second term, Mr. President," said Price.

"Fine," said the President.

Price said, as the President moved away, that his wife Margaret Price, Vice-Chairman of the Democratic National Committee, is recovering nicely from a heart attack and she was very much touched by a beautiful flower arrangement from the President.

To Governor John Burns, of Hawaii, and to Hawaii's Attorney General Bert T. Kabayashi, President Kennedy said:

"You are the ones who have probably come the farthest for this dinner."

Joe Reber, of Miles City, Montana, sitting at the same table with his state's Senator and Mrs. Mike Mansfield, got a real charge when President Kennedy recalled that Reber was the fellow who had lent a horse to his brother, Teddy, at a rodeo. Reber explained that Teddy, now a United States Senator from Massachusetts, rode that bucking bronc over three fences before he was tossed to the dust.

"Have you seen Teddy?" asked the President.

Teddy Kennedy was not there, but his lovely wife, Joan, was. She said that her husband would be at the Gala at the Armory where she later joined Attorney General and Mrs. Robert F. Kennedy and First Lady Jacqueline Kennedy's sister, Princess Radziwill.

At the Indiana table, President Kennedy spotted the lovely Mrs. Birch Bayh, wife of the new Senator from Indiana.

"Why is your husband sitting at another table?" asked the President with a smile.

"Because, Mr. President, he has just flown in from a speech in Indiana, and he got here an hour late."

"Yes, and I know he made a speech in Boston yesterday," said the President.

At the Indiana tables was Indianapolis industrialist Miklos Sperling, whom the President recognized as the man who gave Rembrandt Peale portraits of George and Martha Washington to the new State Department reception suite.

After the President had greeted Sperling and moved away, the former immigrant industrialist confided that he has a special gift for the First Lady's private home, a 14th Century painting.

"It will not fit in with Mrs. Kennedy's White House restoration, but I think she may want to have it for her private family collection," said Sperling.

Speaker of the House and Mrs. John W. McCormack got a special welcome from President Kennedy when he reached their table. The President noted several members of his White House staff at the McCormack table and laughed when the Speaker quipped: "We are melding the legislative and executive branches together tonight."

Nobody discussed the high cost of the dinner with the President, but some of the governors present told a joke on that subject which had occurred earlier in the day at the Governors' Conference.

After reports appeared in the newspapers that government employees were being coerced into buying dinner and Gala tickets, Secretary of State Dean Rusk called a staff meeting, the governors reported.

"Has anyone here been pressured to take tickets for this inaugural celebration?" he asked.

Not a hand went up.

Then after more silence, millionaire Assistant Secretary of State Averell Harriman raised his hand and said:

"Why I haven't even been invited!"

Richard Maguire, a long-time friend of President Kennedy who moved from the White House staff to the post of Treasurer of the Democratic National Committee, created and promoted many of the fund-raising innovations currently on the political scene. The President's Club, created in the fall of 1962 in preparation for the 1963 $1,000-a-plate dinner and $100-a-seat gala, started to spread throughout the country. Its membership grew steadily.

To qualify for membership in the President's Club, a Democrat is required to contribute $1,000 or more to the Democratic National Committee during a given year. The President's Club of New York alone had more than 500 members by May of 1963. The major benefit to club members is an invitation to a dinner with the President and Vice President.

The birthday dinner for the President in New York City at the Waldorf-Astoria on May 23, six days before his actual birthday, netted about $550,000. About $375,000 went to the Democratic National Committee, and approximately $175,000 went to the New York State Democratic Committee.

During the Kennedy Administration, in 1961, 1962, and 1963, there was a move away from the $100-a-plate national dinner toward this somewhat different type of fund raising. Although the $100-a-plate dinners were still used throughout many parts of the country, the national dinner was displaced by the use of professional entertainment at a gala. The $100-a-plate dinner stretched to the $1,000-a-plate dinner as part of the President's Club fund-raising device. A combination of the gala and the $1,000-a-plate dinner provided greater amounts of money than had been raised by any device heretofore. The object of raising greater amounts of money came about as a necessity because of the high cost of campaigning nationally. In 1963, President Kennedy was building up his finances for the 1964 Presidential election. During 1961 and 1962, the profits went toward paying off the 1960 Presidential election debt and toward the cost of the Congressional campaigns in 1962.

The use of President Kennedy's personal touch to raise money for the expensive Presidential campaign worked on the promise of a brief but personal contact between the President and the $1,000-or-more contributor. This contact was usually built around the atmosphere of some social occasion such as his birthday or his January 20th anniversary of taking office. Usually the President moved informally from table to table and shook hands and talked very briefly with the guests. Due to the prestige and personality of President Kennedy, more funds were produced in the short period of his Presidency than ever before in the history of the country.

President John F. Kennedy was assassinated on November 22, 1963, ending the meteoric career of a young, energetic, progressive President who accomplished most of the results of his "1000 days" through his inspirational leadership.

President Lyndon B. Johnson grasped the torch of leadership from the young, fallen leader and carried it forward to victories never dreamed of by even the most ardent admirers of Johnson. So, too, the new President carried on the role of Democratic Party leader at the fund-raising dinners and galas.   ★

1964   ON MAY 26, 1964, President Lyndon B. Johnson was the honored guest at the "Salute to LBJ" affair in Washington,

D.C., at the National Guard Armory. (A "Salute to JFK," planned for early 1964, was cancelled after the assassination.)

More than $1.5 million was raised at the dinner and gala in 1964—a big boost for the campaign chest in that Presidential election year. Two days later President Johnson went to New York where he attended a similar affair and where another $1.5 million was collected.

The Washington events started with a dinner at the International Inn for 750 members of the President's Club, the $1,000 contributors. After the roast beef dinner, these diners and the President joined 8,000 people at the National Guard Armory—the greatest number ever to attend such an affair. The faithful attending the gala forfeited $100 each for the privilege of watching and hearing Richard Adler's production consisting of a star-studded group of entertainers.

Senator John J. Williams (Republican of Delaware) introduced a resolution on the day of the salute which called for the Attorney General to investigate reports that "career employees of the Federal Government have been solicited by the Democratic National Committee to purchase tickets to a political fund-raising dinner." As annual as the dinner are such complaints by the Republican Party.

After praising Presidents Wilson, Franklin D. Roosevelt, Truman, and Kennedy, President Johnson alluded to the Republicans when he said: "Men of little vision and meager vitality—men whose acts are timid and whose aims are tiny—cannot hope to meet the challenge and shoulder the burdens of a mushrooming America."

Following the trend set by President Kennedy at these galas, Johnson spoke for only a few minutes. It appears, temporarily at least, that the contributors are being treated to more entertainment and less political talk for their money. ★

1965

AFTER THE largest landslide of successful Democratic candidates in recent history—all the way from the local and state levels to the federal level—President Lyndon Johnson had a mandate from the people in the 1964 election unlike any that had been given a President since Franklin D. Roosevelt won all but two states in 1936. A top-heavy Democratic House of Representatives and United States Senate gave the President the extra power he needed to fulfill the pledges made in the Democratic platform in August of 1964.

Congress had been in session five months when the House Congressional Campaign Committee, the Senate Campaign Committee, and the Democratic National Committee jointly sponsored a $100-a-plate dinner saluting the members of Congress. More than 8,500 people attended the dinner, forcing it to be held in the Washington Hilton Hotel as well as the National Guard Armory.

Never before had so many convened for a $100-a-plate dinner. This is the first time that the diners overflowed the National Guard Armory into a hotel.

The economy of the country was at its highest peak in several decades. The war in Viet Nam was continuing and increasing in intensity. More people were employed than ever before. Legislation in Congress was being passed with rapid speed. The President's program, the most ambitious since early New Deal days, was well under way.

Vice President Hubert H. Humphrey preceded the President to the podium at the hotel and at the Armory.

From the Battle of New Orleans to the space age, Jefferson-Jackson Day Dinners have been a vital part of the ritual of the Democratic Party. Lyndon B. Johnson as holder of the nation's highest office has taken his place in the line of distinguished custodians of party spirit. (Courtesy of the White House)

After finishing one speech, he moved across the city for the other one.

President Johnson, appearing with Mrs. Johnson and his daughter, Luci, spent much of his time praising the 89th Congress, its members and leaders. He then went on to discuss the substantive work Congress was doing, the opportunities before it, and America's attempts to provide peace for the world.

After the dinner, the President flew to Kansas City, Missouri, where he had breakfast the following morning with former President Harry S. Truman. From there he went on to San Francisco for the 20th anniversary of the founding of the United Nations. ★

1966

THE FIRST SESSION of the 89th Congress, acclaimed by many as the most productive session of Congress in passing substantial legislation, ended on October 22, 1965. In the campaign year of 1966, the question of how to top the previous session became a difficult one. The first three months of the year produced mainly, and almost solely, the public and televised hearings on the Vietnam conflict. Legislative accomplishments of 1965 were all but forgotten in the heat of the discussion on foreign policy led by Senator J. W. Fulbright of Arkansas, the Chairman of the Senate Foreign Relations Committee.

Bombings in North Vietnam ceased for a while but soon began again and even increased. President Johnson's popularity went up and down in almost direct proportion to the number of bombings that were made. The public cried for peace and a cessation of the war; the polls indicated support of a stronger role by the United States in the handling of the conflict.

The whole nation was immersed in the discussion of one topic almost to the exclusion of all others during those first three or four months of 1966—a discussion of the Vietnam situation. The accomplishments of the first session of the 89th Congress were dimmed in competition with the Vietnam issue which dominated the news.

President Lyndon B. Johnson used the $100-a-plate Congressional Campaign Dinner on May 12, 1966, as the forum for telling all Democrats, and especially Congressional incumbents, to stand firmly behind the Administration's record in Vietnam. Referring to his critics on Vietnamese policy, the President said:

> We will have our differences and our disputes and we will do it without questioning the honor and integrity of our fellow man. . . . But we have never abandoned and we will never surrender this world to those who would dominate it and destroy it. If we were to turn our backs on freedom in South Vietnam—if Vietnam were to fall to an aggressor's force—what an empty thing our commitment to liberty would really turn out to be. . . . We will stand there with honor and we shall stand there with patience. It is the stand the free people of the world will respect. It is the stand the vast majority of Americans will demand.

The more than 6,000 Democrats in the National Guard Armory and the overflow of 400 in the Washington Hilton Hotel heard the President tease Senator Fulbright who was sitting at the head table. President Johnson said that he was "delighted to be here tonight with so many of my good and old friends—as well as some members of the Senate Foreign Relations Committee." He further referred to the hearings Senator Fulbright's committee had been holding: "You can say one thing about those hearings—but I don't think this is the place to say it."

President Johnson, speaking for 15 minutes, spent most of his time trying to refresh the public's memory on the major legislation the 89th Congress had already passed. He recalled that the 89th Congress had already enacted "between 80 and 90 per cent of the pledges" the Democratic Party had made in its 1964 platform.

"The American people are not going to disown the most productive Congress under the greatest leadership ever assembled in this city," the President concluded.

Significantly, for the first time since 1953 the Democratic National Committee did not participate in a major fund raiser in Washington, D.C. The House and Senate Democratic Campaign Committees held this dinner without the aid of the Democratic National Committee. President John F. Kennedy had kept the fund raising centrally located in the National Committee. This was the first departure from that policy of having the National Committee control the funds. Early in the year the Democratic National Committee dismissed most of its staff, keeping only a skeleton working crew. Congressmen and Senators became disenchanted with the National Committee and thus helped break the central control of the National Committee over the funds of Congressional campaign committees.

Because Congress had failed to repeal section 14b of the Taft-Hartley Act, and because labor placed much of the blame on the Administration, the AFL-CIO refused to buy tickets and to advertise and support the Congressional dinner. Some unions and union officials still bought tickets although most followed the federation's lead. The labor organizations stressed their desire to distribute their political action funds to those Congressional candidates whose voting records they liked without going through the Democratic National Committee.

The Democratic National Committee initiated a unique and controversial fund-raising device at the end of 1965. Movie houses were rented for first showings of movies where a contribution served as the price of admission. In addition to this contribution, the National Committee collected between $600,000 and $700,000 from advertisements that companies had placed in a quality party publication which was distributed at these shows. This money was to aid "voter education" in those districts of cooperating Democratic Congressmen. Because of adverse publicity, although the Republican Party picked up the idea quickly and started to use it also, the money raised was not used as originally planned. So far its use still has not been determined.

A. B. Krim, a New York lawyer and President of the United Artists Corporation, took over the task of raising funds for the Democratic National Committee after Richard Maguire resigned as treasurer of the party in early 1966. Krim, who helped start the President's Club in New York State, became head of the finance committee on April 20, 1966. The party was $2,400,000 in debt at this time, and Krim aimed to raise $5,000,000 for the 1966 Congressional campaigns. He sought to broaden the base of contributors through direct mail campaigns and door-to-door drives. In addition, the President and the Vice President began holding President's Club affairs in the large metropolitan centers of the country to bolster the National Committee treasury. ★

WHAT FUTURE COURSE the Democratic fund-raising events will follow is left only to the imagination of those provided with the duty and responsibility of raising funds to pay the party's debts.

Although it is true that raising party funds is a major reason for holding dinners today, it is just as true that, in addition to this objective, results are seen in national publicity and policy statements, in morale and organizational advantages to those attending, in sharing problems, and in spiritual inspiration. Dinners for Democrats as well as for dollars renew faith in the old democracy of Jefferson and Jackson. ★

EPILOGUE

SPEAKING to the Democratic National Committee, the State Chairmen and Vice Chairmen of the fifty states in the East Room of the White House on Saturday, January 19, 1963, President Kennedy recalled the fact that the Founding Fathers, in drafting the Constitution, made no provision for political parties. The President pointed out that it had been these political parties that had made the American system work and had "served us well."

President Kennedy, agreeing with former President Harry S. Truman, vowed that a President has no greater responsibility than that of leader of a political party—"especially this political party, the oldest in our country's history, the oldest in the world.

"A party is of no use unless it fulfills some national purpose. I said the other day, in the State of the Union message, that we were not on the top of the hill but on the side of the hill. I don't think in this Administration or in our generation or time will this country be at the top of the hill. But someday it will be, and I hope when it is, they will think we have done our part."

Appendix A

CAPSULES OF
$100-A-PLATE
DINNER SPEECHES,
1936-1966

WASHINGTON, D.C., is the scene of the annual $100-a-plate dinners which began in 1936 and continue today. This is the one time in the year when the Democratic Party faithful from throughout the country gather in the nation's capital to contribute financially to the party's treasury and to listen to the party leaders speak on the issues of the day.

The following pages contain sentence capsules of the major speeches given each year from 1936 through 1966. Themes are shown through the words of the speaker. The key sentences in each major paragraph of a given speech have been taken verbatim from the reading copies of the speeches or from press releases in a few cases. This provides a quick reference for the substance of each speech. Presented in this way this section provides the reader with an overall view of the dinners and speeches.

FRANKLIN D. ROOSEVELT
January 8, 1936

THE MEETING tonight is in honor of the memory of Andrew Jackson.

The real issue is the right of man to a better life.

I speak honestly to all groups [*Democrats, Republicans, Progressives, Independents, farmers, laborers, businessmen*].

I will consider common problems from the American point of view.

I fight for the ideals and policies of the common man despite heavy odds . . . just as Jackson and Jefferson did.

The Democratic Party by positive action has proved its devotion to recovery and well-being of the citizenry.

The basic issue in the election is retention of popular government. Thus, organization of all wanting progress is essential.

You must get the facts underlying the charges of the misleaders.

The people are behind me in solving problems of the nation. A minority of business and finance would "gang up" against the people's liberties.

You and I will fight businessmen and financiers for a better deal. Government needs your opinions to support it.

Despite the Supreme Court decision [*AAA decision two days prior to the speech*], justice and prosperity for American agriculture are objectives of this Administration.

Like Jackson, I will encourage widespread interest in public affairs.

Youth is necessary for fulfillment of America's destiny.

We must fight forces of privilege and greed.

Like Jackson, the American people know the purpose of their government and will not retreat.　　　　★

FRANKLIN D. ROOSEVELT
March 4, 1937

[*Reference to March 4, 1933.*]
I WANT to talk about a crisis today.

I speak as the representative of all Americans.

The Democratic Party is today the majority party.

The Democratic Party will remain in office as long as it solves the problems of the nation.

Our opponents' roars indicate that we have kept our promises.

We have just begun to fight for better conditions.

[*He told a story of possible third term and his desire to turn the government over in good shape.*]

I want to help the nation progress.

All of you want the nation to progress.

I feel concern for the future.

Appeals from all classes for economic freedom of the wage earner, farmer, and small businessmen come to the President.

There are insistent demands upon the government to meet human needs.

Royalist, parliamentary, and democratic governments have failed to meet human needs in other countries.

Leaders of the Democratic Party do not propose that democracy fail to meet human needs.

There is no definite assurance that the three-horse team of the American system of government will pull together.

The New Deal has brought political and economic progress.

Congress and the President have tried to help the farmer through the AAA. You know who vetoed the program.

We have just begun to fight for the farmers.

We have an obligation to fight the Supreme Court on the farm problem.　　　　★

FRANKLIN D. ROOSEVELT
January 8, 1938

I AM HAPPY that there is less unthinking partisanship in the country today.

[*Letter from a woman wanting to vote for FDR, but she's a Republican.*] My answer . . . "I voted for a Republican, Theodore Roosevelt, because he was the best man."

The Democratic Party represents the unity of our country.

Like the great men of the past, I am fighting to restore and maintain the moral integrity of democracy.

Jefferson preached for government responsive to the public will.

Jefferson fought for freedom of the press, even though most of it was against him.

Later, the government was in the hands of a small group of bankers.

Jackson fought the Bank and the press for the integrity and morals of democracy.

Lincoln fought Wall Street for integrity and morals of democracy.

There was a period of commercialization after 1865.

Theodore Roosevelt preached the morals of democracy.

Wilson carried on his fight.

Today, as before, a few maintain privileges harmful to the body politic.

We are striving to uphold the integrity of the morals of democracy by serving the needs of the people and curbing the abuses of power and privilege.

Some contravene this fight against minority abuses into an attack upon the exploited majority itself.

We confirm our traditional democratic antagonism to concentration of control over large areas of industry beyond the needs of operating efficiency.

The utility holding companies are evil because of the control of a few.

We will prevent this utility holding company evil.

[*Story of a 4-inch tail wagging a 96-inch dog . . . illustrates the idea of only a few controlling the utilities.*]

Give me and the government credit for the intention to eradicate these evils.

Help to eradicate these evils of big business is welcome.

I will fight this small group of bankers and industrialists.

I, like Jackson, am fighting to uphold the integrity of the morals of democracy. ★

FRANKLIN D. ROOSEVELT

January 7, 1939

I AM GOING to have a good time tonight.

[*Story appealing to party unity.*]

The Democratic Party should examine itself.

The Republican Party gave the people a "do-nothing" government in the 1920's.

The Democratic Party had a program of action and was elected in 1932.

The Democratic Party kept its pledges and was re-elected in 1936. Millions of non-Democrats helped elect the party to power. Today, as in Jackson's era, people just want the President to serve them.

The Democratic Party must work for the people.

The Republicans have entered the Democratic Party with the intent to divide and conquer.

We *liberals must unite* to give service to the people.

The Republicans are opportunists.

The Republican first New Deal went along with our New Deal.

The Republican second New Deal . . . supports objectives but opposes legislation.

The Republican third New Deal . . . promises voters all sorts of benefits but ignores costs.

Republican tactics are wrong.

We Democrats must unite.

Discussion on differences within the party is helpful.

If we deliver to the American people, we will win.

The American Liberty League is for shopworn propaganda.

Jackson delivered for the common people.

Jackson's successor did not deliver to the people.

Harrison made Biddle, the money-changer, his Secretary of the Treasury.

Democracy came to life under Lincoln, the Democrat.

American people have changed their attitudes toward the government in this generation.

We take politics less seriously, government more seriously.

In the old days, elections were seasonal diversions.

Today, the public scrutinizes every move of government officials.

People can no longer be completely fooled.

The new generation believes in realities; it is national in outlook.

The younger generation intends to "go places" with the New Deal.

Workers of liberal government give service to their country and do a good job.

[*Story of cooperation within the party.*]

We will maintain a united front against the enemies of America. ★

FRANKLIN D. ROOSEVELT
January 8, 1940

YOU ARE legally here.

[*Story of a Republican's nonacceptance to attend banquet.*]

[*Menu of 1934 dinner.*]

Republicans are of little faith.

Great men of history have a common denominator of service to the country despite party allegiance.

People active in politics may lose sight of the true purposes of parties.

Parties are only instruments through which to achieve government.

I hold to party ties less than some of my predecessors.

Parties are for explaining issues, drumming up interest in elections, and improving the breed of candidates in office.

Growing independence of voters indicates more interest in government than party.

Independent voters are needed to win an election.

Some citizens vote strictly party line.

Great statesmen are remembered for big jobs they did.

Hamilton is a hero to me because he did his job [*Bank*].

Jefferson is a hero to me because he did his job [*universal suffrage*].

Lincoln is a hero to me because he did his job [*saving the Union*].

Jackson is a hero to me because he did his job [*popular government*].

To great men, the nation stood above party.

My motives of government have been primarily motives of service.

A President must take criticism and not worry.

It is fun to sift truth through the information arriving at the White House.

The optimists of 1929 are the pessimists of 1940.

World outside our hemisphere is in bad shape.

We have made great gains in economic prosperity and in the security of our individual citizens.

The Democratic Party has provided energy to steer government away from selfishness.

People are glad: moving in the right direction, better farm conditions, better economy, more conservation of natural resources; government is becoming more useful.

Some complainers enjoy bad health.

[*Story of Uncle Jed . . . not caring whether he hears anything or not since what he hears is not very good.*]

Most Congressional struggles wind up amicably.

Some do carry over struggles into private life.

Motive and good manners and knowledge are requirements of good leaders.

Also, a good leader must contribute $100 for a meal, eat it, and then speak.   ★

FRANKLIN D. ROOSEVELT
March 29, 1941

I REGRET having to talk from the *Potomac* off Florida.

The rest at sea is good because of the many demands on the President.

We cannot rest too much or peace will become unattainable.

Jackson placed devotion to country above adherence to party.

In Jackson's day the threat to the Union was internal.

The threat to the Union today is external.

Most of us have risen above party politics.

The two-party system has value for open discussion of issues, formulating policies to meet conditions, free elections.

Totalitarians can't understand the two-party system in a unified country.

Dictatorships afford only one path to follow.

In America, differences are expressed in the polling place.

We must defend our democratic principles from dictatorships.

Nazism would not let us keep these principles.

We shall help those who block dictators.

Enemies of democracy are trying to destroy our unity.

Nazis murder their own helpers.

Communists betrayed the workers of France.

The Nazis have attempted to exploit our love for peace.

Like Lincoln and Jackson, we protect ourselves with deeds.   ★

FRANKLIN D. ROOSEVELT
February 23, 1942

[*Celebration of Washington's Birthday.*]

WASHINGTON faced many defeats.

Washington provided us with a model of moral stamina.

We fight for rights, liberty, and justice.

This is a worldwide war. That is why I want you to take out a world map. Oceans protecting us in the past are now battlefields.

We must fight at vast distances to protect our supply lines. Some advocate that we must pull back and protect our shores.

It is obvious that we can't isolate ourselves from resources of other powers.

We must continue to send aid to China.

The Southwest Pacific is needed to stop Japanese aggression.

The North Atlantic supply line is needed by the British and the Russians.

We don't want an ostrich or turtle policy; we must fight in other lands.

We will and must maintain our four main lines of communication.

Air and naval bases are necessary to protect these lines.

Control of the air requires long-range bombers and light bombers.

Many bombers and men are already fighting in the South Pacific.

The Japanese have the strategic advantage in the battle area.

The Philippines were surrounded by the Japanese.

Because of treaties, we did not add fortifications to Guam or the Philippines.

Because of the encirclement of the Philippines, we could not help the defense.

Our strategy in this area has been of necessity a delaying action.

We knew we could outbuild Japan and overwhelm her.

MacArthur's army and the rest in the South Pacific area are fighting this delaying action very well.

Even if Japan hadn't attacked Pearl Harbor, we could not have stopped their success in the Philippines.

Our losses at Pearl Harbor are greatly exaggerated by the Axis and our own people.

Many details can't be given because of giving aid to the enemy.

Discretion and confidence in war information are necessary in these times.

[*Factual account on damage at Pearl Harbor.*]

We are yielding ground, but we will take the offensive and win.

A decent future depends on victory of the United Nations.

Our special task is uninterrupted production.

We are increasing production to win the war.

These are high purposes . . . not to stop work, no special privileges, give up conveniences.

We are willing to sacrifice ourselves for our nation.

Axis propagandists try to destroy our determination and morale.

Their constant theme has been that Americans are soft and rich and will not fight or work . . . tell that to the Marines.

The United Nations has cooperation, comradeship, and a unified command.

Americans will contribute unified production and acceptance of sacrifice.

The United Nations agrees on certain broad principles of peace.

The Russians and British have fought valiantly.

The Dutch and the Chinese fight bravely.

A great effort is before us.

Paine's words to Washington's army in 1776 . . . "the harder the sacrifice, the more glorious the triumph." ★

FRANKLIN D. ROOSEVELT
February 22, 1943

WE ARE FIGHTING today to maintain freedoms which Washington achieved.

Washington had trouble at the front and at home.

Skeptics and cynics of Washington's day sneered at principles of freedom.

Washington's faith overcame bickering and confusion.

People should not believe in quick victory.

Most Americans follow Washington's ideas, but some lead the Axis to believe America is disunited.

[*Reading of Beatitudes . . . words behind feelings at Valley Forge.*]

We shall follow these truths in our quest for victory, freedom, and peace. ★

SAM RAYBURN
January 22, 1944

JACKSON would rest assured if he saw the two great figures fighting for freedom today.

FDR and Hull are the heroic figures of whom I speak.

Although our land has not been ruined in the war, our Nation is marked by greatness of spirit.

American people, under FDR's leadership, have carried on the job of war ahead of schedule despite some defeatists.

There is still a small number of hecklers but the enemies have learned to respect a fighting America.

Let us see what has been done.

[*Summary of guns, ammunition, explosives, airplanes made.*]

In spite of defeatists and hecklers, we delivered the goods.

Some few think that feats on the home front and in the field of battle just happen.

They don't just happen . . . we have had great leadership.

I should mention what we of the Democratic Party are not going to do.

First, we are not going to let fighting boys go jobless when they return.

We are not going to deprive our people of the right to work.

We are pledged to preserve for our country its system of free enterprise. "Free enterprise" does not mean the same to us as it does to cartels and domestic monopolies.

We are not going to hold out to our people the sorry mirage of isolationism . . . our leader refused to let isolationists prevail.

The Democratic Party is not torn apart by conflicting ideas of foreign policy and we don't intend to let isolationists have their way.

We can tell people the kind of candidate we will not nominate.

We will not palm off an imitation liberal.

People will not entrust the Presidency to one who has no proved ability in the field of foreign policy.

America has seen much trail-blazing in foreign affairs since 1940.

Here is what we are going to do.

First, we are going to crush America's enemies.

Some believe that reconversion from war to peace is easy.

The Democratic Party wants to keep factories running with jobs for the people.

Employers and labor will help us in this effort.

The Democratic Party is going to find a way to internal security as well as world security.

[*Roosevelt quote . . . "I felt it my duty to arouse countrymen to the danger of the new forces let loose in the world."*]

The Democratic Party pledges itself to give armed forces the right to vote.

The Democratic Party has always been the party of courage and vision.

We should not complain of our little inconveniences compared to the sacrifices our boys have made and are making.

We must remain unified.   ★

HARRY S. TRUMAN
March 23, 1946

WE GATHER to reaffirm our faith in the ideals of democracy.

We pay honor to Jackson.

Jackson made democratic doctrines a living reality.

Roosevelt was the champion of social justice and was a great humanitarian.

We must continue to fight for our basic objectives . . . human freedom and human security.

The Democratic Party is a progressive party.

Political parties are instruments through which democracy works.

Leadership of all political parties must face the issues frankly and act in accordance with our national welfare.

The Democratic Party has a long record of achievement, but our policies must remain dynamic.

The Democratic Party's domestic program has been to make the system of free enterprise work.

We are seeking to establish higher standards of living.

The aftermath of war has brought problems of depression and inflation.

We Americans can check inflation and get production going.

Progress toward checking inflation has been delayed by reconversion to peacetime and selfishness.

Administration policy on wages and prices will be successful.

All groups in the country are assured a fair and equitable deal.

When conflicts between selfish and national interests arise, the country must come first.

The Democratic Party must be bound by unity of purpose.

The Democratic Party must keep faith with the American people.

Congress and the President must unite to carry out the party program.

The Democratic Administration has planned the largest home-building program in history and also in a way that prices will not skyrocket.

Price controls on housing are aimed at halting inflation.

Veterans deserve homes at reasonable prices.

Congress must decide between veterans' rights and real estate lobbying.

The Democratic Party's financial policies are being adapted to meet peacetime needs.

We are on our way to a balanced budget and a reduction of debt.

World trade must be returned to private enterprise.

The world needs to cooperate with the UN in developing trade.

Our financial policies are adapted to the needs of our time.

The Democratic Party, the party of enlightened internationalism, is mainly responsible for U.S. achievement of world leadership.

Isolationists debated and almost defeated Democratic efforts to improve national defenses before the war.

The record shows our opponents voted against defense measures.

The Republicans then charged the Democratic Administration with failure to prepare.

Let us be tolerant, however, of inconsistencies of man.

We shall strengthen the foundations of the UN for a prosperous and peaceful world.

At home we must devote ourselves to problems of peace.

Solutions of social problems cannot be a partisan affair.

Let us rededicate ourselves to the cause of peace.

We should emulate the valor and determination of our forefathers.

Free men can solve the big political and social problems of today. ★

HARRY S. TRUMAN
April 5, 1947

THIS MEETING carries forward an old party custom.

The spirit of Jefferson lives in America . . . the spirit of freedom.

No class, party, or nation has a monopoly on Jefferson's principles.

Jefferson's advice to Monroe urged adoption of the Monroe Doctrine.

We, like Jefferson, know how aggression starts, and we must stop it.

The burden of our responsibility today is much greater than in Jefferson's time.

Our responsibility is to stand by the UN, man's hope for peace.

Our foreign policy, the most important question before us today, must not be wrecked on the rocks of partisanship.

I commend the efforts of both parties who have worked toward this goal.

The United States must be strong and united to meet these responsibilities.

We must maintain sufficient military strength to convince the world that we will meet our responsibilities.

Domestically, we are more prosperous than ever.

Predictions last year of economic failure came from men who have little confidence in our system of free enterprise.

We emerged from the war with our financial leadership greater than before.

We have cut down expenditures and made progress toward the elimination of deficits . . . without Republican help.

I am determined that stringent economy shall govern all peace-time operations of the government.

I cut departments' budgets to the tune of 7 billion dollars.

In the public interest, sacrifices of some government services had to be made.

Reductions were made without entering "false economy."

Any further reduction of the budget by Congress will be a venture into false economy . . . and a waste, not a saving.

We must start reducing our debt.

We must decide either to reduce the debt or cut taxes.

In these prosperous times, we should start paying off our debt.

The tax burden is too heavy, but the appropriate time for the reduction of taxes has not come.

High prices, resulting mainly from selfishness, must be lowered if the economy is not to suffer.

Moral responsibility rests on those affecting our markets.

Americans must accept responsibility of world leadership thrust upon them.

We cherish and defend freedom as did our great forefathers.

We Americans must help preserve freedom and the peace.   ★

HARRY S. TRUMAN
February 19, 1948

GREETINGS to meetings everywhere.

This is the 100th Anniversary of the Democratic National Committee.

Jefferson and Jackson were fathers of liberalism.

The party system is the most effective means of presenting issues of the day to the American people.

The party of progressive liberalism is the Democratic Party.

This is the year of choice for Americans . . . choice between progressive liberalism or conservatism.

This is a choice people have had to make since the earliest years of the Republic.

Political parties started in Washington's Cabinet.

Hamilton believed government should be controlled by the rich and well-born and should operate mainly in the interest of wealth and privilege.

Jefferson believed government should be run by the whole people and for the whole people.

Jefferson organized a party of progressive liberalism.

Hamilton's party of conservatism and for the privileged few has its counterpart today.

Conservatism is party rule for the benefit of the privileged few while progressive liberalism is for the benefit of all the people.

Jefferson's term as President benefited the common man . . . especially by means of his Louisiana Purchase.

Jackson, elected by the men of New England's factories and farmers of the West, continued Jeffersonian liberalism.

Influence of concentrated wealth was a common problem to Jefferson, Jackson, Wilson, and FDR.

Proper use of the nation's resources for the benefit of all was a problem of Jackson's as it is today.

The forces which Jefferson, Jackson, and all progressive liberals have had to fight have been forces of selfish wealth and privilege.

The Democratic Party believes that the government must protect and promote interests of all groups of the nation.

The Democratic Party believes vigilance and action are necessary for protection of people from wealth and power.

The pursuit of profits at the expense of welfare of industry caused the breakdown in 1929.

High tariffs prevented trade with us after World War I, causing the worst depression in history.

Government run for the benefit of the few will destroy all; government run for the benefit of all will benefit all.

Some quarters are afraid to look ahead . . . criticized the State of the Union address because of the goals set forth.

[*Story of a backward-flying "floogle bird" . . . not knowing where he is going . . . likened to critics.*]

As in Jefferson's and Jackson's time, critics are afraid to make farsighted preparations.

The common people owe present status to farsighted men in the 1930's who could generate forces of recovery, not the timid who were afraid of the nation's credit.

With the aid of the party of progressive liberalism, farm income grew to its highest point in history.

As pronounced in the State of the Union address, we of the forward-looking faith can increase the farmer's lot.

The Democratic Party lifted man in 1932 out of depths of despair and desolation.

Employment and wages increased greatly.

Critics say we can't have 75-cent minimum wage, 64 million jobs, and raise our standard of living by 27 per cent.

We of the forward-looking faith must see that it is done.

Business failed under reactionary government in 1932.

Business flourished under "hostile" Democratic Party.

Timid people say that business earnings can't grow and cut down inflation at the same time.

The Democratic Party has remained true to its faith.

People will rally around the Democratic Party because it is the best-fitted fighting force for the achievement of goals.

My ten-year program outlined for American prosperity is based on America's ability to plan for the future and if this is called politics, it is that of Jefferson, Jackson, Wilson, and Theodore [*sic*] Roosevelt, and it is good enough for me. ★

HARRY S. TRUMAN
February 24, 1949

I APPRECIATE the introduction.

Greetings to all diners on this happy occasion.

I am glad to be back and to know that our party has served well.

Like some of Jackson's friends, some quarters were planning on burying the Democratic Party.

[*Story of the sarcophagus offered Jackson; he rejected it.*]

Moral of the story: before you offer to bury a good Democrat, make sure he is dead.

You can't bury the Democratic Party as long as it is working for the welfare and advancement of the nation.

The central issue of the past campaign was the privileged few versus the welfare of all the people.

The only justification for the Democratic Party is its usefulness to the American people in achieving the government that they desire.

The Democratic Party is dedicated to a program of interest to all the people.

Special interests, ignoring elections, are fighting the program of the people in Congress.

Special interests, always at work, are calling measures socialism . . . as they have for 16 years.

All that the Democrats have on their side is the people.

People are more informed on government issues than ever, and if we keep them fully informed, they will help fight the special interests.

Americans should know of the tactics used to obstruct the programs.

Special interests are using every trick to defeat our labor policy of repeal of the Taft-Hartley Act . . . an insult to the working men and women.

I thought after elections that Republicans would help get rid of the Taft-Hartley Act, but I was wrong.

The Democratic Party will still work for the repeal of the Taft-Hartley Act.

Reactionaries have started a campaign of confusion against other measures for the welfare of the people.

They say they are for improving social security, housing, rent controls, good wages, developing river basins, but their actions speak differently.

Despite their efforts to confuse, we will enact programs to which we are committed.

We can and will provide a better life for all of our people.

Special interests have fought our determination to preserve the health of our economy.

Some selfish groups tried to destroy our farm price support program.

Collapse of farm prices helped to bring on the depression in the 1920's. Farm price supports prevent such a collapse.

We have submitted to Congress proposals for maintaining full production and full employment.

Proposals are designed to aid business, keep price movements balanced, prevent shortages from driving prices high while farm prices are leveling off.

Special interests are attacking these proposals.

Selfish demands of special groups must not blind us to the common good.

A government able and willing to act in the interest of the whole economy is a better friend of free enterprise than a do-nothing government.

The great problem is that of boom and bust.

As Jefferson said, we are in "a great experiment" . . . today an experiment of achieving economic abundance and basic human rights.

So long as people understand the issues of the day, the special interests cannot prevail against the general welfare. ★

HARRY S. TRUMAN
February 16, 1950

THIS IS the most remarkable dinner I have ever seen.

Dinners throughout the country show our growing strength.

More interest is being shown in Congressional elections.

Dinners are a great tradition . . . first was in 1830.

As in Jackson's time, we meet to discuss some of the country's problems.

There are very grave issues before us . . . national defense, foreign policy, protecting the economy, the national debt.

The Democratic Party is meeting questions squarely.

The Democratic Party has confidence that the U.S. will meet its responsibilities.

We must move forward by modern means . . . not by outmoded concepts of 50 years ago.

Both foreign and domestic programs are necessary to meet demands.

Some want us to turn our backs on the rest of the world.

These people are blind to the problems confronting us.

The Democratic Administration is working toward a balanced budget . . . 70 per cent of the budget goes for past wars and work for peace in the future.

I do not propose to weaken the strength and security of this country to satisfy advocates of false economy.

The do-nothing 80th Congress made the cut over my veto and now we feel the effects of it on our economy . . . a tax cut is not forthcoming.

In this election year, the Democratic Party will not play politics with the federal budget . . . people are entitled to the plain facts.

The Democratic Party can be truthful because it is working for the general welfare of all citizens . . . not one special group.

The main difference between the Republican and Democratic Parties is that the Democratic Party is the party of affirmative values and action and the Republican Party is always against things.

The main thing the Republicans are against is the Democratic Party.

The Republican Party has no affirmative program of its own. Republicans wait for us to present a program; then they react.

The main problem of the Republicans seems to be to find some new scare words.

The newest scare word is "socialism" which they will not make the people believe.

As history shows, our proposals for improving the conditions of people have been greeted with the same scare word for many years.

Conditions of 1933 were met by Democratic plans for recovery and Republicans said that the U.S. was in its greatest danger in history.

Such talk didn't frighten the people.

In 1936, Republicans thought the danger to America was worse. People didn't believe that, either.

In 1940, Republicans said the Democratic regime had deprived the individual of his freedom . . . the New Deal was a failure.

The New Deal had saved America and also won the war.

In 1944, Republicans said: "American economic life is being destroyed."

Apparently, Republicans never learn anything.

Ten days ago, Republicans said the major issue was liberty versus socialism.

The country, seeing such contradictions of facts, won't let them get away with it.

Republicans have cried out against these proposals for 17 years.

In 1944, Joe Martin called Democratic progressive measures "totalitarian, socialistic."

They said that in 1944, 1948, and today.

The Democratic platform, approved by voters in 1948, has been called socialistic.

They knew more about the real wishes of workers, farmers, and businessmen than the Republican National Committee did.

The program of the Democratic Party is not socialistic but is aimed to promote the prosperity and welfare of the American people.

Programs of our party have helped workers, farmers, old people, and seek to foster medical care, education, economic opportunity, political liberty.

The American people will look at themselves to see what freedom they have lost.

The only freedom we have limited is the freedom of the Republicans to run the country.

The scare of socialism by Republicans is an insult to the intelligence of the American people.

Republicans have learned nothing despite the great progress made.

The Democratic objective is to meet the needs of the people.

The real strength of the country lies in the freedom of citizens and their faith in democracy.

The Democratic Party must present its program in very clear terms. If we do, people will again voice their approval.   ★

HARRY S. TRUMAN
April 14, 1951

I APPRECIATE the good things said about me.

It is a meeting of Democrats . . . Americans who put the welfare of the country first.

This is not a time for business as usual or politics as usual.

Some are playing petty politics instead of trying to prevent another world war.

Everyone must put national interest above personal interest at this time.

The only way to establish peace is to bring about international law and order . . . as Jefferson and Jackson knew.

Jefferson and Jackson knew the U.S. couldn't be safe unless it was willing to fight for what was right.

Pope Pius praised Americans for this deed.

Jefferson did not submit to piracy in the world and neither do we.

Now, as then, we fight for law and order.

The danger we face threatens every person. The threat of the Kremlin is to conquer the world by dividing nations one by one.

We must meet the threat as firmly as Jefferson did . . . there is no higher purpose.

We have been checking and countering Communist expansion for five years and finally the Communists resorted to aggression.

This called for a showdown and we went to the defense of Korea.

When we did it, nearly everyone in the U.S. but Communists thought it was the only thing to do . . . now, some say we should get out.

These people are mistaken in that the fight would stop if we got out of Korea.

Our choice lies in fighting in Korea or somewhere else . . . maybe closer to home.

Our struggle in Korea has had profound effects.

First, it is preventing Communists from carrying out their plans.

Second, it has been made clear that the free world must prepare to defend itself.

Third, our firm stand has placed a strain on dictatorships.

Men are fighting in Korea to save us from having to fight on our own soil.

They are fighting to prevent World War III.

Our purpose in Korea is to restore peace and to prevent a world war which would occur if Communist aggression were to go unchecked.

Peace must be settled on a basis that will protect objectives for which the UN is fighting.

We want peace with freedom and justice . . . not by appeasement.

That is why we support the UN, aid free countries, and build up our own military defenses.

Our foreign policy, which is bipartisan, is a policy for world peace. Some, without a foreign policy of their own, are attacking the bipartisan foreign policy in order to confuse us in hopes they will win the next election.

Let me give you a few examples of the thinking of the confusers.

They want powerful defense systems . . . but are against universal military training.

They want other nations to resist aggression . . . but not us.

They want us to get out of Korea, but urge war against China.

They say Russia wouldn't attack if we carry the war to the Chinese.

They want to crush Communism, but they want us to go back in our shell.

They worry about Russians outnumbering us . . . but are not interested in keeping allies.

They want defenses at no cost, war without an army, victory without risks, to run the world without friends.

Confusers blame the President . . . not the enemy.

Such political attacks run off me like water off a duck.

We have built up our defenses tremendously in the past few months.

With European partners, we are building a strong defense in the North Atlantic area.

Americans must and will sacrifice comforts to defend freedoms.

The Democratic Party has provided a better life for all people because of our basic belief that every individual should have a fair deal.

A fair deal today means an equal sharing of responsibilities and sacrifices for our defense program.

Our men fight together in Korea for a common purpose, and we must have that united approach at home.

As in Jefferson's day, we can enjoy freedom only by accepting responsibilities accompanying it.

People everywhere look to us for leadership and we will not fail them.

Jefferson's and Jackson's ideals have helped us before and will help us now. ★

HARRY S. TRUMAN
March 29, 1952

I AM HAPPY to be here.

I have spoken at seven Jefferson-Jackson Day Dinners.

These dinners are political meetings and I like politics.

Good politics is a public service . . . the most rewarding job.

Since you are interested in this Presidential election year, I will give you an analysis of the political situation.

I have been in politics more than 30 years and I am proud of it.

Republicans have been wandering in the political desert for 20 years.

Republicans have been out of office for 20 years and are desperate to get in.

Since I want to keep the Republican Party alive, I offer them advice.

There are good reasons why the Republicans have been out of office so long.

First reason . . . they brought the country to ruin in 1932.

Republicans in the 1920's helped the rich get richer and paid no attention to the welfare of the workers and farmers and brought on the depression.

Second reason . . . the Democratic Party has been giving the country good government.

We have raised incomes of the vast majority of people instead of just building up the prosperity of the few.

Third reason . . . they have no sensible program.

In 1936, they said the New Deal was no good.

In 1940, they admitted the New Deal had some merit, but Republicans ought to run it.

In 1944, Republicans said the New Deal was old and tired.

In 1948, they didn't take a position on anything.

The new Republicans don't know what to do and various theories have arisen.

One theory is against all advances in the country since 1932.

This dinosaur school wants to help only big business.

Republicans would be telling the truth but they would get only the dinosaur vote.

Then there is the theory that Republicans can win if they oppose foreign policy, even though they can't agree on how to oppose it.

Some would like to pull out of Korea, abandon Europe, and let the UN go to smash.

The trouble with this theory is that the American people are smarter than the Republicans who thought it up.

People know we must resist Communism and keep allies.

Then there is the "all-out" theory of expanding fighting in Korea.

Voters know that peace is harder to work for than war.

None of the Republican theories holds much promise of success this year.

Republicans saw themselves in half and put part on each side of the fence.

Republicans are going to wage a campaign of phony propaganda, not on issues; they are going to use "black and white" strategy.

Since Republicans know that the Democratic Party has worked for the good of the people, they will try to make the people think that the facts aren't so.

Republicans think they will succeed because they get the support of newspapers, radio commentators, and poll takers.

Republicans have lots of money and slick advertising experts who don't have too many scruples.

Republicans, by "black and white" technique, will try to make people believe that everything the government has done for the country is socialism.

People won't be fooled by such tactics.

The next part of the "black and white" campaign is to make people believe the Democratic Party is in favor of Communism.

[*Events and wars of the Democratic fight against Communism are cited.*]

Republicans will try to get around facts by claiming that the government is full of Communists.

Some political fakers try to pull the wool over people's eyes with this nonsense.

The real test of anti-Communism is a willingness to devote strength and resources to halt Communism.

Beware of those who pretend to be against Communism and at the same time vote to appease Communism abroad.

The next part of the "black is white" Republican campaign is to fool voters into thinking the Democratic Party is dishonest.

I and my Administration stand for honest government as shown in its organization.

Morality in government means a government that is fair to all . . . not favoring the few.

We recall the scandals and corruption of Republican officeholders in the 1920's, but legislation favoring greed of monopoly and trickery of Wall Street was worse for the country.

Private selfish interests are always trying to corrupt government.

The Democratic Party has fought these interests for the benefit of the public.

Most Republicans vote for special interests.

Republicans yell about honesty in federal employees, but they are the first to ask for special favors for private interests.

I hate injustice to good federal government employees.

We Democrats always work to keep government clean, and help is needed from everyone.

I am sending up plans to Congress to put more federal officials under Civil Service . . . see how the Republicans vote.

All Republican tricks and propaganda cannot make people forget that the Democratic Party has been working for their welfare.

The Democratic Party is working for farmers, free enterprise, welfare of labor, fair opportunities for decent living, chance to educate children, good medical services, provision for retirement.

Above all, the Democratic Party is working for peace, as shown by our willingness to sacrifice to stop aggression.

That is the record of the Democratic Party. . . a record of progress, of actions that are right because they are solidly founded on American ideals.

The Democratic Presidential nominee will have this record to run on.

I shall not be a candidate; I have served efficiently and honestly; I do not feel it is my duty to spend another four years in the White House.

If we hold true to the high ideals of the Democratic Party, there will be a Democratic President in the White House for the next four years. ★

SAM RAYBURN
May 6, 1954

I AM PROUD to be a Democrat and to have served Woodrow Wilson, Franklin D. Roosevelt, and Harry S. Truman.

The Republicans have demonstrated that they cannot function.

Voters are looking to us because we can do the job.

People are wondering when the Eisenhower Administration will start working.

Republicans have created messes of their own.

The McCarthy mess would be played up more if he were a Democrat.

We hear no more complaints about Yalta and Potsdam.

Because of poor foreign policy of the Republicans, we have fewer friends abroad.

I will not criticize Eisenhower personally, like the Republicans did to Roosevelt.

I wonder if Ike doesn't regret his decision to become a Republican.

Eisenhower's messages on health and social security would be hailed as socialistic if they were Democratic.

We Democrats would do something to carry out the policies if we were in charge.

The record of Congress is very poor this session.

Republicans won't balance the budget.

Republicans still believe in the old Hamiltonian theory of "trickle down."

The Democratic theory is to make farmers and workers prosperous.

Democrats tried to pass a bill giving the poor man a break but the Republicans defeated it.

The Republicans claim Lincoln, but I doubt if he would claim them today.

The Republicans are not living up to campaign promises.

Farm problems, high prices, unemployment, small business failures have been brought about by the Republicans.

Republicans claim that the Democrats are prophets of gloom and doom.

[*Story of how Rayburn sold his cattle this year for one-third the price of two years ago.*]

I hope the Eisenhower Administration doesn't follow Hoover's issuance of statements to fool the people.

Americans still hold the President responsible for the conduct of the government.

Eisenhower's popularity is fading as the Republican Party decreases in favor.

Eisenhower's advisers are uncertain, unsure, and unknowing.

Republicans tried a hard money policy which failed.

The Republican Party lacks unity and strong leadership.

Proposals in Congress are bogged down in controversy.

Republicans will ask the people to return them to enact the President's program of the last two years of his Administration.

Republicans should be judged by past performance.

We Democrats performed and did a constructive job for twenty years.

People wanted a change in 1952; now they want another change.

The United States needs a bold and fearless leadership in this time of danger. ★

SAM RAYBURN
April 16, 1955

THANKS for the honor on this occasion.

The party of Jefferson and Jackson is the party of responsibility.

FDR and Wilson, in their inaugural addresses, proclaimed a true change in government.

Wilson was responsible for federal laws reflecting social responsibility.

Wilson fought for ordinary people against private, selfish purposes of some people.

The Democratic Party tries to attain a better life for all of our people.

Truman: "We will improve the lot of the common people." Truman, like other great Democratic leaders, had a humane heart for helping the common people.

Moral change, as well as economic, was recognized and performed by the Democratic Party . . . the people come first.

In the Republican eclipse between Woodrow Wilson and FDR, the nation almost lost its way.

Profound changes wrought by recent Democratic Administrations have made the nation strong.

We improved conditions, not because of fear of Communism, but because it was right to move.

Democratic reforms have made the nation strong.

Democratic leaders like Jefferson, Jackson, FDR, and Harry Truman were humanitarian and cared for the ordinary man.

The President has little discipline in the rank and file.

Republicans are not in step with the President.

Republicans haven't changed in 100 years from the Hamiltonian "trickle-down" theory.

Democratic theory is to assure working man and farmer the earning and purchasing power to produce prosperity for all.

Our theory proved right in 20 years of Democratic Administrations.

Present prosperity, claimed by Republicans, is the result of previous Democratic Administrations.

The Eisenhower program is just an extrusion of Democratic measures.

Republicans have ignored farmers.

There is a growing number of small business failures.

In 1952, Republicans charged Democrats were socialistic. But Republicans have not replaced one law the Democrats passed in 20 years of rule.

Thus, Republicans are as socialistic as the Democrats.

Through negation and nullification, Republicans have prevented Democratic programs from protecting small business and farmers.

Republicans have helped big business and concentration of wealth in the few. Small farmers and businesses are being squeezed by favored corporation-owned farms and big business.

The Eisenhower Administration has turned its back on farmers.

As proven many times, Republican policies are bad for the country. [*Accomplishments of Wilson's Administration.*] . . . Wilson: "Control of banking must be public, not private." [*More accomplishments of Wilson's Administration.*]

Republican isolationism thwarted Wilson's aims of peace.

Wilson's dream of world peace was brought about by Roosevelt and Truman.

Democrats brought prosperity and strength to our country during 20 years' rule.

Democratic foreign policy was respected; Eisenhower's is not.

The Democratic Party must unite for the forthcoming campaign.

The Democratic Party is the best party to govern the nation because of its ability and vision to find solutions and meet the needs of the people. ★

HARRY S. TRUMAN
May 4, 1957

I AM GLAD to be back in Washington since I like it and since I wanted to check on the budget.

The President's budget, largest in peacetime history, is to be balanced and adjusted to meet the needs of people . . . so he says.

I made tight budgets and submitted what I thought it would take to run the government.

Through the budget, the President controls the executive branch, expresses his policies, and renders an account of finances to the people.

The budget must be treated seriously.

The Secretary of the Treasury said Congress should cut the budget or face a depression that would curl your hair.

I had a Cabinet officer or two and a general who disagreed publicly on major policy and I wondered how long the Secretary of the Treasury would keep his job.

The President tried to shift the blame for the size of the budget to Congress by saying one day that Congress had the duty to cut the budget and saying on another day that Congress should not cut it . . . Congress would be wrong whatever it did.

Because my Democratic friends in Congress got so much mail on the size of the budget, they asked the President to explain where the budget should be cut.

The Administration got confused . . . the President said

there was no chance for a cut of $2 billion while Under Secretary of the Treasury said the cut should be about $2 billion.

The next day the Under Secretary said that the President and he were in perfect agreement.

Two weeks later, figures showed that the Under Secretary was right and some said this showed the President wasn't running the government at all.

The President's $2 billion cut is illusory since he is robbing Peter to pay Paul . . . just a means of putting Congress on the spot.

This buck-passing is making it difficult for Congress to deal with the budget on a rational basis.

Thus, Congress must carry on the legislative function and fill a vacuum left by failure of executive leadership.

We can afford to spend what is necessary for the welfare of the people and their safety.

Republican tight money and high interest rate policies can bring on a depression.

One of the worst results of a tight money policy is increased costs of federal government . . . Secretary and Under Secretary of the Treasury should stop trying to run the whole government.

Members of the Cabinet won't manage public debt properly to help the public.

A showdown is coming on the economic issues of government.

Manipulators of special privilege are going to try to take over economic control of the country before they are thrown out of office in 1960.

However, Democrats, with the help of the people, will resist concerted offensive of private greed. ★

HARRY S. TRUMAN
February 22, 1958

Washington and the Senate had disagreements and he told the Senate where to go.

He was abused by the press and sought after by privileged coteries.

Washington was really a Jeffersonian.

American people are fed up with Republican changes for the benefit of persons needing no special benefit, and Democrats will win in 1958 and 1960. Pollsters and recent elections show the Democrats will win the next election.

The people are tired of being bamboozled by Republicans.

The present Republican illusion is coming to an end.

Republicans have failed to cope with the problems of America.

Unemployment is increasing. Farmers are told to get off their land and join the ranks of the unemployed.

School programs, colleges, hospitals, highways, and slum clearance are lagging.

New Deal and Fair Deal programs of security have been neglected.

Republicans have inflation and recession going at the same time.

The Republican program has punished almost everyone.

The Republican Administration has not even helped big business.

The Republican Administration has made nations lose confidence in our leadership.

The Democratic approach to problems of national security is realistic and all funds necessary should be made available for defense, health, and education.

Democratic Advisory Council: "Foreign and defense policy should not suffer for fear of economic weakening."

Republican leadership is always timid and weak . . . only one strong President, Lincoln.

Republican complacency has allowed the Russians to drive ahead.

Principles to guide the Democratic Party are:

The Democratic Party is the party of the people . . . the little man.

The Democratic Party must stand for full enjoyment and protection of civil rights and liberties of every citizen, regardless of race, creed, or nationality.

The Democratic Party must work for constant economic growth and a rising standard of living.

In foreign policy, the Democratic Party must stand firmly for cooperation and concerted action with other free nations.

The Democratic Party must support an adequate national defense, whatever the cost.

The Declaration of Independence . . . "We pledge to each other our lives, our fortunes, and our sacred honor."

Republican leaders have not arrived at any answer to problems.

Good government is good politics . . . let's follow these principles.

They will dispel the fears of American people and justify the hopes they placed in us. ★

SAM RAYBURN

February 28, 1959

I'M HAPPY to break bread with Democrats of all shades of opinion and beliefs, but Democrats with a single, guiding purpose—the safety and well-being of the American people.

The longer I serve under the Republicans, the prouder I am to be a Democrat.

I am proud to be a Democrat for many reasons.

First, our party is a party with a heart.

It was our party that wrote into law the great reforms of the 20th century.

It was our party that successfully piloted this nation through the dark days of the depression and the fateful struggle of World War II and its aftermath.

There is another reason I am proud of the Democratic Party.

It has always been the party of responsibility.

The Democratic Party puts its responsibility to the people first.

We welcome the opportunity to write sane, financially sound legislation to meet the needs of a rapidly growing population which has a rising productivity, requiring more homes, more highways, more schools, more factories, and more food.

The Democratic Party is ready to act responsibly to help our young families, our veterans, our elder citizens, and our poor to have decent homes that they can afford.

We accept the task of saving the independent farmer, of conserving our soil and water and natural resources, of bringing the blessings of electricity and good roads to those who till the soil which feeds our nation and many underprivileged peoples in other lands.

The responsible Democratic Party is going to give the Republican President such sinew of defense that, if wisely used, this nation cannot be driven from position to position by any power on earth.

The Democratic Party has been, and will continue to be, the party of financial responsibility.

In the last four years of Democratic Congresses, we have cut eight billion dollars out of the Republican President's budget.

I think the American people have proved, by their vote at the polls in three successive elections, that they like the rate of forward progress the Democratic Congress has been making.

This new Republican line about reckless spending reminds me of their old propaganda line which has fallen flat. They went up and down the land in 1952 crying alarm about all the socialistic laws enacted under the New Deal and the Fair Deal. If the

Democrats were socialistic for putting them on the statute books, then the Republicans are just as socialistic for leaving them there.

Ours is the only national party, strong and active in every state, embracing people of every type of economic interest.

We do agree on the basic fundamentals that have been the tenets of the Democratic Party from its earliest days.

I have no patience with people who claim to be Democrats who say they want to run other people who claim to be Democrats out of the party.

There are more forces of evil and destruction stalking the earth than at any time in 20 centuries.

Thus we accept the responsibility for guiding this great land and its friends into the wonderful world of tomorrow.

Inspired by the memory of Jefferson, Jackson, Woodrow Wilson, Franklin D. Roosevelt, and Harry S. Truman, we Democrats gladly face the challenge of leading a prosperous, strong, solvent America—and with it free men everywhere—into what Woodrow Wilson foresaw long ago—"pastures of quietness and peace such as the world never dreamed of before." United as good soldiers, we cannot fail. ★

HARRY S. TRUMAN
January 23, 1960

THE NEXT PRESIDENT of the United States is going to have his hands full.

The job of the President is enough to tax the full energy and capacity of the strongest man.

The next President will have the additional burden, which he will inherit, as a result of the indecision and neglect of the present Administration to deal with a number of crucial problems and issues.

There is a growing concern not only among the people but with the experts that all is not as it should be with our space and defense situation.

As things stand, under this Administration we have surrendered an important advantage, including an embarrassing psychological advantage, to the Soviet Union.

I tell you that in this field alone the next President is going to be hard put to get this country back on the track. And let us make no mistake about it, we can only look to a Democratic President to get that done.

One certain way we can squander away this opportunity is to get into contest among ourselves instead of concentrating our attack on the Republican Party.

Let us make sure that we do not default on our obligation to put a Democrat in the White House.

Because we are Democrats, we always have differences among ourselves.

I hope that in this great hour of our call to duty, we can work as a united party so that we can be equal to the challenge.

The Democratic Party, unlike the Republican Party, has an abundance of able men qualified for the high office of Chief Executive of the Nation.

No differences that we might have among ourselves can be as important as the differences we have with the Republicans.

I have at this time no commitment to any candidate. But ahead of any inclinations I may have, I place the overriding consideration of the needs of the country and the world. Against those needs, I would weigh first whether any man having the necessary qualification for office has the ability as well to arouse the support of the people to vote him into office and to be able to live up to the duties of that office in every sense and in every way.

No matter what you hear—and no matter what you read—I have just given you my true position on the big question at this time. ★

JOHN F. KENNEDY
May 27, 1961

It is a great pleasure to be here, and I want to express my appreciation to the members of the Committee who made this dinner such a success.

The success of any President of the United States who has the distinction of being a Democrat is due to the fact that he is supported by a strong, democratic, progressive party.

And I believe in the Administrations of Woodrow Wilson and Franklin Roosevelt and Harry Truman, and now the Democratic Party has a great national purpose—to move this country forward.

I will say on becoming President that the only thing that really surprised us when we got into office was that things were just as bad as we had been saying they were; otherwise we would have been enjoying it very much.

When we became free, sovereign, and independent, there was a King of France, a Czar of Russia, and an Emperor of Peking. They have all gone, and this country remains.

The groundwork for that trip was laid in the Administration of a predecessor of mine, Harry Truman, whose vision and activity in the 1940's helped make it possible to build a Europe which is our strong ally in difficult days.

From 1945 to 1961 was the most extraordinary growth in the individual liberty of individual countries that the world has ever seen.

I do not believe that meetings between heads of state, either allies or those whose purposes make them our adversaries, are designed to solve a series of specific problems or bring about a fundamental change in relationships.

We do not lack for communication with France, or the Soviet Union, or any other nation.

These meetings can play a real and helpful role in the quest for peace.

I believe it is indispensable for leaders of nations to have an understanding of the men with whom they must deal.

Moreover, such meetings are symbolic. They symbolize the deep unity of the Western World.

And the meeting with Mrs. Khruschev is also the symbol and expression of our intention to leave no path to peace unexplored.

I shall tell those who do not agree with us that our desire for peace is matched by our determination to resist all those who seek the destruction of freedom. ★

JOHN F. KENNEDY
January 20, 1962

I SHOW, on behalf of all of us, our great appreciation to Miss Clooney, Miss Remick, and Danny Thomas for coming from a far distance to help us tonight.

I also want to express my appreciation to President Truman.

And I also want to express my appreciation, and the appreciation of us all, to the Vice President for his tribute to Speaker Rayburn.

And as a loyal and faithful friend, I think we have worked together better than any President and Vice Presidential team in history, at least since Roosevelt and Truman.

We observe tonight not a celebration of freedom but a victory of party.

Our deficit will not be paid off in the next hundred days, nor will it be paid off in the first one thousand days, nor in the life of this Administration, nor, perhaps, even in our lifetime on this planet, but let us begin—remembering that generosity is not a sign of weakness and that Ambassadors are always subject to Senate confirmation, for if the Democratic Party cannot be helped by the many who are poor, it cannot be saved by the few who are rich. So let us begin.

What we are attempting to do tonight is to lay the groundwork for the Congressional campaigns of 1962.

In this century only in 1934, during the period of the great preeminence of the Democratic Party, did the party in power ever win seats, let alone hold its own.

This is the oldest Republic in the world.

We are also members of the oldest political party on earth; when we attempt, in this Administration, to rebuild our ties with Latin America, to strengthen our Alliance for Progress, we tread in the same steps that Franklin Roosevelt trod in, nearly 25 or 30 years ago.

When we attempt this year to build more closely the Atlantic Community, we tread in the same steps that President Truman trod in nearly 14 years ago, when he developed the Marshall Plan and NATO.

When we stand with the United Nations against the desires of those who make themselves our adversaries, and even against our friends, we stand where Woodrow Wilson stood nearly 50 years ago.

When we make a great national effort to make sure that free men are not second in space, we move in the same direction that Thomas Jefferson moved in when he sent Lewis and Clark to the far reaches of this country during his term of office.

The reason the Democratic Party has outlived all the other parties has been because it has believed in moving out, in moving ahead, in starting on new areas, and bringing new programs here and abroad.

That is the function of our party.

I believe that the interests of this country will be served by our party as it has on so many vital occasions in the past—and the fire from our effort can light the world.   ★

JOHN F. KENNEDY
January 18, 1963

I WANT to express all of our thanks to all of those who were so generous with us tonight—Mr. Gene Kelly, who is a veteran of the first Inaugural Gala, Kirk Douglas, those talented people in show business at home and abroad who have been so generous, beginning with Franklin Roosevelt, and who have sustained us. I want to thank all of you.

Matt McCloskey was the originator 30 years ago of the $100 dinner. We have revolutionized that by removing the dinner, but we are hanging on to the $100. The day will come when we will let you go.

Actually, I have been asked by Mr. Wynne to announce the man who sold the most tickets tonight. It is Mr. Jerry Kluttz, of the *Washington Post*. Actually, I was called, invited to a cocktail party by Mr. Kenny O'Donnell, and that is the way I happened to get my ticket. In any case, I want to thank you for your help.

A party is of no use unless it fulfills some national purpose. I said the other day, in the State of the Union message, that we were not on the top of the hill but on the side of the hill. I don't think in this Administration or in our generation or time will this country be at the top of the hill. But someday it will be, and I hope when it is, they will think we have done our part. ★

LYNDON B. JOHNSON
May 19, 1964

THE VALIANT MAN who should have been here tonight would be the first to enjoy this occasion.

What we have to do is to remember our duty and try to do it by always putting our country first and our party second.

Tonight we honor the chairmen of the standing committees of the Senate and the House, and those who were first elected in 1936.

This Congress has done much for the prosperity of our Nation.

Thanks to the men at the head table, and in this room, this Congress is the greatest education Congress in the history of the Republic.

This Congress has done more for the common defense of freedom.

This historic Congress is well on its way to doing more than any other for the rights of all of our citizens. . . . It will not be done in a day or a year, or perhaps in this generation, but we have declared war on poverty and we will accept nothing less than total victory.

This Congress has the opportunity to reverse the upward trend of government spending.

This Congress has done more than any other Congress to protect the life of our Nation, to preserve the liberty of our people so that we may all pursue happiness with our families.

With great pride, I have come here tonight to salute the Democratic majority.

Tonight in honoring the great Democrats first elected to Congress in '36, we commemorate the year of our party's greatest victory.

But in these somber and confusing times with their complexities, their challenges, and their change, it is all too easy for the individual to be forgotten, for the plight of the average man to be overlooked.

We of the Democratic Party care what happens to the average family and we care what happens to all Americans.

In Panama or Guantanamo, in Cyprus or Viet Nam or in Zanzibar, our traditional love of freedom will always be reflected, and our interests will also always be protected.

As the party of all the people, Democrats are dedicated to doing all the work that the well-being of our people may require whether it is at home or whether it is abroad.

So I speak as I do tonight from a strong and a growing conviction that in this year of 1964 there may well be a turning point in the conduct of our political affairs.

I believe that the American people have had their fill of partisanship just for the sake of partisanship; that they have had enough of opposing just for opposition's sake.

In that moment of cruel tragedy last November, we all saw that the American Presidency and all of the offices of American leadership are not prizes for partisans but represent the greatness and the glory of the people themselves.

So I believe that in that moment of nightmare, there was ignited a new flame of unity and seriousness and soberness of purpose as is reflected at this head table tonight, the like of which I have not seen in more than 30 years in Washington.

I want our party to fan that flame, to lead and light the way for American democracy this year.

With the record that you write in this Congress, with the platform that we are going to write at that convention, with the purpose we as a nation write in history, let us go to the people this year with a decent campaign, with a unifying campaign, with an inspiring campaign.

Let us go to those who have never been members of any party and to those who have grown weary of the divisions and the diversions of the other party.

Let us invite all of the people to unite with us, to work with us in this truly national party which is a stranger to no region; an open party closed to none, welcoming all; a unifying party which knows no color, knows no creed, knows no North, no South, no East, no West.

I want to call on you tonight, not just one segment of our society but everyone in our society.

Let labor and business and housewife and farmhand, corporation and community, the farmer and the rancher on the land, the worker in the suburb—let them all join with us in doing what needs to be done for this glorious land in which we live.

Let free government, free labor and free enterprise be partners in the creation of free and new opportunity, in the march of progress that is prudent, in the bidding of a prosperity that can be permanent, and in the search for peace that can be universal and secure.

It is our obligation for our party to guide this nation, to lead this nation and through this nation lead the rest of humanity in the world toward a finer life, as Mr. Roosevelt put it, toward a happier life, as the President put it, and toward a better deal for all of us. ★

LYNDON B. JOHNSON
June 24, 1965

I AM ENJOYING this night much more than you really know.

I am very proud to join in this salute to the 89th Congress and to all of the Democratic members in both the House of Representatives and the Senate. I came out here tonight not to bury the Congress but to praise it.

I am a child of the Congress.

And as if to give towering substance to my words tonight, the Congress in one day—today—moved on many fronts toward even higher achievements.

Today the Education and Labor Committee of the House of Representatives reported the higher education bill to the House, and that is a bill which will be one of the enduring monuments of this Congress.

Today this same Committee, under the chairmanship of Chairman Powell, reported the arts and humanities bill, and the mine safety bill, and the disaster relief bill.

Today the Senate Finance Committee voted out our medical care bill for the aged.

Today the Senate Banking and Currency Committee voted out the housing bill.

And today the Senate Labor and Public Welfare Committee reported out the heart and cancer and stroke health measure, and the community mental health center, and the health research facilities amendments, and all three of these bills will be on the Senate floor tomorrow, and I hope before the sun goes down they will have passed that body.

Today the Government Operations Subcommittee voted out the Department of Urban Affairs bill in the Senate—and the House has already passed that bill, I need not tell you.

Today the Senate passed, by a vote of 74 to 9, the silver coinage bill.

Today the House passed the juvenile delinquency bill; and the House passed the extension to the Area Redevelopment Administration bill.

And today the conferees of the House and the Senate agreed on the Presidential Disability and Succession Bill; and the conferees reported the Post Office, Treasury, and Executive Office appropriation bill—and that is a real important bill.

All this happened in just one day—17 bills.

We are proud of all the Congress, and no wonder—this 89th Congress will leap into history as the most effective and the most rewarding Congress for all the people in all the history of America.

And no one knows better than I do that the record of any Congress—and the record, for that matter, of any President—depends finally upon the quality of the leadership in both Houses of the legislative branch.

I am very proud to say that this 89th Congress has leadership—good, strong, wise, experienced, progressive Democratic leadership of the very highest quality.

When some day the world lives in peace, and when the peoples of this hemisphere live together in justice and prosperity, men will honor the name of the good and gentle man who leads the Democratic Party in the Senate of the United States, Mike Mansfield, the Majority Leader.

And, likewise, when Americans see the ideals of their system fulfilled, and when they live in a society that is made great by the people's will, they will give their credit to the man who led the historic legislative breakthrough—the Majority Leader of the House of Representatives, Carl Albert of Oklahoma.

. . . the wise and the diligent and the conscientious warmhearted friend of all the people of the United States, Speaker John McCormack of Massachusetts.

I paid my respects to that young progressive from the South, Russell Long, at the other dinner, but all these measures that we have talked about had to have votes to pass them.

George and Hale are not only the two best looking men in the Senate and the House, and the country, but they are also the most effective.

Now, at this point I think I should announce that I have only 357 Democrats to go before I begin the speech of the evening.

I came here tonight because I wanted to say to you that as Americans—and as Democrats—we are an honored generation.

No other Americans—certainly no other Democrats—can have entrusted into their hands the substance of history just like this moment has placed in ours now.

The more than 50 major bills enacted last year were presented to the Congress by that fearless, outstanding, beloved late President of ours, John Fitzgerald Kennedy. . . . It is an enduring victory for all the people when their Congress is moved and motivated, as the people themselves are, by conscience, and by courage, and by an abiding conviction.

It is a victory for the people when conscience moves their Congress—moves their Congress to declare war on human poverty in this land and to do something about it. . . .

Yes, this is a very great victory for the people of America when conscience and courage and conviction move their Congress . . . a victory for the people when Congress is moved by courage to lift off the burden of wartime tax rates on incomes and place its confidence in our economy to produce the growth that produces jobs to keep America's promise to our growing population. . . .

Yes, it is, finally, a victory for the people when Congress is moved by abiding convictions, deep within the heart and soul of this nation, to stand up before the world to declare the will of the United States of America to resist aggression. . . .

In a very short while I shall be leaving this hall to fly across the continent—first to meet with a man whose name is written forever among the heroes of freedom, Harry S. Truman, and then to fly on to San Francisco to renew there the pledge of support that President Truman gave 20 years ago this week to the United Nations.

For 20 years now—20 years of trial and testing—the purpose of this nation has never wavered for a moment, and I want to tell you that it is strong, and it is steady, and it is sure tonight.

For 20 years we have journeyed a road of danger—and neither the journey nor the danger is near an end.

And I take with me the assurance of the Congress—and my own determination—that so long as peril remains we shall remain prepared; so long as peace is weak we shall remain strong; and so long as Communist aggression challenges freedom we shall meet it.

I remember that a great Democrat, Woodrow Wilson, once told us that there is "something better . . . that a man can give than his life."

Well, you are giving such a living spirit—and, in so doing, you are honoring your party by honoring first your country.

My heart bursts with pride tonight when I look at this head

table and come back to the scenes of my childhood, so to speak.

And so as we return to our homes this evening I hope that each of you that has made this sacrifice to buy a ticket and come out here to help reelect Democratic Congressmen and Democratic Senators . . . I hope that you know that we are grateful to each of you for taking away from your families some of the things that you could give them and giving it to your party and, I hope, to the benefit of your country.

We appreciate it, and it is absolutely necessary.

Instead of suffering losses in the off year we are going to bring you back gains for your sacrifices here tonight—gains that you and your children will be proud of.   ★

May 12, 1966

LYNDON B. JOHNSON

WILL ROGERS once said: "I'm not a member of any organized political party. I'm a Democrat."

I ran across that quotation just the other day in a magazine article. It went on to say: "This week, any Democrat in the U.S. could borrow Will Roger's words and describe his own status with as much accuracy as humor." That article appeared shortly before the Congressional campaign in 1954.

Well, the voters thought otherwise.

I bring this up tonight because we are in an election year.

I know that when election time rolls around again this year, the American people are not going to disown the most productive Congress ever assembled in this city.

Our old people will not forget that, working together, we passed the Health Insurance for the Aged Act, which meant Medicare, and the Older Americans Act, which means new security and hope.

Our young people will not forget that we passed the Elementary and Secondary Education Act and the Higher Education Act.

Our servicemen will not forget that we passed the Veterans Readjustment Benefits Act.

Our poor will not forget that we passed the Economic Opportunity Act Amendments of 1965; or the Appalachian Regional Development Act; or the Public Works and Economic Development Act. They will not forget Project Head Start, the Job Corps, the Neighborhood Youth Corps, VISTA, the Urban and Rural Community Action Programs.

Our immigrants and their families will not forget we passed the Immigration and Nationality Act.

Our workers will not forget that we passed the Manpower Act —or the Job Development Program—or the Vocational Rehabilitation Amendments.

Our minorities will not forget that we passed the historic Voting Rights Act—the first effective Voting Rights Act in a hundred years.

Our city dwellers will not forget the Housing and Urban Development Act—or the pioneering program of Rent Supplements for low-income people—or the new grant programs for the urban growth and renewal projects, and low-rent public housing construction.

Our travelers and conservationists will not forget the Highway Beautification Act—or the Water Pollution Control Bill and the Air Pollution Control Bill.

Our farmers will not forget the Food and Agriculture Act, or the omnibus benefits it will bring them.

Our sick and suffering citizens will not forget the Heart and Stroke measure.

All this was only a promise when this Congress met for the first time. It was all in our platform. And I am proud tonight that the promise has been redeemed; the platform has been fulfilled—more than 80 per cent of the pledges in that platform are now laws of the land!

This Congress did it. We did it. Together we have passed more laws for the good of more men, women, and children than any one Congress since our Nation was founded.

But the task is not yet finished. We still have work to do. . . . the country needs all of you back here next January to build on the foundation you have laid—to move our people forward.

There are some who tell us how troubled and frustrated they are about Vietnam. . . . the people of our country have not lost the spirit or the courage or the wisdom which have kept us a free people.

Americans have learned, at painful cost, that freedom is indivisible. They have learned that aggression in any part of the world carries the seeds of destruction to our own freedom.

But we have never abandoned and we will never surrender this world to those who would dominate it and destroy it. If we were to turn our backs on freedom in South Vietnam—if Vietnam were to fall to force—what an empty thing our commitment to liberty would be!

We shall stand with honor. We shall stand with courage. We shall stand with patience. That is what this Congress expects. It is the stand the vast majority of Americans will respect. Go out and tell them this fall that America will presevere until peace comes to Vietnam.   ★

MENUS OF SELECTED JEFFERSON-JACKSON DAY DINNERS

THE MENUS at the Jefferson-Jackson Dinners have varied not too greatly with time. A connoisseur in the delicacies of the table, a gourmet, an epicure, could easily be enticed to partake of the edibles served at these celebrations.

The earlier dinners especially displayed an enormous diversity of delicacies and tasty dishes. More modern affairs have retained the quality of the food, but the vast variety is missing.

Several selected menus will suggest the succulence of such repasts:

MENU OF THE JACKSON ERA

SOUPS

Consommé   Pureé aux Croutons

FISH

Cod's Head and Oyster Sauce   Pickerel   Bass, Sauce Hollandaise
Baked Codfish, Sauce *au vin de Madere*

RELEVÉS

Turkey, Sauce *aux Huîtres*   Ham, Sauce *au Vin de Champagne*
Filet de Boeuf, Garni d'Attelettes

PIÈCES FROIDES

Salade de Volaille Jardinière   *Perdrix aux Choux*
Huîtres en aspic   *Pâté de Foie Gras Périgueux*

ENTRÉES

Tête de Veau en Tortue
Casserole de Pommes de Terre, Garnie Volaille
Suprême de Volaille Vol au Vent aux Huîtres Fricandeau de Veau
Sauce *aux Petits Pois*   *Anguille à la Tartare*
Timbale de Macaroni à la Milanaise
Ris de Veau en Casserole   *Caneton de Volaille à la Royale*

HORS D'OEUVRES

Salade de Homard   *Choucroute, Garnie Volaille*
Cornichons   Olives   Sardines

ROASTS

Beef   Saddle of Mutton
Turkey   Chicken   Duck   Mongolian Goose
Partridge   Quail   Brant   Canvasback Duck

275

ENTREMETS DE LÉGUMES

Petits Pois   *Céleri au Jus*   *Choux-fleurs au Gratin*   *Épinards*
Pommes de Terre au Gratin   *Navets Sucrés*

ENTREMETS SUCRÉS

Tartelettes de Pommes Omelettes Soufflées Charlotte Russe Conti
Charlotte Russe *au Marasquin*   *Gelée au Rhum*
Blanc-manger à la Crème d'Amandes

DESSERTS

Fruit   Ice Cream   Roman Punch   Iced Orange Water

CAFÉ ET LIQUEURS

Wines (Sherry Sack, Champagne, Claret, Port, Brandy)

MENU IN 1936,

The $50-a-plate dinner

Tomato Stuffed with Fresh Lobster, Crabflakes and Shrimp Rachel
Diamondback Terrapin Soup *au Madère Rastegais*
Celery   Olives   Nuts
Breast of Capon with Irish Bacon, Southern Style
Broccoli Polonaise   Rice Croquettes with Guava Jelly
Hearts of Romaine Lettuce with Hearts of Palm
Artichoke and Alligator Pear   Lorenzo Dressing
Graham Bread and Cheese Sandwich
Gâteau Jackson
Demitasse

MENU IN 1937,

The first $100-a-plate dinner

Diamondback Terrapin Soup, *Croûte aux Choux Farcis*
Madeira Wine
Celery   Olives   Pecans
Fish Course (Pompano) with Eggplant and Almonds
Sherry
Breast of Capon on Ham
Artichokes   Cateline (with chestnuts)   New Peas with Mint Sauce

Sweet Potatoes with *Oranges Triomphe*
Champagne
Salade Victoire, Port Salut Cheese Sandwiches
Coupe Nougat Quarante-Six (an ice symbolic of the 46 states
supporting Mr. Roosevelt)
Gateau Parfait   Coffee

JACKSON DAY DINNER, 1939

Canapé of Anchovy and Deviled Egg
Hearts of Celery
Green Turtle Soup with Sherry
Green and Ripe Olives   Pecans
Buttercrust
Broiled Rock Bass with Grilled Tomato and Eggplant
Graves Rosechâtel, 1929
Filet Mignon with Fresh Mushrooms Bordelaise
New Peas, French Style   New Brown Potatoes
St. Julien, 1933
Mixed Fresh Vegetable Salad with Cheese Wafers
Nougat Ice Cream and Pineapple Granite
Chocolate Leaves and Demitasse

JEFFERSON-JACKSON DAY DINNER, 1940

Diamondback Terrapin Soup with Amontillado
Hot Buttercrusts
Hearts of Celery
Graves Rosechâtel, 1933
Lobster, Crabflakes and Scallops à la Newburgh, with Madeira
Old Fashioned Corn Bread
Cucumber Sandwiches
Margaux, 1933
Heart of Filet Mignon, Excelsior
New String Beans *à l'Anglaise*   Potatoes Macaire

Hearts of Romaine Lettuce, with Melon, Grapefruit and
Asparagus Tips, Vinaigrette Sauce
Cheese Wafers
Spumoni Ice Cream Royal with Spun Sugar
Madeleine à l'Anis
Demitasse

JEFFERSON-JACKSON DAY DINNER, 1945

Half Grapefruit with Crushed Strawberries
Diamondback Terrapin Soup with Sherry, *en tasse*
Pirogues
Celery, Olives
Beaulieu Chablis
Canapé of Shrimps and Crabflakes Lorenzo with
Fresh Mushroom Sauce
Coleslaw
Vaillant Burgundy
Broiled Swordfish Steak, Tartar Sauce
New String Beans   Parsley Potatoes
Mixed Green Salad with Tomato, Escoffier Sauce
Wafers
Frozen Boston Chocolate Eggnog Ice Cream
Demitasse

JEFFERSON-JACKSON DAY DINNER, 1946

Essence of Tomato
Celery   Olives   Carrots
Widner's Rhine Wine
Baked Half Chicken
New Peas   Parsley Potatoes
Beaurosé, B.V.
Mixed Green Salad with Sweetened Vinegar Dressing
Melon, Grapefruit, Pineapple and Orange Coupe
Oatmeal Molasses Cookies
Demitasse
Cigars and Cigarettes

JEFFERSON-JACKSON DAY DINNER, 1949

Diamondback Terrapin Soup with Madeira Rastegais
Celery, Olives
Lobster and Crabflakes *Sauté Américaine*
Old Fashioned Corn Bread
Château-Lejon White Wine
New String Beans Forestière
Broiled Filet Mignon Rossini, Sauce Bordelaise
Potatoes Dauphine
Château-Lejon Red Wine
Mixed Green Salad with Endive and Avocado
Lorenzo Dressing
Brown Bread and Liptauer Cheese Sandwich
Chocolate Mousse with Black Cherries
Madeleine à l'Anis
Moka
Cigars and Cigarettes

JEFFERSON-JACKSON DAY DINNER, 1950

Pink Grapefruit *au Kirsch*
Celery   Green Olives
Broiled Filet Mignon, Bordelaise
Pommes Rissolées
New String Beans, Provençale
Great Western American Burgundy
Hearts of Lettuce, Roquefort Cheese Dressing
Fancy Ice Cream
Petits Fours
Demitasse

NOTES

PREFACE

1. The degree to which political parties are necessary in a democracy has been argued by American leaders and political writers since the United States was formed. A classic book on American parties which is critical of the looseness, decentralization, and faults of such parties is E. E. Schattschneider's *Party Government* (New York: Rinehart and Company, 1942). The Committee on Political Parties of the American Political Science Association aroused much comment and stimulated many articles with its report, *Toward a More Responsible Two-Party System* (New York: Rinehart and Company, 1950), in which it suggested that parties needed to be more responsible, centralized, and tightly controlled. For more than a decade now, articles both praising and attacking the suggestions of the committee can be found in political science books and magazines. Two standard texts, both comprehensive and authoritative, describing the role of political parties in a democracy and analyzing new and old theories of parties as a catalyst in the functioning of the United States government are: Austin Ranney and Willmoore Kendall's *Democracy and the American Party System* (New York: Harcourt, Brace and Company, 1956), and V. O. Key's *Politics, Parties, Pressure Groups*, 4th edition (New York: Thomas Y. Crowell, 1958). Although political parties in America have been under attack since the formation of the United States because of their vagueness of party platforms and party issues, most of the basic books acknowledge the vital part they play in the stability of the American government. Note especially Chapter 11, "The Strength of Our Political System," by Allan Nevins in A. N. Christensen and Evron Kirkpatrick's *The People, Politics, and the Politician*, revised edition (New York: Henry Holt and Company, Inc., 1950), pp. 294–98.

2. C. W. Cassinelli, *The Politics of Freedom: An Analysis of the Modern Democratic State* (Seattle: University of Washington Press, 1961), p. 20. The author points out that "every democratic state has at least two political parties, and its party system—the organization, operation, and interrelationships of the parties—is an integral part of its institutional structure." Maurice Duverger's *Political Parties* (New York: John Wiley and Sons, 1954) is still the most definitive work on the relationships between political parties and the democracies of the world. It provides a valuable insight into the role political parties play in American democracy.

3. A letter from Thomas Jefferson to President George Washington, dated May 13, 1792, mentions the Republican Party for the first time. The present-day Democratic Party evolved from this Republican Party. For 28 years the party was known as the Democratic-Republican Party, or simply the Republican Party. In 1810 the word "democrat" was accepted as meaning the same thing as "republican," according to Frank R. Kent in *The Democratic Party* (New York: The Century Company, 1928), p. 14. The party dropped "Republican" from its name in the period of Andrew Jackson and became the Democratic Party, the name by which we know it today. See Herbert Agar's *The Price of Union* (Boston: Houghton Mifflin Company, 1950), pp. 117–25; and David L. Cohn's *The Fabulous Democrats* (New York: G. P. Putnam's Sons, 1956), pp. 9–13 for explanations of reasons for changing the name of the party.

4. Cassinelli, pp. 31–32, states that "the dynamics of the democratic party system strongly encourages the members of all parties to develop a sense of group identification." The four points mentioned

here are neither all inclusive nor exclusive. The psychology of mass movements and of membership in organizations applies to political parties as well as other groups. Eric Hoffer's *The True Believer* (New York: Harper and Brothers, 1951) and any number of basic psychology texts explain the motivation of ingroups and the needs for maintaining the membership of any organization, including a political party. No set of characteristics fully and neatly applies to American political parties. See Agar, p. 89: "The national party is always a loose alliance of local parties held together precariously by self-interest or by a shared hostility . . . the best policy for the nation may be a troublesome and unpopular policy in certain districts." Loose party discipline is probably the most efficient way to function. Political parties may have learned to minimize such discontent, but the party system is usually given little credit. However, this does not obviate the fact that members of a political party seek to promote their party through identification with it.

CHAPTER 1

A Party Is Born

1. Frank R. Kent, *The Democratic Party* (New York: The Century Company, 1928), pp. 15–20. The Jefferson Manuscripts, Henry Minor's *The Story of the Democratic Party* (New York: Macmillan Company, 1928), Richard Hofstadter's *The American Political Tradition and the Men Who Made It* (New York: Alfred A. Knopf, 1948), and Herbert Clancy's *The Democratic Party: Jefferson to Jackson* (New York: Fordham University Press, 1962) are also good sources of description of the people and events surrounding the birth of the Democratic Party.
2. Herbert Agar, *The Price of Union* (Boston: Houghton Mifflin Company, 1950), pp. 117–21. A comprehensive study of the struggle between Hamilton and Jefferson is found in Claude Bowers' *Jefferson and Hamilton* (New York: Houghton Mifflin Company, 1925). Knowing the role of aristocracy in America, real and imagined, is an aid to understanding the struggle between Jefferson and Hamilton. See Francis J. Grund's *Aristocracy in America* (Gloucester, Mass.: Peter Smith, 1959), where he describes America's tendency "to destroy self-selected aristocrats."
3. Agar, p. 118, quoting Jefferson from the *Anas* papers.
4. Wilfred E. Binkley, *American Political Parties: Their Natural History* (New York: Alfred A. Knopf, 1943), p. 31. This is a standard history of electoral coalitions and national party elections. It is especially good on the origins of Federalism.
5. Kent, p. 14.
6. Alexander Hamilton, John Jay, and James Madison, *The Federalist* (New York: Modern Library, 1937), p. 56.
7. Clancy, p. 4.
8. A. J. Beveridge, *The Life of John Marshall* (Boston: Houghton Mifflin Company, 1929), Vol. 2, p. 410.
9. David S. Muzzey, *A History of Our Country* (New York: Ginn and Company, 1941), p. 205.
10. *Ibid.*, p. 288

CHAPTER 2
The History of an Expensive Meal

1. *Washington Post* (Washington, D.C.), Jan. 8, 1939, p. 1.
2. Telephone conversation with James A. Farley in New York City on July 15, 1958.
3. Marie Chatham, "The Role of the National Party Chairman From Hanna to Farley" (unpublished Ph.D. dissertation, University of Maryland, 1953), p. 133.
4. *New York Times* (New York), Jan. 12, 1936.
5. Personal interview with Governor Orville Freeman in his Executive Office in St. Paul, Minn., Aug. 12, 1958.
6. Personal interview with Sam Rayburn in the Speaker's Chambers, Capitol Building, Washington, D.C., Jan. 21, 1959.
7. Personal interview with Stephen A. Mitchell at his home on Michigan Avenue in Chicago, Aug. 16, 1958.
8. Personal interview with Governor Orville Freeman in his Executive Office in St. Paul, Minn., Aug. 12, 1958.
9. Personal interview with Senator Estes Kefauver of Tennessee in his Senate office in Washington, D.C., Jan. 22, 1959.
10. Personal interview with Stephen A. Mitchell at his home on Michigan Avenue in Chicago, Aug. 16, 1958.
11. *Ibid.*
12. Personal interview with Samuel A. Brightman, Deputy Chairman of Public Affairs of the Democratic National Committee, at the National Headquarters in Washington, D.C., Dec. 22, 1958.
13. Personal interview with Governor Orville Freeman in his Executive Office in St. Paul, Minn., Aug. 12, 1958.
14. Personal interview with former President Harry S. Truman at his office in the Truman Library, Independence, Mo., Aug. 28, 1959.

CHAPTER 3
Incredible Victory

Any number of American history books give the general history of the Battle of New Orleans in the War of 1812. Most of the information in this chapter came from letters and newspaper reports.

1. *Daily National Intelligencer* (Washington, D.C.), Feb. 6, 1815, p. 2.
2. *Ibid.*
3. *Ibid.*, Apr. 19, 1815, p. 3.
4. *Ibid.*, Jan. 15, 1816, p. 3.
5. *Ibid.*, Jan. 11, 1817, p. 3.
6. *Ibid.*, Jan. 10, 1824, p. 3.
7. *Ibid.*, Jan. 15, 1824, p. 3.
8. The records at the Democratic National Committee Library indicated that the first Jackson Day Dinner was in 1828. They did not show that the first dinner really was held in 1827 as was discovered by this author in researching this book. Also, the skimpy records there had

no indication of the many affairs held in the first half of the 19th century.

9. *United States Telegraph and Commercial Herald* (Washington, D.C.), Jan. 6, 1827, p. 2.

10. John Spencer Bassett, editor, *Correspondence of Andrew Jackson* (Washington, D.C.: Carnegie Institution of Washington, 1926–33), VI, pp. 489-90.

11. *Daily National Intelligencer* (Washington, D.C.), Jan. 6, 1827, p. 1.

12. *Ibid.,* Jan. 9, 1828, p. 3.

13. *United States Telegraph* (Washington, D.C.), Jan. 9, 1828, p. 3.

14. *Ibid.,* Jan. 12, 1828, p. 2.

15. *Ibid.* Continuous battles over the partisan nature of political dinners began with the 1828 dinner. Newspapers have always played a prominent role in declaiming and acclaiming the dinners. The *Daily National Intelligencer,* an anti-Jackson paper in 1828, printed a very strong editorial on the partisanship of the second dinner. The *United States Telegraph,* a pro-Jackson paper at this particular time, answered in kind. The battle between parties and papers continues today.

16. *Daily National Intelligencer* (Washington, D.C.), Jan. 14, 1828, p. 3.

17. *United States Telegraph* (Washington, D.C.), Jan. 15, 1828, p. 3.

18. Maud Burr Morris, *Records of the Columbia Historical Society, Washington, D.C.* (Washington, D.C.: The Society, 1935), 35–36, pp. 126-28.

19. *Daily National Intelligencer* (Washington, D.C.), Jan. 9, 1829, p. 3.

20. *Ibid.,* Jan. 20, 1829, p. 3.

21. *Ibid.*

CHAPTER 4
"Our Federal Union: It Must Be Preserved"

1. *United States Telegraph* (Washington, D.C.), Apr. 15, 1830, p. 1.

2. *Daily National Intelligencer* (Washington, D.C.), Apr. 19, 1830, p. 3. Both the *United States Telegraph* and the *Daily National Intelligencer* carried full accounts of the famous 1830 Jefferson Dinner.

3. *Ibid.*

4. *Ibid.*

5. *Ibid.*

6. *Ibid.*

7. *Ibid.*

8. *Ibid.*

9. James Parton, *Life of Andrew Jackson* (Boston: James R. Osgood and Company, 1876), III, p. 284.

CHAPTER 5
In the Days of Jackson

1. *Globe* (Washington, D.C.), Jan. 25, 1834, p. 1.

2. *Ibid.,* Jan. 10, 1835, p. 2.

3. *Daily National Intelligencer* (Washington, D.C.), Jan. 17, 1835, p. 3.
4. *Washington Star* (Washington, D.C.), Jan. 5, 1940, p. 2.
5. *Globe* (Washington, D.C.), Jan. 20, 1835, p. 3.
6. *Daily National Intelligencer* (Washington, D.C.), Jan. 13, 1838, p. 3.
7. John Spencer Bassett, editor, *Correspondence of Andrew Jackson* (Washington, D.C.: Carnegie Institution of Washington, 1926–33), VI, pp. 41–42.
8. The *Globe* explanation is in its Jan. 20, 1840, edition, p. 3; the *Daily National Intelligencer* in its Jan. 24, 1840, edition, p. 3.
9. Bassett, p. 254.
10. *Globe* (Washington, D.C.), Jan. 11, 1844, p. 1.

CHAPTER 6

"Intervention for Nonintervention"

1. *Daily National Intelligencer* (Washington, D.C.), Jan. 11, 1847, p. 2.
2. A complete and very detailed account of the 1852 dinner is found in the *Daily Union* (Washington, D.C.), Jan. 10, 1852, p. 3.

CHAPTER 7

Remembered Forever

1. Both the celebration and the dinner in 1853 were reported in the *Daily Union* (Washington, D.C.), Jan. 11, 1853, pp. 3–4.
2. *Records of the Columbia Historical Society, Washington, D.C.,* compiled by the Committee on Publication and the Recording Secretary, Vol. V, Washington, D.C., 1902, pp. 116–18.
3. *Ibid.*

CHAPTER 8

The End of an Era

1. *Daily National Intelligencer* (Washington, D.C.), Jan. 9, 1854, p. 3.
2. *Daily Union* (Washington, D.C.), Jan. 7, 1855, p. 3.
3. Both the *Daily Union* and the *Washington Sentinel* reported the 1855 anniversary—Jan. 9, 1855, p. 2 and Jan. 9, 1855, p. 3, respectively.
4. *Daily National Intelligencer* (Washington, D.C.), Jan. 8, 1865, p. 2.
5. *Daily Morning Chronicle* (Washington, D.C.), Jan. 9, 1867, p. 2 had a complete account of this dinner.
6. *Daily National Intelligencer* (Washington, D.C.), Jan. 9, 1868, p. 2. This was an extra edition devoted especially to the 1868 dinner. More than 10,000 extra copies were printed.

CHAPTER 9
Revival and Remembrance

1. *Washington Post* (Washington, D.C.), Jan. 8, 1894, p. 4.
2. *Ibid.,* Jan. 9, 1896, p. 3.
3. *Ibid.,* Jan. 9, 1897, p. 1.

CHAPTER 10
A Changing Celebration

1. *Washington Post* (Washington, D.C.), Jan. 17, 1911, p. 1.
2. *Ibid.,* Jan. 18, 1911, p. 1.
3. Both the *Washington Post* and the *Washington Star* (Washington, D.C.) on Jan. 9, 1912, carried pages of stories about the 1912 Jackson Day affair. The headlines came from both papers.
4. *Washington Star* (Washington, D.C.), Jan. 9, 1912.
5. *Ibid.,* Jan. 5, 1912, p. 20.
6. *Ibid.,* Jan. 9, 1912.
7. *Washington Post* (Washington, D.C.), Jan. 9, 1912, p. 6.
8. *Ibid.,* Jan. 8, 1912, p. 1.
9. *Washington Star* (Washington, D.C.), Jan. 9, 1912, p. 5.
10. *Ibid.*
11. *Washington Post* (Washington, D.C.), Jan. 8, 1915, p. 2.
12. *Ibid.,* Jan. 10, 1915, p. 1.

CHAPTER 11
Talkathon Times of the Twenties

1. *Washington Star* (Washington, D.C.), Jan. 4, 1920, p. 1. (The *Star* and the *Post* carried every detail of the 1920 dinner in their columns and pages on Jan. 9, 1920.)
2. *Ibid.*
3. *Ibid.*
4. *Washington Post* (Washington, D.C.), Jan. 10, 1928, p. 1.
5. *Washington Star* (Washington D.C.), Jan. 13, 1928, p. 1.
6. *Washington Post* (Washington D.C.), Jan. 10, 1928, p. 1.
7. *Washington Star* (Washington, D.C.), Jan. 13, 1928, p. 4.
8. *Ibid.*
9. *Ibid.,* p. 1.
10. The titles of these articles were taken from the *Washington Star* and the *Washington Post* (Washington, D.C.), Jan. 13, 1928, p. 1.
11. *Washington Post* (Washington, D.C.), Jan. 8, 1932, p. 6.
12. *Washington Star* (Washington, D.C.), Jan. 9, 1932, p. 1.
13. *Ibid.,* Jan. 13, 1928, p. 4.

CHAPTER 12
Genesis of the $100-a-Plate Dinner

1. Marie Chatham, "The Role of the National Party Chairman From Hanna to Farley" (unpublished Ph.D. dissertation, University of Maryland, 1953), p. 131.
2. *Washington Star* (Washington, D.C.), Jan. 8, 1936, p. 1.
3. *Ibid.,* Jan. 9, 1936, p. 3.
4. *Washington Post* (Washington, D.C.), Jan. 9, 1936, p. 1. The *Washington Star* (Washington, D.C.), Jan. 9, 1936, also contains reports of this historic 1936 dinner.

CHAPTER 13
Reprise by Roosevelt

Any number of books written about the Roosevelt era contain information on the New Deal programs, the issues, and the personalities surrounding the Jefferson-Jackson Day affairs. See Bibliography.
1. Franklin D. Roosevelt's Speech at the Victory Dinner, Mar. 4, 1937.
2. *Washington Star* (Washington, D.C.), Mar. 3, 1937, p. 2.
3. Arthur Schlesinger, *Political and Social Growth of the American People* (New York: Macmillan Company, 1941), p. 581.
4. Basil Rauch, *Franklin D. Roosevelt* (New York: Rinehart and Company, 1957), p. 197.
5. *Washington Post* (Washington, D.C.), Jan. 9, 1940, p. 1.
6. *New York Times* (New York), Dec. 31, 1939, p. 1.
7. *Ibid.*
8. *Ibid.,* Jan. 2, 1940, p. 12.
9. *Washington Post* (Washington, D.C.), Jan. 10, 1940, p. 10.
10. Franklin D. Roosevelt, *Foreign Policy* (New York: Wilfred Funk, Inc., 1942), pp. 318–24.
11. Samuel I. Rosenman, *Working With Roosevelt* (New York: Harper and Brothers, 1952), p. 274.
12. David Lawrence, *Washington Star* (Washington, D.C.), Feb. 23, 1942, p. 9.
13. Rosenman, p. 330.
14. *New York Times* (New York), Jan. 23, 1944, p. 1.
15. *Washington Post* (Washington, D.C.), Jan. 21, 1944, p. 1.
16. *New York Times* (New York), Feb. 26, 1945, p. 21.
17. Part of a confidential memorandum sent by Robert Hannegan, Democratic National Chairman, to National Committeemen, Committeewomen, State Chairmen, and Chairmen of Jefferson Day Dinner Committees of 1945.

CHAPTER 14
Testimonials in Truman's Time

1. *New York Times* (New York), Mar. 25, 1946, p. 1.
2. *Washington Star* (Washington, D.C.), Apr. 7, 1947, p. 8 (Editorial).

3. *Washington Post* (Washington, D.C.), Feb. 23, 1948, p. 1.
4. Personal interview with former President Harry S. Truman at his office in the Truman Library, Independence, Mo., Aug. 28, 1959.
5. *Washington Post* (Washington, D.C.), Feb. 20, 1948, p. 1.
6. *Ibid.,* Feb. 25, 1949, p. 1.
7. *Ibid.,* Feb. 16, 1950, p. 1.
8. *New York Herald Tribune* (New York), Mar. 29, 1952.
9. Personal interview with former President Harry S. Truman at his office in the Truman Library, Independence, Mo., Aug. 28, 1959.

CHAPTER 15
Fund Raising in the Fifties

1. *Washington Post* (Washington, D.C.), May 5, 1957, p. 1.
2. *Ibid.*
3. *Washington Star* (Washington, D.C.), Feb. 21, 1958, p. 3.
4. Harry S. Truman's Speech at the Jefferson-Jackson Day Dinner, Feb. 22, 1958.
5. *Ibid.*

CHAPTER 16
Jefferson, Jackson, JFK, and Johnson

Again the best sources for the Democratic dinners in the 1960's can be found in the Washington, D.C., newspapers.

★

BIBLIOGRAPHY
AND SOURCES

T HE BASIC RESEARCH for this book was completed by the use of seven different types of sources: actual study of the speech manuscripts of the speakers at the Democratic Dinners, the usual research through pertinent books, the study of magazine articles, the comprehensive and exhaustive search through all of the newspapers of Washington, D.C., from the early 1800's through 1965, the scanning of unpublished theses and dissertations, the working in the personal and official papers of Franklin D. Roosevelt, Harry S. Truman, and Sam Rayburn, and the intensive interviewing of a dozen key Democratic officials.

A: SPEECH MANUSCRIPTS

Franklin D. Roosevelt

Jackson Day Dinner Address, Jan. 8, 1936; Democratic Victory Dinner Address, Mar. 4, 1937; Jackson Day Dinner Address, Jan. 8, 1938; Jackson Day Dinner Address, Jan. 7, 1939; Jackson Day Dinner Address, Jan. 8, 1940; Jackson Day Address, Mar. 29, 1941; 210th Anniversary of George Washington's Birthday Address, Feb. 23, 1942; George Washington Day Address, Feb. 22, 1943; Jefferson Day Dinner Address, to have been delivered by President Roosevelt on Apr. 13, 1945.

Harry S. Truman

Jackson Day Dinner Address, Mar. 23, 1946; Jefferson Day Dinner Address, Apr. 5, 1947; Jefferson-Jackson Day Dinner Address, Feb. 19, 1948; Jefferson-Jackson Day Dinner Address, Feb. 24, 1949; Jefferson-Jackson Day Dinner Address, Feb. 16, 1950; Jefferson-Jackson Day Dinner Address, Apr. 14, 1951; Jefferson-Jackson Day Dinner Address, Mar. 29, 1952; Jefferson-Jackson Day Dinner Address, May 4, 1957; Harry S. Truman Dinner, Feb. 22, 1958.

Sam Rayburn

Jackson Day Dinner Address, Jan. 22, 1944; Jefferson-Jackson Day Dinner Address, May 6, 1954; Rayburn Testimonial Dinner Address, Apr. 16, 1955; Woodrow Wilson Centennial Dinner Address, Apr. 21, 1956.

John F. Kennedy

John F. Kennedy Birthday Dinner, May 27, 1961; First Anniversary of Kennedy Administration, Jan. 20, 1962; Inaugural Salute Celebration, Jan. 18, 1963.

Lyndon B. Johnson

Salute to LBJ Dinner and Gala, May 26, 1964; Congressional Dinner, June 24, 1965.

Drafts, stenographic copies, reading copies, and electrical transcriptions of all of the speeches of Roosevelt and Truman were studied. Only one of Rayburn's speeches, the 1944 speech, was studied by electrical transcription. Some drafts and all news releases of the speeches of Rayburn, Kennedy, and Johnson were analyzed.

B: BOOKS

Adams, James Truslow, *The March of Democracy*. New York: Scribner's Sons, 1932–33.

Alsop, Joseph, and Catledge, Turner, *The 168 Days*. Garden City, N.Y.: Doubleday, Doran and Company, Inc., 1938.

Alsop, Joseph, and Kintner, Robert, *Men Around the President*. New York: Doubleday, Doran and Company, Inc., 1939.

Bailey, Stanley, *Mr. Roosevelt's Experiments*. London: L. and Virginia Woolf at the Hogarth Press, 1935.

Baird, A. Craig, *Representative American Speeches, 1939–40*. New York: H. W. Wilson Company, 1940.

Barnes, William Robbins (ed.), *The Supreme Court Issue and the Constitution*. New York: Barnes and Noble, Inc., 1937.

Bassett, John Spencer (ed.), *Correspondence of Andrew Jackson*. Washington, D.C.: Carnegie Institution of Washington, 1926–33.

———, *The Life of Andrew Jackson*. Garden City, N.Y.: Doubleday, Page and Company, 1911.

Binkley, Wilfred E., *The Man in the White House*. Baltimore: Johns Hopkins Press, 1958.

Bowers, Claude Gernade, *The Party Battles of the Jackson Period*. New York: Houghton Mifflin Company, 1922.

Buell, Augustus C., *History of Andrew Jackson, Pioneer, Patriot, Soldier, Politician, President*. New York: C. Scribner's Sons, 1904.

Busch, Noel, *What Manner of Man*. New York: Harper and Brothers, 1944.

Byrnes, James, *Speaking Frankly*. New York: Harper and Brothers, 1947.

Clancy, Herbert J., *The Democratic Party: Jefferson to Jackson*. New York: Fordham University Press, 1962.

Clemens, Cyril, *The Man From Missouri*. New York: J. P. Didier, 1945.

——— (ed.), *Truman Speaks*. New York: J. P. Didier, 1946.

Daniels, Jonathan, *The Man From Independence*. Philadelphia: J. B. Lippincott Co., 1950.

Day, Donald, *FDR'S Own Story*. Boston: Little, Brown and Company, 1951.

Delano, Daniel, *Franklin Roosevelt and the Delano Influence*. Pittsburgh: J. S. Nudi Publications, 1946.

Dows, Olin, *Franklin Roosevelt at Hyde Park*. New York: American Artists Group, 1949.

Dumond, Dwight, *Roosevelt to Roosevelt*. New York: Henry Holt and Company, Inc., 1937.

Erickson, Aaron, *Roosevelt Albums: Highlights of Life and Work*. New York: Knickerbocker Publishing Company, 1945.

Farley, James, *Behind the Ballots*. New York: Harcourt, Brace and Company, 1938.

———, *Jim Farley's Story: The Roosevelt Years*. New York: Whittlesey House, 1948.

Faulkner, Harold, *American Political and Social History*. New York: Appleton-Century-Crofts, 1948.

Feis, Herbert, *The Road to Pearl Harbor*. Princeton: Princeton University Press, 1950.

Flynn, John, *Country Squire in the White House*. New York: Doubleday, Doran and Company, Inc., 1940.

————, *The Roosevelt Myth*. New York: Devin-Adair Company, 1948.

Freidel, Frank, *Franklin D. Roosevelt*. Boston: Little, Brown and Company, 1952. Three vols.

Gallup, George, *The Pulse of Democracy*. New York: Simon and Schuster, 1940.

Geddes, Donald (ed.), *Franklin Delano Roosevelt, A Memorial*. New York: Pocket Books, Inc., 1945.

Gosnell, Harold, *Champion Campaigner: Franklin D. Roosevelt*. New York: Macmillan Company, 1952.

Greer, Thomas, *What Roosevelt Thought: The Social and Political Ideas of FDR*. East Lansing: Michigan State University Press, 1958.

Gunther, John, *Roosevelt in Retrospect*. New York: Harper and Brothers, 1950.

Halter, Ernest, *Collecting First Editions of Franklin D. Roosevelt*. Chicago: Private edition for subscribers, 1949.

Hardman, J. B. S., *Rendezvous With Destiny*. New York: Dryden Press, 1944.

Hassett, William D., *Off the Record With FDR, 1942–1945*. New Brunswick, N.J.: Rutgers University Press, 1958.

Hatch, Alden, *Franklin D. Roosevelt, An Informal Biography*. New York: Henry Holt and Company, Inc., 1947.

High, Stanley, *Roosevelt . . . and Then?* New York: Harper and Brothers, 1937.

Hillman, William, *Mr. President*. New York: Farrar, Straus and Young, 1952.

Hinderaker, Ivan, *Party Politics*. New York: Henry Holt and Company, Inc., 1956.

Hofstadter, Richard, *The American Political Tradition and the Men Who Made It*. New York: Alfred A. Knopf, Inc., 1948.

————, Miller, William, and Aaron, Daniel, *The United States*. Englewood Cliffs: Prentice-Hall, Inc., 1957.

Hull, Cordell, *Memoirs*. New York: Macmillan Company, 1948.

Ickes, Harold, *The Secret Diary of Harold L. Ickes*. New York: Simon and Schuster, 1954.

James, Marquis, *Andrew Jackson, Portrait of a President*. New York: Bobbs-Merrill Company, 1937.

————, *Andrew Jackson, The Border Captain*. Indianapolis: Bobbs-Merrill Company, 1933.

Johnson, Gerald W., *Andrew Jackson, An Epic in Homespun*. New York: Minton, Belch, and Company, 1927.

Kavinoky, Edward, *My Friends: Twenty-eight History Making Speeches*. Buffalo, N.Y.: Foster and Stewart Publishing Company, 1945.

Key, V. O., *Politics, Parties, and Pressure Groups*. New York: Thomas Y. Crowell Company, 1959.

Kingdon, Frank, *As FDR Said*. New York: Duell, Sloan and Pearce, 1950.

————, *That Man in the White House*. New York: Arco Publishing Company, 1944.

Kinnaird, Clark (ed.), *The Real FDR*. New York: The Citadel Press, 1945.

Knowles, Archibald, *A Rendezvous With Destiny*. Philadelphia: David McKay Company, 1946.

Koenig, Louis, *The Presidency and the Crisis*. New York: King's Crown Press, 1944.

———, *The Truman Administration*. New York: New York University Press, 1956.

Kohn, Hans, *Force or Reason*. Cambridge, Mass.: Harvard University Press, 1937.

Lindley, Ernest, *Franklin D. Roosevelt*. Indianapolis: Bobbs-Merrill Company, 1931.

———, *The Roosevelt Revolution: First Phase*. New York: Viking Press, 1936.

MacKenzie, Compton, *Mr. Roosevelt*. New York: E. P. Dutton and Company, Inc., 1944.

Meyersohn, Maxwell, *The Wit and Wisdom of FDR*. Boston: Beacon Press, 1950.

Michelson, Charles, *The Ghost Talks*. New York: G. P. Putnam's Sons, 1944.

Moley, Raymond, *27 Masters of Politics*. New York: Funk and Wagnalls Company, 1949.

Morris, Maud Burr, *Records of the Columbia Historical Society, Washington, D.C.*, Washington, D.C.: The Society, 1935.

Novins, Allen, *The New Deal and World Affairs*. New Haven: Yale University Press, 1930.

Ogg, Frederic Austin, *The Reign of Andrew Jackson*. New Haven: Yale University Press, 1921.

Parton, James, *Life of Andrew Jackson*. Boston: James Osgood and Company, 1876. Three vols.

Perkins, Dexter, *The New Age of Franklin Roosevelt, 1932–45*. Chicago: University of Chicago Press, 1957.

Perkins, Frances, *The Roosevelt I Knew*. New York: Viking Press, 1946.

Rauch, Basil, *Franklin D. Roosevelt*. New York: Rinehart and Company, Inc., 1957.

———, *History of the New Deal, 1933–1938*. New York: Creative Press, Inc., 1944.

———, *Roosevelt: From Munich to Pearl Harbor*. New York: Creative Press, Inc., 1950.

———, *The Roosevelt Reader*. New York: Rinehart and Company, 1957.

Robinson, Edgar, *The Roosevelt Leadership: 1933–1945*. Philadelphia: J. B. Lippincott Co., 1955.

———, *They Voted for Roosevelt*. Stanford, Calif.: Stanford University Press, 1947.

Roosevelt, Eleanor, *If You Ask Me*. New York: Appleton-Century Company, Inc., 1946.

———, *My Days*. New York: Dodge Publishing Company, 1938.

———, *On My Own*. New York: Harper and Brothers, 1958.

———, *This I Remember*. New York: Harper and Brothers, 1949.

———, *This Is My Story*. New York: Harper and Brothers, 1937.

Roosevelt, Elliott, *As He Saw It*. New York: Duell, Sloan and Pearce, 1946.

——— (ed.), *F.D.R.: His Personal Letters*. New York: Duell, Sloan and Pearce, 1947–50. Four vols.

Roosevelt, Franklin D., *Foreign Policy*. New York: Wilfred Funk, Inc., 1942.

———, *Our Democracy in Action*. Washington, D.C.: National Home Library Foundation, 1940.

———, *The Public Papers and Addresses of Franklin D. Roosevelt*. New

York: Random House, 1938–50. Thirteen vols. Volumes 6–9 have the imprint of the Macmillan Company.

Rosenau, James, *The Roosevelt Treasury*. New York: Doubleday and Company, Inc., 1951.

Rosenman, Samuel I., *Working With Roosevelt*. New York: Harper and Brothers, 1952.

Rose, Leland, *This Democratic Roosevelt, The Life Story of Franklin Delano*. New York: E. P. Dutton and Company, Inc., 1932.

Rossiter, Clinton, *The American Presidency*. New York: Harcourt, Brace and Company, 1960.

——, *Parties and Politics in America*. Ithaca, N.Y.: Cornell University Press, 1960.

Ruskowski, Casimir, *Is Roosevelt an Andrew Jackson?* Boston: Bruce Humphries, Inc., 1939.

Schlesinger, Arthur Meier, *The Age of Jackson*. Boston: Little, Brown and Company, 1946.

——, *The Age of Roosevelt*. Boston: Houghton Mifflin Company, 1957–60. Three vols.

——, *Political and Social Growth of the American People, 1865–1940*. New York: Macmillan Company, 1941.

Schnapper, M. B. (ed.), *The Truman Program: Addresses and Messages*. Washington, D.C.: Public Affairs Press, 1949.

Sherwood, Robert E., *Roosevelt and Hopkins, An Intimate Story*. New York: Harper and Brothers, 1950.

Smith, Edward Conrad, and Zurcher, Arnold John, *Dictionary of American Politics*. New York: Barnes and Noble, Inc., 1957.

Smith, Merriman, *Thank You, Mr. President*. New York: Harper and Brothers, 1946.

Sumner, William Graham, *Andrew Jackson*. New York: Houghton Mifflin Company, 1910.

Syrett, Harold Coffin, *Andrew Jackson: His Contributions to the American Tradition*, Indianapolis: Bobbs-Merrill Company, 1953.

Truman, Harry S., *Memoirs*. Garden City, N.Y.: Doubleday and Company, Inc., 1955.

——, *Mr. Citizen*. New York: Geis Associates, 1960.

Tugwell, Rexford Guy, *The Democratic Roosevelt*. Garden City, N.Y.: Doubleday and Company, Inc., 1957.

Tully, Grace, *F.D.R., My Boss*. New York: Charles Scribner's Sons, 1949.

Walker, Alexander, *Jackson and New Orleans*. New York: J. C. Derby, 1856.

Ward, John William, *Andrew Jackson, Symbol for an Age*. New York: Oxford University Press, 1955.

Zevin, B. D., *Nothing To Fear: The Selected Addresses of Franklin Delano Roosevelt, 1932–1945*. Boston: Houghton Mifflin Company, 1946.

C: ARTICLES

Arnall, Ellis, "Democrats Can Win," *Atlantic Monthly* (Oct., 1948), 182: 37–38.

Braden, Waldo W., and Brandenburg, Earnest, "Roosevelt's Fireside Chats," *Speech Monographs* (Nov., 1955), 22:290–302.

Brandenburg, Earnest, "Franklin D. Roosevelt's International Speeches: 1939–1941," *Speech Monographs* (Aug., 1949), 16:21–40.

——, "The Preparation of Franklin D. Roosevelt's Speeches," *Quarterly Journal of Speech* (Apr., 1949), 35:214–21.

Brembeck, Cole, "Harry Truman at the Whistle Stops," *Quarterly Journal of Speech* (Feb., 1952), 38:42–50.

Randolph, Jennings, "Harry S. Truman," *Quarterly Journal of Speech* (Oct., 1948), 34:300–302.

———, "Truman—A Winning Speaker," *Quarterly Journal of Speech* (Dec., 1948), 34:421–24.

Ratcliffe, S. K., "President Truman's Triumph," *The Contemporary Review* (Dec., 1948), 174:321.

Roosevelt, Eleanor, "If You Ask Me," *Ladies Home Journal* (Oct., 1948), 65:45.

Ross, Charles G., "How Truman Did It," *Collier's* (Dec. 25, 1948), 122:88.

Schiffman, Joseph, "Observations on Roosevelt's Literary Style," *Quarterly Journal of Speech* (Apr., 1949), 35:222–26.

White, Eugene E., and Henderlider, Clair R., "What Harry S. Truman Told Us About His Speaking," *Quarterly Journal of Speech* (Feb., 1954), 40:37–42.

D: NEWSPAPERS

The following newspapers contain significant commentary on the Jackson Day events.

Baltimore Sun, Apr. 16, 1951.
Brooklyn Eagle, Sept. 22, 1940.
Christian Science Monitor, Mar. 3, 1948.
Cincinnati Times Star, Mar. 29, 1952.
Dallas Morning News, Jan. 11 and Mar. 11, 1911; May 6, 1913.
Des Moines Register, Mar. 1, 1952.
El Paso Herald Post, Mar. 5, 1959.
Milwaukee Journal, Apr. 15, 1951.
Nashville Post, Apr. 6, 1945.
New York Newspapers:
New York Herald Tribune, Apr. 6, 1945; Mar. 22, 1946; Mar. 25, 1946; Apr. 16, 1951; May 7, 1954.
New York Times

1932: Jan. 3, 9.	1941: Jan. 5, 23; Mar. 23, 28, 29.
1936: Jan. 3, 6, 8, 9, 10, 12, 14, 19; June 4; Aug. 12; Nov. 6; Dec. 31.	1942: Jan. 4, 7; Feb. 2, 12, 19, 22, 23, 24, 25; Mar. 24.
1937: Jan. 6, 17; Feb. 23; Mar. 4, 5, 6, 7; Dec. 16.	1943: Jan. 28; Feb. 17, 21, 23, 27.
1938: Jan. 4, 9, 11, 12, 19; Feb. 13; Mar. 11.	1944: Jan. 23, 24.
1939: Jan. 3, 7, 8, 10; Mar. 12; Nov. 29.	1945: Feb. 26; Apr. 6, 13, 14.
1940: Jan. 2, 3, 4, 7, 8, 9, 10, 14; Feb. 6; Dec. 21, 31.	1946: Mar. 25.
	1948: July 14.
	1949: Jan. 30.
	All years, 1950–65

St. Louis Post Dispatch, Jan. 5, 1941.
Washington, D.C., Newspapers:
Daily Morning Chronicle, Jan. 10, 1866; Jan. 8 and 9, 1867.
Daily National Intelligencer

1815: Jan. 19; Feb. 2, 6, 13, 15; Mar. 25; Apr. 19.	1836: Jan. 8.
	1838: Jan. 13.
1816: Jan. 15.	1839: Jan. 9.

1817: Jan. 11.
1823: Jan. 7.
1824: Jan. 10, 15, 21, 31.
1826: Jan. 17.
1827: Jan. 6, 9, 11.
1828: Jan. 1, 9; Feb. 4, 6.
1829: Jan. 7, 8, 9, 14, 20.
1830: Jan. 5, 6, 11; Apr. 13, 19, 20, 21, 24.
1831: Jan. 7, 15, 18.
1832: Jan. 3, 5.
1833: Jan. 7.
1835: Jan. 17.

1840: Jan. 20, 24.
1844: Jan. 11.
1846: Jan. 8, 12.
1847: Jan. 6, 11.
1848: Jan. 5.
1852: Jan. 9.
1853: Jan. 6, 10, 11.
1854: Jan. 9.
1865: Jan. 8, 10.
1866: Jan. 8, 11.
1867: Jan. 5, 7, 8, 9, 10.
1868: Jan. 4, 6, 8, 9.
1869: Jan. 9.

Daily Union
1847: Jan. 2, 4, 5.
1849: Jan. 9.
1852: Jan. 1, 10.
1853: Jan. 11, 15.

1855: Jan. 2, 6, 7, 9.
1857: Jan. 9, 14.
1858: Jan. 3, 9, 10, 12.
1859: Jan. 9.

Globe
1832: Jan. 2, 7, 8, 9, 20.
1833: Jan. 3, 8; Feb. 5.
1834: Jan. 6, 8, 18, 25.

1835: Jan. 10, 14.
1840: Jan. 7, 20, 29.
1844: Jan. 5, 6, 9, 11.

National Intelligencer and Express, Jan. 7, 1870.
Times Herald, Mar. 25, 1946.
United States Telegraph
1828: Jan. 7, 9, 12, 15, 16.
1829: Jan. 13, 14, 15, 18.

1830: Jan. 8; Apr. 8, 12, 15.
1834: Jan. 10.

United States Telegraph and Commercial Herald
1827: Jan. 6, 8, 11, 13.
Washington News, Mar. 25, 1946.
Washington Post
1883: Jan. 8.
1885: Jan. 8, 9.
1888: Jan. 8.
1890: Jan. 9.
1891: Jan. 9.
1892: Jan. 9.
1893: Jan. 7, 8, 10.
1894: Jan. 8, 9.
1895: Jan. 8, 9.
1896: Jan. 9.
1897: Jan. 8, 9.
1898: Jan. 9.
1899: Jan. 8, 9.
1900: Jan. 9.
1902: Jan. 9.
1903: Jan. 9.
1904: Jan. 9.
1907: Jan. 9.
1908: Jan. 7, 9.
1909: Jan. 9.
1910: Jan. 9.
1911: Jan. 17, 18.
1912: Jan. 8, 9, 10.

1915: Jan. 8, 9, 10.
1920: Jan. 7, 8, 9, 10.
1924: Jan. 8, 9.
1926: Jan. 9.
1928: Jan. 9, 10, 13.
1932: Jan. 8, 9, 17.
1936: Jan. 9.
1938: Jan. 8, 9, 10.
1939: Jan. 8, 9.
1940: Jan. 8, 9, 10.
1944: Jan. 21, 22, 23.
1946: Mar. 21.
1947: Apr. 5, 6.
1948: Feb. 19, 20.
1949: Feb. 25.
1950: Feb. 16, 17, 18.
1951: Apr. 15, 16.
1952: Mar. 29, 30.
1956: Apr. 22.
1957: May 5.
1958: Feb. 23.
1959–65: Excellent coverage

Washington Sentinel, Jan. 9, 1855.
Washington Star

1868: Jan. 9.	1943: Feb. 21, 23.
1880: Jan. 5.	1944: Jan. 23.
1892: Jan. 9.	1946: Mar. 23, 24.
1896: Jan. 8, 9.	1947: Apr. 5, 6.
1912: Jan. 5, 9.	1948: Feb. 20.
1920: Jan. 4, 5, 6, 7, 9, 11, 12.	1949: Feb. 24, 25, 26.
1928: Jan. 11, 13.	1950: Feb. 14, 17.
1932: Jan. 9.	1951: Apr. 15.
1936: Jan. 8, 9.	1952: Mar. 23, 25, 29, 30.
1937: Mar. 1, 3, 5, 6.	1954: May 7.
1938: Jan. 8, 9.	1955: Apr. 16, 17.
1939: Jan. 7, 8.	1956: Apr. 21, 22.
1940: Jan. 5, 9.	1957: May 4, 5.
1941: Mar. 30.	1958: Feb. 21, 23.
1942: Feb. 23, 24.	1959–65: Excellent coverage

E: UNPUBLISHED MASTER'S THESES AND DOCTORAL DISSERTATIONS

Allen, Edna. "Franklin Delano Roosevelt as a Speaker." Thesis, Baylor University, 1951.

Bach, Earl. "An Objective Analysis of the Speech Style of Franklin D. Roosevelt." Thesis, Marquette University, 1938.

Brandenburg, Earnest. "An Analysis and Criticism of Franklin D. Roosevelt's Speeches on International Affairs Delivered Between September 3, 1939–December 7, 1941." Dissertation, University of Iowa, 1949.

Brembeck, Cole. "The Persuasive Speaking of Truman and Dewey in the 1948 Presidential Campaign." Dissertation, University of Wisconsin, 1951.

Brooks, George. "A Rhetorical Comparison of Woodrow Wilson and Franklin D. Roosevelt, Based Upon Aristotelian Criteria." Dissertation, Ohio State University, 1945.

Cameron, Turner C. "Political Philosophy of Franklin D. Roosevelt." Dissertation, Princeton University, 1940.

Chatham, Marie. "The Role of the National Party Chairman From Hanna to Farley." Dissertation, University of Maryland, 1953.

Coffey, Virginia. "Franklin D. Roosevelt and the Fireside Chats." Thesis, University of Redlands, 1947.

Cowperthwaite, L. LeRoy. "A Criticism of the Speaking of Franklin D. Roosevelt in the Presidential Campaign of 1932." Dissertation, University of Iowa, 1950.

Flory, Margaret. "An Analysis of the Oratory of President Franklin D. Roosevelt." Thesis, Ohio University, 1938.

Freeley, Austin. "A Comparison and Analysis of the Factors of Rhetorical Invention in Selected Wartime Speeches of Franklin D. Roosevelt and Winston Spencer Churchill." Dissertation, Northwestern University, 1955.

Henderson, Bancroft. "The Democratic National Committee." Dissertation, University of Minnesota, 1958.

Hill, Howard A. "The Study of Persuasive Factors in the Speeches of Harry S. Truman in the 1948 Presidential Campaign." Thesis, Marquette University, 1949.

MacColl, E. Kimbark. "The Supreme Court and Public Opinion—A Study of the Court Fight of 1937." Dissertation, University of California, 1953.

Norton, Laurence E. "A Symbol Analysis of Roosevelt and Dewey Speeches in the 1944 Presidential Campaign." Dissertation, University of Wisconsin, 1947.

Parker, Daniel P. "The Political and Social Views of Harry S. Truman." Dissertation, University of Pennsylvania, 1951.

Pennington, Paul Jordan. "A Rhetorical Study of the Gubernatorial Speaking of Franklin D. Roosevelt." Dissertation, Louisiana State University, 1957.

Phelps, Bernard Fred. "A Rhetorical Analysis of the 1937 Addresses of Franklin D. Roosevelt in Support of Court Reform." Thesis, Ohio State University, 1957.

Quimby, Rollin. "Franklin D. Roosevelt and Harry Truman—The Preparation and Delivery of Their Public Addresses." Thesis, University of Michigan, 1948.

Ray, Robert F. "An Evaluation of the Public Speaking of President Franklin D. Roosevelt and Governor Thomas E. Dewey in the Presidential Campaign of 1944." Dissertation, University of Iowa, 1947.

Rogge, Edward. "The Speechmaking of Harry S. Truman." Dissertation, University of Missouri, 1958.

Schrier, Charlotte. "The Public Speaking Techniques of Franklin D. Roosevelt in Selected Occasional Addresses." Thesis, University of Iowa, 1939.

Wilson, John. "An Analysis of the Criticism of Selected Speeches by Franklin D. Roosevelt." Dissertation, University of Wisconsin, 1955.

F: PERSONAL AND OFFICIAL PAPERS

The following sources were studied in the Franklin D. Roosevelt Library at Hyde Park, N.Y., and in the Harry S. Truman Library at Independence, Mo. Information was also gathered from the Sam Rayburn Library in Bonham, Tex., from the Democratic National Committee Library and from the Library of Congress in Washington, D.C.

FRANKLIN D. ROOSEVELT LIBRARY

President's Personal File:

1A President's Personal Life
33 Davis, Norman H.
40 Astor, Vincent
46 Cross, Guernsey T.
64 Rosenman, Samuel I.
65 Democratic Party
86 Daniels, Josephus
88 Baruch, Bernard
98 FDR's Correspondence with Publishers
100 O'Neal, Edward A.
159 Lindsay, Prof. Samuel McCune

200B Radio Addresses of the President, 1933–1945
222 House, Col. Edward M.
259 Jefferson, Thomas
309 Farley, James A.
313 Fayerweather, Charles S.
321 Mundelein, George Cardinal
477 National Broadcasting Company
482 Hooker, Henry S.
576 Clark, William
603 Democratic National Committee

605 Stevens, Raymond B.
684 Barton, George Sumner
853 National Association of Broad-
 casters
984 Paley, William S.
1023 Roper, Daniel C.
1069 Jackson, Andrew
1180 Tobin, Daniel J.
1409 Dickerman, Marion
1487 Sheppard, Morris
1637 Powys, Llewelyn
1788 Elkus, Abram I.
1792 LaFollette, Robert M., Jr.
1817 Marsland, Charles H.
1820 Correspondence
1820 Speech Material and Suggestions; Transcripts of Speeches
2178 Villard, Oswald Garrison
2332 Baker, Ray Stannard
2432 Morley, Christopher
2501 Schlesinger, Arthur M.
2609 University of Virginia
2668 Lorenzen, Gen. A. F.
2816 Byrnes, James F.
2856 Houston, Herbert S.
2915 *New York Herald Tribune*
3119 Oliphant, Herman
3319 Seswell, Emmett

3435 Good Neighbor League, Inc.
3884 Ludwig, Emil
4083 Knox, Col. Frank
4096 Hopkins, Harry
4484 Fahey, John H.
4509 Sandburg, Carl
4715 Willert, Lady Florence
4721 American Institute of Public
 Opinion
4951 Carlson, Capt. Evans F.
5107 *The Nation*
5739 Jackson Day Dinner Committee (D.C.)
6242 Lockley, Fred
6426 Buck, Gene
6448 Mooney, James D.
6650 Thompson, Dorothy
6721 Corcoran, Thomas G.
6741 Sforza, Count Carlo
7096 Slattery, Harry
7356 Sherwood, Robert E.
7489 Lewisohn, Sam A.
8488 Wright, James L.
8601 Kerr, Robert S.
8617 Butcher, Harry C.
8966 Biow, Milton
9026 Reinsch, J. Leonard

Official Files:
234 Jefferson, Thomas
299 Democratic Party
300 Democratic National Committee
576 Government of Albania
576A Miscellaneous
576B Endorsements for Minister
593 Jackson, Andrew

856 Republican Party
857 Straw Votes
1060 Securities and Exchange Commission
1370 Second Term
2443 Good Neighbor League
4117 Hopkins, Harry

Master Speech File (Speeches given on the following dates):
Jan. 8, 1936   Mar. 29, 1941
Mar. 4, 1937   Feb. 23, 1942
Jan. 8, 1938   Feb. 22, 1943
Jan. 7, 1939   Apr. 13, 1945
Jan. 8, 1940

Samuel I. Rosenman Papers: Speech drafts from 1940–44.
Press Conferences: All from 1936 through 1945.
Microfilms: Various studies on Roosevelt were studied in this manner.
Boxed Manuscripts of Public Papers: 1933–36.
Boxed Documents: 1936–40.
Recordings: Various speeches delivered by Roosevelt. The following
are the library numbers of the recordings heard:
40, 41, 54, 58, 96, 97, 98, 131, 132, 199, 200, 201, 262, 263, 264,
276, 355, 372, 385, 396, 387, 424.

Harry S. Truman Library
President's Personal Files:
200 President's Messages, commendatory of Jackson Day Dinner
Address, Mar. 23, 1946

259 Jefferson, Thomas (concerning Jefferson-Jackson Day Dinners)
Message to Congress, Mar. 12, 1947
Jackson Day Address, Apr. 5, 1947
    Pro and Con Breakdown
Jefferson-Jackson Day Address, Feb. 19, 1948
Jefferson-Jackson Day Address, Feb. 24, 1949
    Pro and Con Breakdown
Address at U.S. Conference of Mayors, Mar. 21, 1949
Jefferson-Jackson Day Address, Feb. 16, 1950
    Pro and Con Breakdown
Jefferson-Jackson Day Address, Apr. 14, 1951
    Pro and Con Breakdown
Jefferson-Jackson Day Address, Mar. 29, 1952
1F Speech Drafts (of all speeches under study)

Official Files:

      1 Agriculture Department
  136 Radio Matters
 136B Television
  144 Newspapers, the Press, Correspondents
  234 Jefferson, Thomas (concerning Jefferson-Jackson Day)
299F Third Term Announcement
  505 Straw Votes, Polls
505A Gallup Poll
  550 Mail Reports
693–698 Radio Matters
713–717 Clipping File
1154–1156 Democratic National Committee
1184–1192 Democratic Party
 1680 Mail Reports
 2935 Speech Suggestions

Files of the Official White House Reporter:
Transcripts of President's Speeches, Ribbon Copies, 1945–53.

Rosenman Files: Drafts of speeches on which he worked.
Lloyd Files: Drafts of speeches on which he worked.
Murphy Files: Drafts of speeches on which he worked.

G: OTHER SOURCES

The following persons were interviewed:
Samuel C. Brightman, Deputy Chairman of Public Affairs of the Democratic National Committee, Dec. 22, 1958.
Mrs. India Edwards, former Executive Director of the Women's Division of the Democratic National Committee, Jan. 22, 1959.
Oscar Ewing, adviser to Truman, May 10, 1959.
James A. Farley, former Chairman of the Democratic National Committee, July 15, 1958.
Governor Orville Freeman of Minnesota, Aug. 12, 1958.
Senator Estes Kefauver of Tennessee, Jan. 22, 1959.
Stephen A. Mitchell, former Chairman of the Democratic National Committee, Aug. 16, 1958.
Sam Rayburn, Speaker of the House of Representatives, Jan. 21, 1959.
Edward Roddan, news correspondent, Jan. 23, 1959.
Harry S. Truman, former President of the United States, Aug. 28, 1959.
Letter: From James A. Farley, Sept. 3, 1959.

★

Index

E

Eaton, John Henry, 44
Economic Aid, 176
Economic growth, 201
"Economic royalists," 4, 21, 148
Edmondson, J. Howard, 29, 204
Edwards, Mrs. India, xvii, 26, 27
Ego-involvement, xv
Eighth of January celebrations: 1816, 39; military ball, 1817, 39; public and private balls, 1823–1824, 40–42; 1828, 43–48; 1829, 48–49; 1830, dinner and ball, 51; balls, 1831–1833, 59; public dinner, 1834, 59; extinguishment of national debt, 1835, 59–62; laying cornerstone of Jackson City, 1836, 62–63; parade, 1839, 63; 25th anniversary of Battle of New Orleans, 1840, 63–64; celebration of Bill of Reversal, 1844, 64–67; balls, 1846–1849, 69; dinner, 1852, 69–72; dinner, 1854, 79; 40th anniversary of Battle of New Orleans, ball, 1855, 79–80; balls, 1858–1859, 80; 50th anniversary of Battle of New Orleans, 1865, 80; dinner, 1867, 82; dinner, 1868, 82–83; 1880, 87; banquet, 1885, 87; banquet, 1893, 87–88; 1895, 90; reception, literary reading, music, 1896, 90–91; banquet, 1897, 91–92; dinner in Baltimore, 1911, 95–96; banquet, 1912, 96–102; centennial of Battle of New Orleans, 1915, 102–3; banquet, 1920, 107–14; banquet, 1928, 114–23; banquet, 1932, 124–28; $50-a-plate dinner, 1936, 134–38; $100-a-plate dinner, 1937, 141–47; banquet, 1938, 147–51; dinner, 1939, 151–53; dinner, 1940, 153–58; dinner, 1941, 158–60; dinner, 1944, 166–68; 700-calorie dinner, 1946, 173–76
Eisenhower, Gen. Dwight D., 185, 191–95, 197, 198, 200
Elections:
—Congressional, 1946, 169, 176; 1950, 182; 1958, 198–200; 1960, 211; 1962, 224; 1966, 231
—direct election of Senators, 100, 102
—general, 110
—presidential, 1824, 9, 16, 83; 1912, 95–102; 1920, 113; 1928, 121; 1960, 207; 1964, 224
Ellis, E. John, 87
Embargo and Nonintercourse Acts, 34
Employment, 201
Enterprise, private, 176
Europe, 8, 103, 155, 213; Eastern, 176
Evans, J. K., 211–12

Everett, Edward, 46
Ewing, Oscar, xvii
Ewing, Gen. Thomas, 83
Excise Tax Bill, 192
Executive Department, reorganization of, 152

F

Farewell Address, 6
Farley, James A., xvii, 15–30, 121, 133–35, 138, 149, 155, 216, 217; picture of, 19
Fascism, *see* Germany
Federal Employment Bureau, 102
Federalism, 5
Federalist, The, 7
Federalist Party, xv, 3–12, 34
Fifth Regiment Armory, 95
"Fireside Chat," 161–64
Flynn, Edward J., 24, 161
Folk, Joseph W., 98
Formosa, 193
Forrestal, James V., 25
"Four Freedoms," 159
France, 8
Freeman, Orville, xvii, 17, 18, 21, 29, 212
French Revolution of 1789, 3
Fulbright, J. William, 28, 204, 228–30
Fund raising, 15–23, 30, 121, 141, 151–52, 165, 169, 170, 188, 191, 216–17, 219, 220; at Democratic dinners, 133–38; by campaign book, 133–34; "750 Club," 196; $10 sustaining fund, 196, 204, 207; "Dollars for Democrats," 211; President's Club, 223–24; movie innovation, 230–31

G

Gadsby's Hotel, 48
Gala, 223, 224–25; $100-a-seat, 1963, 217; Salute to LBJ, 1964, 29; 1965, 30
Gardner, O. Max, 15, 24, 27
Garner, John N., 127, 150, 151, 155
Garret, Finis J., 116
George, Walter, 152
Georgetown Invincibles, 63
Gerard, James W., 107, 112, 127, 128
Germany, 158–70
Ghent, Treaty of, 34
Gillette, Guy, 152
Globe, 48, 60, 64
Goleta, California, 164
Government: British, 5; representative, 9
Grasso, Ella, 28, 204
Gray, George, 88
Great Britain, 158–70

161–64; 1943 dinner speaker, 165–66; preparation for 1945 dinner, 169–70; picture of, 143; death of, 169
Roosevelt, Franklin D., Library, xvii
Roosevelt, Mrs. Franklin D., 24, 28, 145, 153, 161
Roosevelt, Theodore, 97, 180; death of, 104
Rosenbloom, Carroll, 216
Rosenman, Samuel I., 151, 160
Ross, Nellie, 116, 127
Rural Electrification Administration, 208
Rusk, Dean, 222
Russia, 165, 176, 185, 200

S

Saint-Memin, Charles Fevret de, 52
Satellite, 200
Saulsbury, Eli, 87
Scott, Maj. Gen. Winfield, 40, 75
Secession, 34
Self-preservation, 194
Self-sacrifice, xv
Shaver, Clem, 116
Sheraton Park Hotel, 198, 202, 207; Sheraton Hall, 204
Ship purchase bill, 103
Shoreham Hotel, 96
Shouse, Jouett, 128
Singapore, 162
Slavery, abolition of, 12
Slum clearance, 208
Small, Robert T., 110
Smith, Alfred E., 116–28; pictures of, 117, 118
Smith, Ellison D., 152
Social cohesion, 22
Social security, 181, 208
Socialism, 182
Socialization, 131
Soil bank, 195
Southeast Asia Treaty Organization, 193
Speakers at dinners, 132
Speaking, political, 22–23; purposes of, 23
"Special interests," 4, 7, 197
"Special privileges," 128
Speech capsules: 1936, 235–36; 1937, 236; 1938, 237; 1939, 238–39; 1940, 230–40; 1941, 240; 1942, 240–42; 1943, 242; 1944, 242–43; 1946, 244–45; 1947, 245–46; 1948, 246–48; 1949, 248–49; 1950, 249–51; 1951, 251–53; 1952, 253–56; 1954, 256–57; 1955, 257–59; 1957, 259–60; 1958, 260–61; 1959, 262–63; 1960, 263–64; 1961, 264–65; 1962, 265–66; 1963, 266–67; 1964, 267–69; 1965, 269–72; 1966, 272–73

Speeches, *see also* Public addresses
—by FDR, 1936, 134–38; 1937, 141–47; 1938, 147–51; 1939, 151–53; 1940, 153–58; 1941, 158–60; 1942, 161–64; 1943, 165–66; 1945, preparation of, 169–70
—by Sam Rayburn, 1944, 166–68; 1954, 191–93; 1955, 193–94; 1956, 194–97; 1959, 202–5
—by Harry S. Truman, 1946, 173–76; 1947, 176–78; 1948, 178–80; 1949, 180–82; 1950, 182–83; 1951, 183–85; 1952, 185–88; 1957, 197–98; 1958, 198–202; 1960, 207–12
—by John F. Kennedy, 1961, 212–14; 1962, 214–17; 1963, 217–24
—by Lyndon B. Johnson, 1964, 224–25; 1965, 226–28; 1966, 228–31
Sperling, Miklos, 222
"Spoils system," 89
Stansberry, Henry, 83
State of the Union Address, 1942, 162
Statler Hotel, 26, 178–80, 182
Steel strike, 210
Stevens, Thaddeus, 87
Stevenson, Adlai, 15, 28, 192, 194, 195, 197, 199, 207; picture of, 195
Stevenson, Andrew, 49
Stewart, Andrew, 46
Stimson, Henry L., 159
Stinnett, Lillian M., vii
Stinnett, Owen E., vii
Storrs, Henry Randolph, 46
Stratton, Samuel, 28, 204
Suffrage, right of, 102, 108
Sullivan, Gael, 25
Sullivan, John L., 27, 28
Supreme Court, 135–38; "packing" of, 136, 141–47, 148–53; Court Bill, 144; reorganization of federal judiciary, 144; and racial integration, 200
Sutherland, Joan, 219
Symington, Stuart, 29, 204, 207, 208

T

Taft, Robert A., 184
Taft-Hartley Act, 181; repeal of section 14b, 230
Tariff, 103
Tawes, J. Millard, 28, 204
Taylor, Robert, 98
Television, 179, 180, 182, 186, 199; closed-circuit, 211
Tennessee Valley Authority, 152
Thompson, Juston, 116